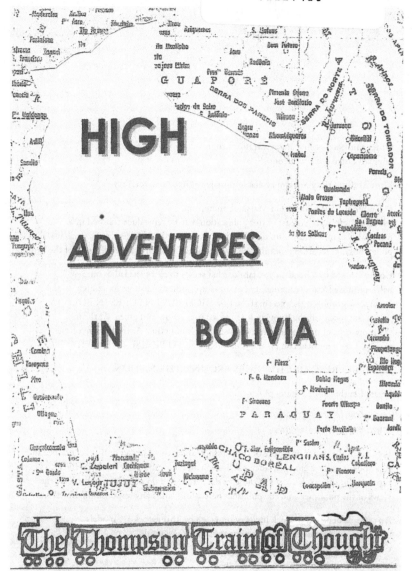

HIGH

· ADVENTURES

IN   BOLIVIA

The Thompson Train of Thought

BY
Hazel & Marshall Thompson

Order this book online at www.trafford.com
or email orders@trafford.com

Most Trafford titles are also available at major online book retailers.

Cover: Backed by a hand-woven fabric, (that serves to carry the ladies burden:
baby, produce from the market, or her dress-up clothes and shoes for church, so she
won't look grubby at the meeting) the title HIGH ADVENTURES IN BOLIVIA
stands out nicely, in the Bolivian fl ag colors: red, yellow and green. At the top,
the snow-caps of the Royal Range of the Andes Mountains. At the bottom of the
page you see a musical combo at a Junta, READY TO PRAISE THE LORD!

Back Cover: RING OF CHURCHES AROUND THE NATION

Printed in the United States of America.

ISBN: 978-1-4907-5152-8 (sc)
ISBN: 978-1-4907-5151-1 (e)

Trafford rev. 01/07/2015

 www.trafford.com

North America & international
toll-free: 1 888 232 4444 (USA & Canada)
fax: 812 355 4082

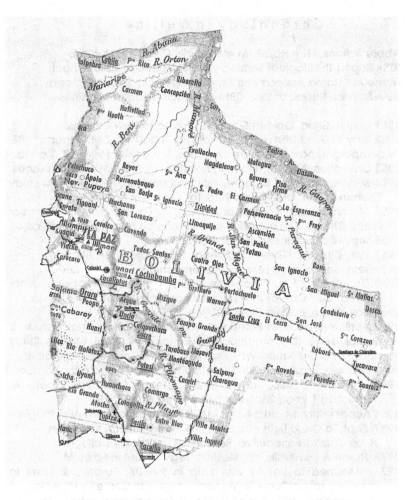

Map of Bolivia with cities, villages, rivers, peaks and railroads marked.
Area: 1,098,580 Km.2 Arable 2%, Pasture 24%, Forested 50%
Population: 4,500,000 est. (1955) Present est. 9,000,000
Ethnic: Aymara 24%, Quechua 30%, Mestizo 30%, Others 16%
Industry: Mining, petrol, animal husbandry and forest products.

Chronology In Outline

Abbreviations: H = Hazel; M =Marshall; Grad.=graduated;
BTS= Baptist Theological Seminary; VBS=Vacation Bible School;
Home A.= Home Assignment; Ev.= evangelistic; Bio.= biography;
BBU=Bolivian Baptist Union; CBM= Canadian Baptist Ministries

1951 May H. Grad. Golden Gate BTS. Posted to New Orleans.
1952 May M.Grad.DenverConservative.BTS.(BD) = MDiv. Canada, VBS,
Ev.campaigns, pastored three churches, Upper Blackville NB, Canada
1953 Ordination, Marriage to H. in Houston, TX. 5/3/53 VBS in 5 places.
1954 May Apppointed to India, July visa denied , redirected to study
Spanish in San Jose, Costa Rica, for service in Bolivia.
1955 March 11, son Borden born. Aug. to La Paz, Bolivia: to pastor
Prado Church. Jail outreach and Ev. church planting around city.
1956 Sept. 4, daughter Krystal born in La Paz.
1957 Jan. Director: Bible-High School, Guatajata, Lake Titicaca
1959 Sept. family time, Nov. 21, Karlene born in Texas, Home A.
1960 Deputation: Jan. Willowdale, Ont.; Mar. New Brunswick; June;
Toronto.: July Camps in West; Sept. prepare for return to Bolivia.
1960 Nov. Oruro, Bolivia; Bible Institute, field missionary.
1962 April: New work in Potosi with Avelino Gonzales. Aug.: Borden &
Krystal away to Carachipampa School. H. wrote Mission Study
book: *Smoke from Bolivian Fires* & edited Ev. paper: *Redencion*.
1964 Mar. elected Executive-Secretary of the BBU Apr. Cochabamba
1965 June: took ship, family time in Texas Sept. 2nd Home A.
Deputation 1 year; 2nd year off salary in Wolfville, NS.
1966 Acadia Univ. M. studied for MA in History .H. earned *BEd*. taught.
1967 Sept. To Oruro field missionary. Bible Institute for five years.
H. on Cruzada executive. Both taught at Reekie College.
1972 Home A. Wolfville, NS, Masters Degree conferred on M.
1973   Returned to Bolivia with visits in the UK, Europe, & Brazil to
spend 4 years in Sucre to start new work with Cornelio Heredia.
The Man You Ought to Know, bio. of Jesus given to rural schools.
1977 Home A, in Wolfville, NS. Visits to churches across Canada.
1978   Research on unreached fields and peoples. CBM   board
decision to investigate opportunities in difficult places. Sept. to
McGill University for Islamic studies in preparation for teaching.
1990 Return to Bolivia for a month of Ev. visits Potosi, Sucre, the South.
1991 Retirement from teaching in the Middle-East. Settled in Moncton.
1998 Return to Bolivia for celebration of 100th year with Mark
Parent tour leader and son of a colleague. Visits to Santa
Cruz, Sucre, Cochabamba, Oruro, La Paz and Guatajata for kudos,
recognition and congratulations from many to the CBM and BBU.

FOREWORD

It is strange which incidents in a long life will stick in your mind and recall in detail when stimulated by pictures, smells, or word triggers that bring to mind the occasion. This book is a collection of such memories, each reflecting the emotions and physical stimuli that accompany that moment in life. Each of us is the receptor and participant in that incident forever recorded in our store of significant moments in our lives; most are shared scenarios, but many are private, some secret, memories to be cherished or avoided in our daily routine. So many memories are lost, yet so many preserved and recalled occasionally or routinely. A few are forgotten only to be resurrected on some significant occasion. We have walked in these paths of recall from the start and to the completion of this book.

We are amazed at the twists and turns that our lives have taken. The hand of God is detected in many of the decisions or lack of that element in some events of our lives. Indeed, choice was clearly not present in many of those recorded moments; something greater is occurring around us and through us every day. Mystery still pervades the world and the words of the old gospel hymn echoes: 'We will understand it better by and by' and brings real comfort to our hearts.

Therefore, we take little credit for the direction and incidents recorded here. We experienced them: to this alone we can testify. The whys and wherefores we leave to the questions of the guidance of the Spirit of Jesus and His will for lives dedicated to his use, honor and glory. Few great advances for God and the church are accomplished alone. Indeed, an army of believers and workers bring about most spiritual growth and changes. One or another may trigger the start of a movement toward God, but many carry out the end results by co-operating with the Spirit. Many co-workers are not mentioned here. Their work will have been as important for the outcome described herein, as those of us who recall and record these incidents. They and not we should receive their commendation of, "Well done good and faithful servant; you have been diligent ... " We can glory only in the privilege of being present and experiencing with them a movement of God in the heart of a people. His Church; both Catholic and Evangelical have benefited the people and nation of Bolivia and received blessings because of the fervor aroused by the faithful living out of the promises and opportunities created by the movement of that Spirit. We have been useful, with a multitude of others, in changing the course of a nation.

We cast any crowns before Him: Jesus the Christ , our Savior.

Faithfully,

Hazel & Marshall Thompson

Table of illustrations:

Table of Contents

Lord... You have the words of eternal life...

John 6:68

"Here's something to read that will help you!"

MİSSIONARY PUZZLE: FINDING OUT WHO'S WHO IN BOLIVIAN HISTORY
Copied from a gelatin pad prepared by Hazel Thompson 1973.

```
B O L I V I A N   M I S S I O N A R I E S
        1898 - 1973
D L A M R O W E P P F I N K C I R R E M
N L C H A N D L E R N E S L E A K I M E
I U R I D G E W A Y A N J B D R A E B R
L B N L L H E M R E B A H A D H F M O R
K N O L C G B R E P K A W K C U B O S I
C R S Y N H O L M E S H A E O L H R O T
N U R E O O L S W I T Z E R O P I R P T
A T E R M O T A O H E Y P R K A L I R I
R E D N E D Y R D A B O O K E R L S I N
F I N D L A Y C D Y O U N G H E E O C D
R N A M R O G C A M S G E X C N N N E A
A E N I C M R L H A R R I N G T O N T L
S P A L O O O A O C I E T T O H S O S L
F H H T H O L R P N A Y E W U O R S I E
R Y C O O R Y K K E T B N Y L M E L U H
E P U N W E A E I I S S E T D P K L Q C
E Y B R U N T O N L E N T A I S C I M T
K P H I L L I P S N N O B E N O I M L I
I E A L L A B Y D O C B S E G N V N A M
E R U G G L E S B S S I G R U T S T P ?
```

ALLABY	DABBS	HILLYER	MITCHELL	SCOTT
AMY	DRYDEN	HOLMES	MOORE	STAIRS
ANDERSON	EPP	HOOD	MORRISON	STURGISS
BAKER	FINDLAY	HOPKINS	PALMQUIST	SWITZER
BEARD	FINK	JAKEWAY	PARENT	TAYLOR
DONKEY	FRANCKLIN	KERFOOT	PHILLIPS	THOMPSON
BOOKER	FRASER	LEMON	PRICE	TINDALL
BRUNTON	GREY	MACGORMAN	PYPER	TOWNSEND
BUCHANAN	GOULDING	MACNEIL	REEKIE	TURNBULL
BUSK	HABERNEHL	MERRICK	RIDGENAY	VICKERSON
CHANDLEY	HADDOW	MERRITT	ROCHOW	WILKERSON
CLARKE	HARRINGTON	MIKAELSEN	ROWE	WORMALD
COOKE	HILL	MILLSON	RUGGLES	YOUNG
FREDERICA	HILLER	MILTON		

When you have marked all the names in the square and the
list, the 37 leftover letters will form Bible message. ___ __ ___

___ ___ _____ ____ _____ _____

_____ ____ __ ____ ___.

"Marry me, and we will go to India together." Well, I had known God wanted me to be a missionary since I was four...and I hadn't even trusted Him as my Savior until I was seven. And though Southern Baptists had worked in China, Nigeria and Brazil, my call was to India. They had never had any missionaries in India.

My first grade teacher had been a missionary in China, and made a great impression on me. But from my first Social Studies in school, and my first hearing "Go ye..." from God, it always pointed me to India.

A month before the above proposal was made, an interview with the Southern Baptist Convention Mission Board personnel secretary had made it clear that they had no visas for India, and even if they did, they wouldn't be sending untried, green ones like me to fill them! I cried for two weeks, then dug through my book shelf to find the *Missionary Digest: Reports of the Canadian Baptist Foreign Mission Board*, which a friend from University days had sent to me the year before. The "Get acquainted card" on the back was duly filled out and mailed. Now that same pleasant friend was sitting in my New Orleans living room, suggesting we make it a twosome.

While the initial shock was wearing off, he hurried on to say that he didn't want my answer right away. He would be a guest in our slum mission Good Will Center for about 10 days, and suggested that I just think on it.

I was teaching kindergarten 9AM to Noon, in charge of Bible Clubs for boys and girls each afternoon (the legacy of a worker who had moved to another job in February) and nursing the director of our Friendship House who was suffering from allergies that put her in the hospital eventually. On the fifth day of his stay, I added taking her husband and daughter to visit her in the hospital each day, and also taught a study course on missions in a church all the way across town each evening.

At the end of the ten days, I still had not come to a decision. So, Marshall went off to visit his family and friends in Texas. He left me the address and phone number of each of the places he would visit with the dates he expected to stay with each one. I had already planned to take time off from May 1st to attend the Southern Baptist Convention in Houston, my home town. Jackie, a friend in New Orleans, and Elizabeth, the former colleague mentioned above were going to stay in my home there. Marshall also made plans to see me there.

A letter came a few days after he left inviting me to his ordination in Waco on April the 29th. When I called him to accept his invitation, I also said yes to his proposal. I was booked for a Seminar on Drama in the Church, and two camps, when my kindergarten teaching year finished a month later. I figured that if we married in July, with all that done; he could come from Canada, and I could go from New Orleans, and we could meet halfway in Chattanooga to marry.

In the south the arrangements for ordination are usually made between the person's home church and the one where he is pastoring. Thus he had wired the Upper Blackville church asking them to communicate with the Seventh and James Baptist Church in Waco, where he had been baptized. Though they did not know what to do with the letter, and never answered, his home church proceeded to call an ordaining council, and ordained him. I was in attendance.

When he picked me up from the bus station on the afternoon of the proposed ordination, he took me to the Baylor campus. There in the middle of the mall, he hoisted me up onto the lap of Judge Baylor's giant bronze statue. With the explanation that he had always heard that one should propose on bended knee; he sat me on one of the statues knees and he sat on the other while he repeated his proposal. Just at that moment, the bell rang for classes to change. and the flood of students came from every direction on their way to the next class. Oblivious of this, he put a ring on my finger, and then was interrupted by a passer-by's question: "What are you-all doin' up there?" People were always climbing up on the statue, but usually there was someone nearby taking a picture of them, and she didn't see anyone. So he answered her and said, "I just asked her to marry me and now I'm going to kiss her!"

We had supper and then went to the prayer meeting at the church where we had sung in the choir for several years. After the regular meeting, those who had come for the examination and ordination constituted as a council privately. I visited with various friends, until we were all called in to witness the ordination.

After the ordination, he took me on a romantic drive out to Lake Waco. Under the beautiful full moon, he told me we would be married on Sunday (this was Wednesday). But, I objected, "We have to make all the plans; clothes, preacher, church, reception, cake, etc."

"This is my vacation," he said, "—a whole month— (nobody in Texas gets a month) and I have to work a whole year before I get another one!" I conceded.

On the way home we stopped at the telegraph office and sent six telegrams. In the excitement, we managed to leave some vital detail out of each one: the town, the name or location of the church, the groom's name, the date, and the hour.

My best friend was attending Baylor University at the time, and with her I went shopping the next day. Actually, we also returned and Fritzi took a picture of us up on the statue, too. We found a marvelous aqua ballet length organdy dress strewn with flocked lilies of the valley, with some wee blossoms anchored with rhinestones. My shoes, with three-inch-high heels, were made of white lace that looked like cobwebs. I had just purchased a few weeks before, an ornate necklace of pearls, that fit in perfectly for a wedding. I felt like Cinderella.

My friend, Fritzi, went home to Houston on Friday, and her mother made her a dress of the same design, in pale pink.

When the girls I had invited to stay at my house arrived in Houston, just hours after we did, they phoned to find out how to get there. I asked if they were sitting down, and if they were braced. They were crowded into a phone booth both trying to hear. When I announced that we were being married at 6 PM the next day, they couldn't believe it. But they got right into the spirit and enjoyed helping us get ready. One of my telegrams had been to my other best friend in Houston., Dalgus. I asked her to book the church, order the cake and hire a photographer. In spite of all the difficulties, she had managed to do it all. She and Fritzi had made all the arrangements for the reception at Fritzi's brother's house, and everything was beautiful. My brother cornered me to ask what name he should put on the wedding gift. Marshall's friend Jack came from Waco, to be his best man, and his wife Nancy played the organ. My friend Pat sang.

After a lovely honeymoon to Corpus Christi, we returned for the last day of Convention. My friends teased me about marrying a "fly by night' as we put Marshall on the plane back to Boston, where he finished his trip to St. John by rail.

Marshall's beginnings go a long way back: High School graduation at 15 years old while living on his Grandfather's plant nursery. While in university he started working in Providence Hospital as an orderly. At 18 he was drafted into the army medical corps after preliminary infantry training. He had overseas experience in the Philippine Islands for 18 months. He returned to Baylor University in Waco, starting in pre-med and finishing in a bachelor of arts course. He studied in Golden Gate Baptist Theological Seminary in California and Denver Seminary in Colorado and tried several times to apply as a candidate for India, but always they said 'you need experience'. He went to Canada with a friend to get it. Let's let him tell it.

I proceeded to the Miramichi River pastorate of Upper Blackville, Underhill and New Zion: a circuit of churches under the supervision of the Home Mission Department of the United Baptist Convention of the Maritime Provinces. I was 26 years old and enjoying my first pastoral experiences. Before that, I had largely been a song leader and soloist. The Seminaries of North America were full of war veterans who wished to study and many wished to serve God in some way. The joke going in Baptist circles was that: "If you are Southern Baptist you must go out, start and build your own church. If another fundamental type of Baptist, go out and split your own church." Since I was neither builder nor splitter, I chose to accompany a Canadian friend to get my experience where, he assured me, there were many churches that needed pastors. My father had worked on a farm on the Niagara peninsula during the First World War. Canadians were short of helping hands because they entered that war earlier than the United States. He was not yet 18. I had seen pictures of dad on the 'Maid of the Mists' by Niagara Falls. Canada was within my heritage.

After helping in evangelistic campaigns in Nova Scotia and daily vacation Bible schools in New Brunswick I got a pastorate in Upper Blackville. I loved it, but it was only a step in the way I wanted to go for God. I had in one sense challenged God. I felt a missionary call, but He had to prove I could be effective in my own language first. I blundered successfully through nearly two years of experience and found help in every situation. I even saw a few things that I and others considered miraculous. We put in a basement in one church. We had a baptism in the Miramichi River: twenty one men and one twelve-year-old girl. My radio program of 'Quiet Talks' was widely accepted. The churches became self-supporting. I was ready for the next step outward. When India proved to be a closed door, we, for I had been married a year by then, were guided to Bolivia.

In preparation, we studied a year in Costa Rica for language. I started preparing sermons and preaching after four months. We were expected to be able to talk about almost any subject on graduation. I wasn't quite that accomplished, but God had again proved that He could get me through anything including fatherhood and emergency surgery for appendicitis; I would soon have the opportunity to prove that hope again. I was called to the largest Protestant church in the largest city in Bolivia; they couldn't agree on anyone else, and I was an unknown factor. No one could object! At least, until after I was installed. I would continue to need God desperately.

We sealed our union with this promise inscribed in our rings:

God will bless us, and all the ends of the earth will fear him. Psalm 67:7

Within two hours of our arrival in Bolivia, I knew I was in trouble. We were sitting at supper at the radio apartment, guests of Art and Sylvia Wormald. In breezed Mary Beard. She asked, "Has anyone seen the keys to Villa San Antonio? I'm due there for a meeting in 10 minutes, and I can't find the key."

Her question was greeted by general, rude laughter (or so it seemed to me). When that died down, no one admitted having used them last, or having seen them: so off she hurried without them. Inside, I was feeling badly, thinking of the frequency with which I found myself unable to lay my hands on my own keys. Would they always be so unkind, rather than helping her look, or offering some other solution? Later, I understand, she held the meeting in the park, and the children who came were not upset at all.

It was two months before they found the key. She cleaned up her desk and there it was; buried under several layers of paper. THEN, having seen it, I could join them in the good natured laughter. I could see the joke. The key was six inches long, a whole pound of iron, threaded through with a two foot length of leather thong!

I DID have some problems with keys, later. Coming on the train from Cochabamba, after a few months, we reached the station at the Alto of La Paz (the Heights) just at dusk. People who live on the Alto or further north on the Altiplano, get off there, and take other transportation for the rest of their trip. Porters get on the train to help them off, or to stay with it and help others get their things ready to get off at the main station in the city.

We were sitting in the next to the last seat on our car. It had a very high back. Our nine month old son had been sleeping with my purse as his pillow. When I leaned across him to see out, he woke up, and we both moved toward the window to get a glimpse of the lights in the bowl of the city below. What a startling sight! The twinkling lights of the city were popping on one at a time, and we were enchanted by the sight. While we were thus occupied, someone reached over the back of that seat, and made off with my purse. I didn't have a lot of money in it to lose, but I had my ID, temporary driver's license, and, of course, a BIG bunch of keys. The street gate, the patio gate, our apartment door (with a couple of locks on each) were only a few of the many I was trusted with. People locked EVERYTHING there. The locks had to be replaced at considerable expense.

From the first incident on the train, I began pinning my keys just inside the top of my purse, when I bought a new one. Of course, if they took the whole purse, as they had that time, they would still get the keys. However, that kept them from gravitating to the bottom of the purse, and usually I lost a lot of time digging for them until I started that practice. It put them right at my finger-tips, and I didn't have nearly as hard a time finding them in subsequent years by taking that action. And I might have lost them more times than I did. Most of the time when I lost them, they were somewhere in the house, and they turned up after a search.

This wasn't the last time I lost my keys. You'll read about some in other chapters. And not all of them were about losing them.

Another time I was supposed to meet Marshall downtown and we would go home together. When my meeting was over, I went to the little park near the central plaza, where I was supposed to wait for him in the car, until his class was over. We had gone separately, so I hadn't seen where he had parked the Jeep, but I had my own keys, and though it was dusk, found the car easily. I took out my key, and put it in the lock, but it didn't work. I'm straining to see what I'm doing wrong, when a gentleman comes up and asks if I was having some problem. I was thankful that he seemed so ready to help. When I said the obvious—that the key wouldn't open it, he said,"Probably because it's my car." I'm sure my face glowed like a neon sign as we laughed. Looking forward I saw the very next car was another jeep of the same color, make and model. It was ours.

The third incident was when President Paz Estensoro was exiled. Vice President Rene Barrientos led a revolt, and gave him till noon on Tuesday to leave the country. I had to go pick Karlene up from kindergarten, and hurry home to Jordan street with her, then go on to the market to stock up, in case the disturbance lasted a while. Those things done, we were secure behind our doors, and I was telling Karlene where we would hide if someone came hunting us. The door bell rang, and I went to answer it, leaving her in the second patio.

"Who is it?" I asked tremulously. A strong male voice answered, "You don't know me, but I noticed that you left your keys on the outside of the door, and was sure you'd want to take them inside." We laughed as I opened the door, and took them from the lock. I thanked him profusely.

Did I say that we were secure inside? Well, we really were, but no thanks to ME! I do believe that we were secure inside, because we daily put our lives into God's hands. He is able to keep us in his care, whatever our circumstance, whenever we need Him, and wherever we happen to be. . .

I will give to you the keys
of the kingdom of heaven:
What you close is closed;
what you open is open!
Matthew 16:19

You own Heavens' keys; who do you admit and who exclude?

3   Help at Home

"And I was scraping vegetables off the ceiling for a week!"
she giggled.   Maria Luisa, that is.   This conversation began
about 2 years after the event, which happened when she had
first begun working for us.   We were discussing what life was
like before she came to live with us.

She had cooked on some quite primitive stoves using
wood, charcoal, and sheep dung. Early in our stay she had
suggested we buy an interesting kerosene pump stove for
emergencies, in case the power went off. She knew how to
cook on it and the complicated formula for lighting it, though
they had never owned one. We had been in Bolivia for a
couple of months, but had just moved into our newly renovated
apartment behind the church and were on our own: Marshall,
Borden and Hazel. This was the parsonage, and had been
fixed up while we house-sat for the Wormald's as they went to
Panama for a radio course.

The Stairs, another missionary family, were temporarily living
in the apartment above us. Florence offered to help 'break her
in,' (train her, that is). We were at the point where we were
going to spend practically the day at the Customs House,
every day. Our fine big, beautiful electric stove had not been
connected yet, so Florence suggested she could prepare
things with Maria's help on her two burner hot plate, and we
could all eat together. Florence would get Maria to prepare
the vegetables. Then she would put the water in the pressure
cooker and turn on the hot plate, while she set Maria to doing
something else. When the food was cooked, she would come
in, turn off the fire, take the pot to the sink, take the weight off
the top, run the cold water over the lid until the steam was
exhausted, take the top off the pot and serve the vegetables.

This went on for a week. Then one day, Florence was called
away, and had not returned when the things were cooked. We
were still at the Custom's house; so Maria took things into her
own hands. She turned off the fire, took the pot to the sink, and
took off the top. The power of the steam threw the top against
her shoulder, and the vegetables erupted all over the ceiling.
With great presence of mind, she quickly peeled and cut up
more vegetables, put in the water, put on the top, turned on the

17

fire. Then, she got rid of most of the mess around the sink, and part way up the wall. When Florence finished with the duty that took her away, she came in to take off the vegetables, and was hoping that they hadn't gone dry. Maria Luisa assured her that they were doing just fine, scared to death that Florence would look up. That's when she said: "And I was scraping vegetables off the ceiling for a week!" In that wee closet of a kitchen, it had never been detected.

Maria's father brought her a few weeks before this incident, hoping that we would engage her as a maid. He said she was 17, and was a good worker, and would do everything I asked her to. Her sister worked for some Lutheran missionary ladies, and he had heard that we needed someone.

He was right, she was a good worker, and was eager to learn everything new. When I would give her a task when we were preparing a meal, she quickly finished that and was peering over my shoulder to see how I was doing mine. The next time she would do that as well. I taught her to make white sauce, and brown gravy. These were things that we used in many meals. Any red meat was always served with gravy. I had some intolerance for milk, but could eat it cooked into white sauce. So I often had her cream vegetables and make banana pudding, with the basic white sauce sweetened with sugar. It was a favorite dessert for the whole family. She learned to do it better than I did.

I taught her to make cakes and she was soon being asked by her friends if she could make a cake for someone's birthday. Since many people there didn't have ovens, she would ask permission to cook it in my kitchen with the ingredients that her friends brought for her to make it with. I TRIED to teach her to make pies, but she just couldn't see any use in all those different steps: first the crust, then the filling, and then the meringue. Since she did so well on everything else, I didn't insist that she go ahead and do it. When I wanted a pie, I made it myself. In all her work, she went at it with enthusiasm, so she could finish quickly. She was mostly very pleasant to be around.

She noticed that we were frugal in our buying, so when I put tea on the list for her to buy, she brought home an enormous newspaper-wrapped package with five pounds of tea that she bought in bulk at the market. She proclaimed that it was a great bargain. When she made the first pot of it, though, Marshall just hated it. It tasted like green tomatoes! He insisted that I get Lipton's yellow label from then on. I think he even gave her permission to throw it away. However, her own frugality kicked in and she just put it way back on the shelf. After a few months, I found out that when some organization came for a social time, and had forgotten to bring their own tea, that she shared 'our' tea with them. When it was half gone, she mentioned it, and confessed how she had gotten rid of it. Marshall suggested that she take it down to the church kitchen to save them the embarrassment of having to ask for it.

She loved Borden, and observed our ways of disciplining him, and tried to help us maintain that discipline. He was a good little boy and didn't need a lot of correction, but we saw other families whose discipline was undermined constantly by their maids, so we were very fortunate.

One of the things that I figured I'd have a hard time with going to India as a missionary was having to deal with servants. You always read about foreigners in India, with a houseful of them. Having grown up in very humble circumstances myself, I didn't look forward to that. When I couldn't go to India, that was something that I was relieved about -- not having an army of servants. I just treated Maria like one of the family, and for us it worked. She learned the table blessing that we taught our children. Years later, when she married, she taught her children that same blessing.

After working for us a couple of years, she needed an I.D. and went to the Catholic church where her father had registered her at birth (since there was no civil registry at that time). When she showed it to us, it stated that she was 17, meaning that she was only 15 when she first came to us. I was amazed that she showed such maturity in so many things.

We moved to Guatajata after two and a half years at the Prado church, downtown. It was like going to the end of the world! While we lived in La Paz, we had a two block walk to get to the Camacho market. You could find EVERYTHING in that market: fresh fruits, vegetables, meat, clothing, knick-knacks, furniture, kerosene, charcoal, sewing supplies and yard goods! Even the canned goods that you also could buy at the import store, you could often get there for less.

At Guatajata we would have about the same distance to walk to market, but about all you could buy was potatoes, fresh or dried fish, onions, candles, matches, and charcoal. Someone drove into La Paz from the farm every two weeks, and all of us sent grocery lists. The Palmquists lived in the farmhouse, Mary Haddow, Janet Holmes and Doris Millson in the Señoritas' House. We lived in the Igloo, so named because it was so hard to heat. It was NEVER over 8 degrees Celsius in our bedroom. We had electric lights from 6 to 10PM when the generator worked. When it burned out on November first, we were away in town buying for Christmas. The new generator part had to be ordered from somewhere outside the country. We put up our Christmas tree hopefully, anyway. We had bought lights for the tree, and records for everybody. After a candle light Christmas, Marshall declared we would not take down the tree until we had enjoyed it lighted and heard the music on the records.

The part was only installed on Feb. 29th. Doug Moore came out with the parts and together the men worked on the motor. It was pitch dark when they came in to wash up, but they were successful in finishing the repairs, and all of us at Guatajata had light that night.

The Moore family stayed the night. After a holiday dinner we enjoyed a late Christmas celebration with Doug, Flo and the children, satisfied with lights, music and laughter.

When the Stairs moved to Guatajata, they had brought with them an old wood stove that had been converted to use kerosene. They loved it, and Mrs. Stairs had been able to make wonderful meals on it. Maria Luisa had always done just fine with it as well. I only had to deal with it on Sunday all day, and Wednesday afternoon. Having a stove that heats the whole top of the stove at once has a lot of advantages, like the old wood stove we had used on the Miramichi. The meal could be kept warm without extra cost for fuel. Maria, found some large slate slabs (ovals about 3 inches thick and a foot long) that she put on the back of the stove during the day. When she cut off the fuel supply after supper, she would wrap them in towels, and put them at the foot of our beds, in lieu of hot water bottles. There was always hot water for a cup of tea, if anyone came calling. We liked it, too.

The only disadvantage, was cleaning it. Once in every week, she had to spend half a day getting the soot out of it. It was a dirty, smelly job. She usually did it on Tuesday morning, and all done up in with an old scarf and apron, she did this odious job. After about a year of this, one Wednesday, when she was off for the afternoon visiting friends, I went out to the kitchen to start on supper. The fire wouldn't light! I went through all the steps: pouring the alcohol onto the burner, setting fire to it, waiting two minutes for the iron cup to heat, opening the valve to feed in the kerosene: it just wouldn't light! I opened the lid and sure enough, it looked like she hadn't cleaned it. I swathed my head (I already had on my apron) and went to work. Supper was late, everyone was in a bad mood. I did calm my indignation enough, to civilly ask when she came in, what had happened to keep her from cleaning the stove. She said she had, and immediately went to look inside. Remember, I had just spent the afternoon cleaning the stove? Well, in just the two of hours it took to fix supper, it had already built up like a week worth of soot! We both stared in disbelief. The rest of that week, she had to spend half a day cleaning the stove!

Neither Marshall nor I had ever used one of these stoves before, so we didn't know what to do to correct the problem. The next week Marshall went into town, and we were counting on him to speak to someone, in the hope of fixing it. In the rush of doing all the list of chores that he had to do every time he went into town, he forgot. He faced two desolate women upon his return. Two weeks later, I went into town for my book club meeting, and I did all the shopping I had to do when I went. I did talk to some people, but no one knew what to do. Finally, I spoke to some, and wrote to other members of the furniture committee (they met only twice a year during conference) and it was approved that I could have a new stove. The meals during the next two months were scanty. It took that long from the first Wednesday afternoon until we finally had the new one installed and we could use it.

In spite of that and the breakdown of the motor that supplied the electricity we loved living there, and for us, the beauty of the lake and mountains was enough to make up for the hardships.

Though Maria had gone to about eighth grade in school, and was a good diligent student, speaking perfect Spanish, she also had the advantage of knowing how to speak Aymara, the Indian language spoken at Guatajata. She was very excited that she would be able to help us when someone came to the door that couldn't speak Spanish. Both Marshall and I had taken several short courses in Aymara, and were able to greet people, count to 100, tell them where we were going, and ask for some items in the market. We could pronounce it properly when reading it, and recognized key words singing the hymns, hearing the preacher, etc. However, no one ever asked us where we were going and conversation was definitely not an option for us. Fortunately, most of the men and the younger women had been to our schools there and could use Spanish. The older women had not been allowed to go to school, and we often had to call on Maria Luisa to translate for us.

On her day and afternoon off, she made friends in the neighborhood and often brought us some treat that her friends had given her. One of the things that we really enjoyed about Bolivia was the bread. Our favorites were 'pancitos' that were like large hamburger buns; and 'mariketas', six inch long french loaves, but there were many others as well. It was really bad news when we found out that you couldn't buy bread at Guatajata. When we knew that we were going there to live, Mary Beard suggested that we send Maria to learn bread making from Santusa -- her cook. She learned and made WONDERFUL bread. Makes my mouth water just to think of it.

We learned with God's help we could cope with any situation where we were placed.

Jesus said: "I am the bread of life" John 6:35

Marshall wrote an article once on 'Sam, Sam, the Tramite Man.' 'Tramite' is an all inclusive term for what we call 'red tape'. When he had 'tramites' to do, he would take his current book along, and read it until his name was called. As pastor at the Prado Church, he had lots of tramites to do.

Our first experience with tramites in Bolivia was with our entrance visas. Actually, our entrance visas were over a year coming, and caused us trouble every time we had to get more papers done. Before we went, with only a few weeks to go in language school in Costa Rica, we were supposed to send our passports to Panama to be processed as that was where the nearest Bolivian consul was found. Since we were afraid we couldn't get them back in time for the flight we had booked, someone suggested that we enter on a tourist visa, and we did.

Something we had acquired during our stay in Costa Rica at the language school was a medium sized parrot named 'Admiral'. He was Marshall's prized pet, and he wished to take him along with us to our new home in Bolivia. He made inquiries, and found that if he could get some papers and a doctor's certificate that the bird was healthy, we could bring him along. So, at some expense of both time and money, he acquired those credentials. Having a five and a half month old baby, I was very apprehensive about juggling him and all his paraphernalia while Marshall carried a bird cage.

We stopped overnight in Panama. The Customs and Immigration people looked over the papers, and authorized us to take the Admiral with us to the hotel. We had no trouble finding an orange to satisfy his need for food. Our next stop was two days in Lima. So when they said that our papers from Costa Rica were not acceptable, and their own doctors would have to OK his entry, we didn't know what to do. We knew that they would never find a doctor to come all the way to the airport at 4 AM Sunday morning! However, the attendants at the airport offered to feed and look after him for us. We enjoyed seeing the sights in Lima. We came back to the airport Monday to continue our flight, found him doing just fine and were very thankful for their help.

Ironically, when we arrived in Bolivia, they asked what we

had in the cage. When we said a parrot; they never even lifted the cover to look at him, much less the papers! And this was the country where we hoped to spend the rest of our lives!

Back to the visa: the lawyer who did the Baptist Missionaries papers, also did the papers for the Methodist Missionaries. At the same time we were getting ours done, a Dr. Bill Jack Marshall came to the Methodist hospital. The files got all scrambled together, and we found out that he had been working on only one of the Marshall couples' papers. When he DID get around to doing ours, it was revealed that NO CONSULATE OUTSIDE THE COUNTRY HAD AUTHORIZED OUR ENTRY. Every time we got anything official done, the lack of that paper made it take twice as long to process.

When we first went in to get our drivers licenses, about five months after we arrived in Bolivia, I went with Marshall , Grace Anderson and Rubin Bonney. We got one requirement done each month for several months. We asked about their rule book to prepare for the written exam, and they said they were out of print. They didn't actually give us written tests since we all had valid licenses from North America, but it would have been nice to know their rules for the road, anyway. Of course, we quickly learned some things that differed from North America: in daytime, you honked at each intersection, and if you were meeting another car; whoever honked first had the right of way. At night, in the city you did not use your headlights except at intersections. The first one to flash had the right-of-way. On the highway, the car going up-hill has the right-of-way. But if a big truck saw that you were driving a little jeep, he'd just sort of bulldoze you right off the road. In short, the biggest truck won. For that reason I'd rather drive at night. In mountain driving you couldn't always see the size of the vehicle by the headlights, but you can see their lights three curves away.

We had bought a car to take to India, but when we could not go there, we requested that they send it to India – in our place. However, the Board had sent it to Bolivia. There it was being used for the radio staff and only in the city. Marshall and I had driven it for a year and a half in Canada, giving us a real advantage. None of us had driven during the year of language school in Costa Rica, but Grace had not driven for

24

three years. We had permission to use that car for the driving test, but Grace was asked to drive first. It was a grueling exam, and for all of us it was difficult on the steep hills of the city. Where I grew up, the only hills were graded railroad crossings! Being with her during her test drive, we were able to avoid her mistakes. But I had to wince when the insensitive examiner twitted her by saying, "The *señora* drives better than you, doesn't she?"

Since we didn't have a vehicle and lived on the Prado Boulevard downtown, we went up the hill by bus as far as the plaza for each visit. By this time I was pregnant, and really finding that trip to the office hard. Finally, Janet Holmes said that if I didn't stop going on the bus, I'd have the baby on the bus like squeezing out tooth paste. Well , even that teasing didn't stop me, but the offices were two and a half blocks up that hill above Plaza Murillo, and I just couldn't walk it anymore. I gave up, and didn't drive even when we could get a car. We were living in the parsonage – second floor of a three story building behind the Prado church. I was three blocks from the Camacho market – only about six blocks from Plaza Murillo (but straight up the hill, of course) and in easy reach of anything I wanted to buy. All the people came to us. We were there for two and a half years before being transferred to Guatajata.

There, of course, I would NEED that driver's license. By that time Krysi was 15 months and Borden three years old. I could drive around in the country without a license, but to go into town, I would need it. We only found out in mid-December, and we moved the third of January. Asking around, I found out I could trade in my license, because by that time, the papers for the first tramites were no where to be found.

I belonged to the Book Club, which met monthly and hitched a ride with Janet Holmes or Mary Haddow when the club met. I started getting the signatures – again – one at a time.

Then there was a big strike while Marshall was in town. They were burning cars across from the US embassy, but it was the time they had told me to come back to the office next. It was hard to decide alone, but I caught a truck into town. I went to the office, and I couldn't find anyone. I still had to get three signatures and an order to get my picture made-and making the picture, and getting the picture back to them. I figured another five months. I was really despairing. I found a bell (like teachers have on their desks), struck it and waited. Then I heard a voice from the end of the hall – maybe five offices away. "*Pase no mas*, come right in," and started walking that way. When I got there, I found myself in the presence of the '*Jefe*', chief. He looked haggard, but was a real gentleman.

He wondered what he could do for me. I told him I'd come for my driver's license. Begging my pardon, he explained that EVERY person in the Traffic division had been on duty 48 hours straight, and he was no exception. He scanned my papers, and commented on how the process had dragged on (and actually that was only from the second start). "Lets get this over with," he said. He gave me the order for the picture, signed several places (as *Jefe*, he could do that), and told me to bring it back the minute I had the picture. I walked down the hill just a little way, and was back within the hour with the pictures. He said the others would have it all ready for me when I came back the next month. And that's what happened. Only two years and five months to the day after I had taken that original test, my license came through. It had no expiration date, but later they made laminated cards instead of the little book we first got.

Years and years later, I had to use it again. It seems some man who became *Jefe* after that, sold illegally, a lot of laminated *brevetes* (drivers' licenses), and those were ALL invalidated. However, if you had the old book, you could (when in La Paz again) take it in and get a new card. Anyway, I think I still have both of them, and I take them with me when I go back to Bolivia, and I can still drive with them. I won't say that God started the riots, but I'm sure glad that He used them to help me get my license a little sooner.

We pray that as you read about the things the Lord has taken us through, that you will see His great works and glorify Him. We know He can meet your needs, as well. Though, of course He NEVER solves any problem in just the same way.

These things happened long years ago, and we have laughed about what seemed such serious trials at the moment they happened. Whatever the trials are that you are going through now, learn to lean on Him and look to Him for the solution, and you will be able to laugh about the fretting that Satan traps us into. Just go on preparing step by step, and when the moment comes, everything will fall into place. And the marvelous thing is that others will see the miracles it took to bring you through. Hopefully, that will make it quite natural for them to lean on Jesus when hard times come to them.

Look, ... my reward is with me to give to all according to their works. Revelation 22:12

The Prado Baptist Church La Paz, 1955

Antonio Chiriotto had been prosperous, but a dissolute atheist much of his life. He ended up on Skid Row, and found relief from his spiritual unease at the Peniel Hall Gospel Mission in Los Angeles, California. After hearing the Gospel, he felt compelled to travel to South America to spread it among those who had never heard. Finding that he could not legally establish the kind of work he desired in Argentina, he traveled to Bolivia, where he heard it could be done legally. He was 80 years old in 1911 when he made the trip from Argentina and arrived in La Paz.

He wanted to show his appreciation by giving his money for some project beneficial to the Aymara Indians, who he felt were the neediest he had seen. The Gospel would have to be presented to the Indian farmers along with literacy, help in the agricultural field, and health care, as well as Gospel preaching. These four fields were addressed in spite of much opposition and skepticism. He left the money, US$ 30,000 to an interdenominational committee before death and burial in La Paz.

Only the Canadian Baptists seemed to take an interest in the challenge of Peniel Hall Farm. A primary school was started at the purchased farm, and an offer of help for other communities sprang from the success of that first school at Guatajata. Others along the lake appeared with time and the third generation of missionaries enjoyed the benefits of the forerunners' work. A clinic, six grades of school with a few girls now attending, a church building and the farm existed in the time of Dr. Merrick. He began to promise land to the farm *peons* - serfs: the men who worked the land were tied to the land. The completion of certain basic reforms was included in a legal agreement. Most accepted the agreement and eventually got the land. An example had been given and later a political party promised the same to others, if political power was theirs. They were elected eventually. Land reform and turmoil followed, but *peons* got their land after centuries of servitude. New challenges were appropriate to the local and national situation. A radical socialist government ruled in La Paz.

The Bible High School in Guatajata was a solution to an artificial crisis. So great was the desire to get their boy children to be teachers that parents lied about their age and some were 4-5 years old in the first of eight grades. The government had a teacher training school started near Achacachi, whose certificate assured employment at a government school. The entrance age was 16 years old proved by a required birth certificate. But those who had managed to pass the mission financed grade schools found a two or three year wait to admission. The boys were bored with farm work and discovered that hard earned knowledge was easily lost through neglect. Enough appeals provoked an inspiration. Why not combine the Bible training, usually offered to deacons and other adults, with a high school curriculum (modified and reduced). The mission was willing to finance one teacher to help launch the effort.

Remigio Gutierrez was the chosen teacher and the curriculum was divided between the two of us, with my wife Hazel taking some hours. The books were taken from all types of sources. A National Geographic book on the Indians of the Americas allowed glimpses of other American cultures and crops. One picture fascinated them: the Indian, a Hopi, looked exactly like Justino Quispe, the outstanding Aymara evangelical leader from Guatajata. There were always racial similarities as well as diversity among the Amerindians. I tried to give them pride in their origins.

We were both, teachers and students, working in second languages and there were moments of incomprehension in the class. Hazel and I had many chuckles provoked by a mix-up in Bible class between the ten plagues suffered by the Egyptians and the dream of Pharaoh. Studying in the Old Testament, we took up both the ten plagues and the ten, fat and lean cows in Pharaoh's dream. I, Marshall, usually wrote two exams. The students were given alternate papers so there would be no 'sharing' of knowledge during the tests. The difference in the word "skinny" and the word for a car license, was only in the initial letter: *flaca* for skinny and *placa* for license plates for vehicles. The difference between plague *plaga* and license *placa* was the fourth letter. Several students answering the question on the dream put down "*diez vacas placas*" (ten cow's licenses), but when one got mixed up and wrote "*diez placas flacas*" (ten skinny licenses); for the ten plagues, it was even funnier.

There was also the matter of science class. I performed a special experiment on the dangers of alcohol. It started with a jigger of raw alcohol, the kind they drink at the festivals. I pour it over an egg and in about a minute, the egg is cooked, the white and yellow clouding and hardening. Take another jigger and pour it in a beaker of swimming tadpoles, they quiver and die. All the students are visibly impressed. Lectures follow about the sensitive nature of nerve and brain tissue, liver tissue and endocrine systems. In short the damage done by regular alcohol intake: the dangers of alcoholism.

Tests follow lessons, the science test revealed they understood portions of lessons. Question: What can we learn from the experiments with alcohol and the polliwogs? Answer: If we drink alcohol we will never have stomach worms. He got credit for the answer. We got a laugh.

John Palmquist, the other resident missionary, had a separate group of students that only he taught. They had a bulldozer and were a mechanical group learning the use and upkeep of the machine. Likewise, the management of the farm was exclusively under his direction, under a foreman of his selection. Other personnel confined their gardening to their housing lot, inside the wall.

Once he left on vacation and put his colleague -- me, in charge, but left no money to pay wages of workers or foreman. The stored potatoes were starting to go soft so we sold them to local farmers who were short of potatoes to freeze for chunyo, (the dehydrated potatoes used for safe storage). We also sold eucalyptus branches about to break from the weight of the heavy rains on the growth. We sold them to fishermen who had an abundant catch but not sufficient firewood to dry the fish for their preservation. They used an open chimney of stone with the fire beneath and smoke traveling between the rocks to cure the catch, placed on the stepped rocks to dry. I was able to pay the workers and still deliver a large sum to the returned missionary. The largest profit the farm ever earned in a month.

I had a private garden behind our yard walls and tried several different crops like rhubarb, kohlrabi, and southern giant mustard.   Rhubarb interested them and they grew it successfully but the first year they harvested by pulling the plant up by the roots like they do most of their harvests. The giant mustard went to seed but the wind pollinated the local tiny wild mustard and it was twice the usual size the next year. I understand the imported plants had changed the local genetic situation forever. We had completely modified the local flora and unknowingly produced an improved mustard plant that they traditionally used for fodder.

Discipline in our school followed modified traditional lines. Modern redemptive - oriented punishment was mixed with traditional methods or instruments. Application: teachers never whipped or insulted the students. We did deprive them of privileges or play time. Parents were informed of grades and deportment. The parents felt free to scold or punish. The boys (they were all boys) heard and usually responded in improved class behavior. Toward the end of the year we found things were disappearing; largely personal items from the dormitory boys. The national teacher called the boys together. He went through the foot locker and bags of personal possessions and the stolen goods were discovered.

The parents were informed and the father came with a three meter long whip. He was going to punish him publicly in the traditional way. The school boys formed a half circle behind the school and watched with baited breath while the culprit, a large chesty boy with a round face, stood hang-dog in the center and the father stood beside the teachers.

The man held out the whip to the teachers, but both refused to take it. The father then ordered the boy to kneel before them and to apologize. He did so in a few words. The father unwound the whip and caught the boy on the arm and back. There was no force in the blow, but the whimpering boy rose and tried to leave. He was sternly ordered back by the father. As he knelt the father caught him a harder blow on arm and back. The boy started crying as did some of the other students. One light blow more brought father and son to bow before the teachers who raised them up. Each embraced the others and forgiveness was given by each to all. The students breathed a collective sigh of relief, the ordeal was over.

The year ended within the month and the graduates

divided: some were old enough to pass directly to the Teachers' College in near-by Achicachi. Younger boys would want another year. Some transferred to John's mechanical course. The punished boy worked their farm and married. One enterprising boy used the geometry he learned to calculate the number of square meters in their property. He also drew property maps. His fame grew and he measured other men's land for a price. Still others were apprenticed. New boys filled their places, but a politician named Flores from the lake district (who had been trained in the mission schools) prevailed on the education ministry of the government to start a High School in his home town. It was only five kilometers from Guatajata, so we went over for the visit of the President of the Republic when he came to inaugurate the site, by laying the corner stone for the new school.

Mary Haddow, the resident nurse, took her one-ton truck to pick up the President at the lake side and bring him to the ceremony. She arrived at Huarina where the road split toward Copacabana and the farm on one side, Achicachi, where the syndicate (farmers' union) centered its power was on the other. There was an armed barricade at the divide. A convoy of syndicate members blocked the cross road. They stopped the Presidential convoy lead by Mary driving President Paz Estensoro.

"We have a feast prepared and have come to escort our President to our reception," they announced. Mary stopped with a dozen rifles aimed at her windshield. The President was seated on a plank across the open back of her pickup. With dignity he said to them, "I am on my way to dedicate a high school for the lake district. All true followers of the revolution understand this need for education. I will return to your celebration when I complete my duties." Then he leaned forward, rapped sharply on the roof of the cab, and added in a strong voice,"Drive on". She eased forward, and the gunmen scattered. Mary drove through the army of rifles to the village where we waited with all the graduates from the Bible High School. They were to form the nucleus of the new school.

My duties as Treasurer of the Bolivian Baptist Union had completed its year. The convention was at Guatajata. We were in trouble. We worked late the night before, but the books did not balance. Constantino, my assistant, kept repeating the little jingle, "In life, we suffer to learn. So what do we learn? to suffer," while we worked through the years data to find the errors and balance the books.

We were out about $100 and the convention was unusually cheap that year. We knew where the money had gone but didn't have receipts to prove it. The books had gone out of balance during the purchases for the March convention. The convention had to name a commission to examine the books. Miss Holmes did the revision. I paid off the debt at $10 a month till I left for furlough in ten months.

Leaving, we left our furniture and goods in the attic of the 'Igloo,' where we lived. It had lots of attic to hold our goods.

We also left Glover, our large, tan, short-haired dog the guardian of the house for the next occupants. One evening when I was away, Hazel and Maria Luisa were working at the kitchen table. They had been visited by a fisherman earlier, and had bought some of his catch. At sundown they secured the door at the back and the gate at the front for the night. Maria had told Hazel that the man's wife had drowned when she had gone to help him with the fish; rumor had it that he had pushed her. So she was a little scared of him. When there was a knocking at the window, both of them immediately thought of him and wondered how he could have gotten over the wall. Hazel slid along the kitchen wall, so she could peep out and see. It was only Glover! It was a season for big white moths, and Glover had one front paw up on the window sill, while batting at the moth with the other! In that position, he was tall as a man, and really had them both scared. He could run up a steep hill and chase the trespassing sheep from our property. He was feared by careless neighbors who always felt that the property should have reverted to them in the land reform.

The mission ended some years later by giving most of the total Guatajata property to the whole community instead of greedy individuals. The navy occupied a house. The Church through the Bolivian Baptist Union got a building for the hospital. The schools got the school buildings and play grounds. That high school we saw moved while we were there moved back to Guatajata and the new buildings were on mission donated property. Finally the village square, market and municipal buildings were built on donated property.

The will of Antonio Chiriotto stipulated that the ministry include Health care, Educational, Agricultural, and Spiritual dimensions. This was accomplished when a rural community was transformed by the acceptance of Evangelical Christianity, dignity and modernity. His prayer, purchase and patience were rewarded amply. We are promised in the Gospels that what we sow will bring a harvest.

He who sows abundantly shall also reap abundantly

2 Corinthians 9:6

Guatajata schools watch gymnastic displays by seniors

The sixth of August is Independence day, the general public celebrate; usually with a parade, dance and alcohol. In contrast, at the farm and rural school center of Guatajata, the 22 schools parade down the main street and highway, sober and happy. Trucks loaded with people line the road. Some passengers wait to go to other centers of celebration and others climb down to get to the seats near the school grounds where the main performance will take place. The band stand and buildings are decorated with flags and pennants flashing their bright reds, yellows and greens. The children in their white uniforms are marched by grade and schools, into the grassy assembly grounds. The Band enters the band stand and continues to play while the children take their places around the perimeter of the soccer field.

We watched the first six grades do their exercises. They danced in circles, some with flags, others with colored handkerchiefs waving in the breeze. They crisscrossed, traded partners, moved into squares, then circles. Each class had a different pattern: of music, marching order and hand gestures. A kaleidoscope of motions and colors consisted of girls who would normally be illiterate, watching sheep on the hillsides where you now see the old people on duty. School boys whose grandfathers were serfs perform. Serfdom was part of the heritage of the Spanish conquest five hundred years before. Now they are freemen. Proud parents stand by and watch their broods go through their paces.

The farm equipment group with John Palmquist put on a beautiful display with the bulldozer-tractor. They were learning, aside from regular farm duties, to control the dry rivers that flood and cause damage during the rains. The Bible High School boys (no mere girls had reached the heights of seventh and eight grades at that time) preformed gymnastics in pairs and groups. Doing flips, cartwheels, shoulder stands, group pyramids of three or six with tumbling descents: these students showed that physical prowess accompanied mental training. Judges made awards at the conclusion.

After the displays came speeches, acknowledgements, and recognitions. Dignitaries sincerely lauded liberty and the universal vote. They complained about the loss of Bolivia's seaports a hundred years before, and pointed out the need to negotiate an outlet to the sea, as their most important international issue. Chile holds Antofagasta at the southern end of the rail line. Arica at the north end of that republic was once Peruvian territory. Years later, Chile offered to surrender that border part to Bolivia, but Peru forbade it. The people know when to cheer and the argument is decades old. One port would change everything, they maintain. Would it?

Food comes after all the excitement and requires concentration. There is a yard wide cloth in five yard strips placed end to end, whose center is covered with small potatoes, *paplisa (pink polka dotted potatoes)*, *oka* (a local root crop), broad beans, corn and cookies made with quinoa (a local grain). All are steam-cooked in their skins. Bowls of *llah'wha*, a sauce made of tomato, onion, garlic, hot red and green peppers ground and mixed in oil, were strategically placed along the strips for dipping.. Some finger-length, dried, whole fish were scattered among the goodies. (I, Hazel, never cared for them. I just couldn't look those wee fish in their lifeless, gaping eyes.) The ladies filled soup plates for their husbands, and guests first, and then sat apart while each person served himself from the 'finger food' on the cloths. Private dishes were unwrapped, shared with the visitors, and eaten along with the other offerings. Everyone ate until everything was gone or until the leftovers are taken home by the feasters. Independence Day has been celebrated and each proud family herds its children onto a truck headed for their particular village, hurrying to arrive before sunset and dark. Fear still rules the dark, but headlights, electricity, and lanterns are replacing the oil lamps. Light pushes out the blackness, just as the knowledge of God identifies and pushes out evil.

Since the time of Dr. Merrick's land reforms the situation of the rural Indian serfs has changed radically. Government is no longer the exclusive domain of Creole and mixed people. Getting a government job depends now on training, ability, demonstrated performance as well as pull and connections. The rural Indian, that makes up almost half the population, now has the opportunity of influence by voice and vote in the affairs of the nation that has grown up out of its native soil. The Sixth of August, Independence Day, has real meaning for everyone now.

Whatever a man sows that is what he will reap.

Galatians 6:7

Bolivian farmers still use oxen in many rural areas.

The school year was coming to an end and we would be going home. We were due to move into the city of La Paz at the end of the month to prepare to leave Bolivia the 21st of September. Since Hazel was expecting our third child on November 21st this was the last date we could book a flight. We had made arrangements for a doctor, prenatal care and hospital stay in Beaumont, Texas. Her sister-in-law had coordinated everything so we would be staying with Hazel's brother's family. Before home assignment in Canada we would spend our allotted family time with a stop over to visit in Texas. It seemed incredible that we had finished a year of language study and four years working in Bolivia, absent from North America for five years.

Hazel was packing and sorting — what to take, what to store, what to give away, throw away or sell. Several red letter events were to take place before our departure date. First came two holidays: *Dia del Indio,* Indian Day, the first of August, and *Seis de Agosto,* Sixth of August, which is Independence Day. In all the nation there would be parades, athletic events and exhibitions. After this there would be the Bible-High School excursion, closing, church and community farewells at Guatajata. Then in the city, there would be Krysi's third birthday party, more personal and church farewells.

Marshall would be occupied with *tramites:* the legal red tape connected with passports, travel permits, visas, tickets, etc. You wouldn't believe the legal moves necessary to take a child born of foreign parentage out of the country.

The two last events that would be the finale of our rural life in Bolivia was the Bible High School graduation and a farewell by the church. It seemed rather cold to have a graduation ceremony without having some kind of excursion with the class, or better still, with the whole school. There were about thirty students. I, Marshall, suggested we go to Heapy, a tall mountain easily seen from Guatajata. Actually there were two, one peak behind the other, but they appeared as one from our lake-side view. I was told that there existed a rough truck trail that rose half-way up the mountain side. I didn't ask why. I had been often fascinated by the fact that you could probably see the peninsula, the two sides of divided Lake Titicaca, and the whole Royal Range of the Andes, from Illampu in the north to Illimani towering over La Paz city. I was frankly curious, and here was my opportunity to see it.

The excursion was set for the 17th of August. We would meet at school time and I would take the teacher and about eight boys in the Jeep. Those who lived in that direction would meet us at the top of the road. Everyone was to take his own lunch in hand. Our teacher, Remigio Gutierez, was eager to go as well. We knew that not everyone would get permission to come. Mountains are sacred among indigenous people and many are held in reverential fear. Some of the children would probably not appear for the event. We were to meet at 8:30 and we waited for the tardy ones. We set off about nine, full of enthusiasm and passengers. The kids adjusted themselves two and three deep on the seat along the back and sides. It was an open jeep; no doors or windows, just a roof. We searched for the side-road that would take us up near the top of the mountain. We found it an hour up the lake road and the ascent took another stretch of time. We left the car at a spot where the last broad glade offered an easy turn around. We turned, parked the jeep at the end of the road, took our lunches, and went on by foot. There were about fifteen of us by this time. We met a few more along the way. It took another hour to get to the top. So, we were arriving for lunch time. As we ascended we discovered that we were not alone. The sound of a drum echoed softly in the air, then rounding a rise and a turn, we found people near the top. It is hard to say who was more surprised.

Ahead of us a large egg shaped boulder rested naturally on a stone platform, but there was activity below, and it was surrounded by people. It was balanced on its small end and as tall as a truck bed. The expressions the gathered wore indicated that we were not welcome, and not a part of their group. A man dressed in rough city-style, homespun clothes approached to explain that we had our ways of worship and they had theirs, and each had a right to their choice. We were at a shrine devoted to celebrating the consecration of a *brujo*, (brew-ho) a witch doctor. I motioned the boys to go left, climbing to where there was some higher ground free of people, and sloped away from where the worshipers stood. We could be out of sight mutually, but a few steps back up the slope we could see almost everything from a third story building height above the crowd. Another man followed us to argue his case. He said that this was their manner of serving God and explained that the giant egg was the symbol of the Pacha Mama, the Earth Mother, where offerings were made. A group with incense was chanting, and burning incense to the front left of the egg where a small cone-shaped hillock gave them a first story view of the worship grounds. The place of incense offering was called, 'The Glory.'

My teacher remembered his father's stories about the annual dedication of new *brujos*. The mountain shrine used to be full of thousands of spectators and worshipers. Today there were only a few hundred largely from the other, north side, of the peninsula, where we were just beginning to preach. Only one candidate for the vocation of *brujo* (brew-hoe) was moving about near the bottom of the egg. Worshipers had declined. I told the man, who came to explain things, that God had allowed false worship during the time of ignorance, but that the false gods were usurpers. I said that God was repossessing His world, and that they would see Him victorious.

After he left, another man came who knew our teacher and explained that the people below us were angry with him because he was from Guatajata. They thought he had brought us. I said that God brought us; why would he come to a place like this? He said that he was down on his luck, and thought it wouldn't hurt to come, and see if he couldn't change it. I told him the church was closer and better. He left and Remigio expressed a desire to put a stick of dynamite on top of the rock and split it. (The force of the blast is downward.) I said that when Christ was in their hearts it would only be a big boulder again. There was no need for violence.

We decided to turn around to our spot of green grass and eat lunch, turning our backs, figuratively and literally on the worshipers. As we did so, the tempo of the drums and the volume of singing seemed to swell. We ignored it as we got out our lunches.

Suddenly the wind which had been blowing strongly the whole way, dropped, there was only a sunny calm. A horrible smell of purification came to my nose. I wondered what had died and looked around for some corpse. Our teacher was talking, we had formed a circle, and were going to pray before eating. His voice began to weaken and he forced out his last words: "Pastor, pray!" I was shocked by the aspect of my students. They were frozen in place, like rabbits ready to run, but unable to resist the hypnotic effects of the snake or weasel. This was a spiritual encounter! This is why I had been sent to be present on the date that everyone who worshiped here knew to be significant. The mountain spirit was here now. He must empower the candidates for his ministry. I would have to be his adversary in the power of Jesus, the anointed Messiah of God. Force was useless. Only spirit can confront spirit. I prayed.

I was surprised at the volume and confidence of my voice. I thanked God for our food and His protection and blessing. I prayed for the binding of the spirits of oppression, deception and evil. I prayed that all the area that we viewed would be free of the spirit of evil; that all would soon hear the liberating message of salvation in the name of Jesus, as the gospel was proclaimed. Everything had gone quiet about us; no voices, drums, or chanting. I had bound the spirit and finished our prayer. I walked about seeking the source of the earlier smell (just in case I was wrong) as the boys, now relaxed, started to talk, and began eating. I heard a dull rumble and going to the overlook found it empty and I saw the last of a running crowd.

A man cast a look of terror over his shoulder. What could have been their experience? I glimpsed his terror from our hill. The breeze had come up again strong and fresh. Several of our boys shouted and there on the other mountain peak which rose about two hundred meters higher than ours, we saw four boys almost at our level. They were Bible School boys. They had climbed the wrong Heapy and were on the other longer horn of the two peaks. They waved and signaled us happily. A deep valley between the two peaks would prevent their joining us. One set a fire in the *ichu* grass that lay like small haystacks up the slope. Enthused the others did too. One match set fire to a handful of grass and they passed the flame from one boy to the other until a ring of fire spread around the peak . The fire swept upward, the whole peak caught fire in a matter of minutes. Heavy black smoke boiled up from the mountain. It looked like a volcano. The breeze was strong in our faces as we watched, but the smoke seemed unaffected and went straight up in a thick well-defined column a thousand meters up. Suddenly, after rising several thousand feet up it disappeared in a slight slurring like an upside-down comma and the smoke was erased, gone without further trace. As the fuel of grass was consumed the bottom of the column gradually faded out. The boys had retreated down the mountain lest the fire follow them. It didn't, the line between the burned and untouched remained clear. The fire had gone up; created a sign or signal visible for a hundred miles, then out. The cloud dissipated as we finished our lunches and descended to tour the vacant shrine. Under the egg-like rock we found a tunnel-like area where candles were in evidence, melted and hardened wax was spread all over the rock base. A small sacrifice – a guinea pig – lay with its throat cut. Flowers were spilled about. For a moment I caught the echo of the scent that I had smelled on the hill when the wind stopped, the odor of death and decay. We had seen enough and I pray that the rock has become that which it is – stone material, not an object of veneration. There were the contents of medicine bundles scattered about with broken bowls, all part of spirit healing in Aymara culture.

The school boys acted like they wanted to get away, and ran ahead down the slope. It was the opposite direction from that which the worshipers had taken, so I did not discourage them. I walked with the teacher until he decided that the boys might act unruly or fight for the best seats in the jeep and rushed ahead to get them in order. I had worn loafers for the excursion; not very ideal for mountain climbing. The slopes were steep but not vertical. However, the heel strap rubbed my right foot and made a hole in my sock. I stopped to adjust it several times; it was making a bruise. Everyone was out of sight.

Just above the parking place, I increased speed and running down a slope I saw a curious rock like a ball; it had holes as if composed of lava or bone. I noticed it rolling like a hand-bowling ball from the left, toward where I would intercept it in two long steps. I felt spry and thought I should like to kick it like a little beach ball ahead down the trail. At that moment I felt another thought warning me. "NO, JUMP!" I did, just clearing the ball. Pain shot from my heel to my head. I stopped to examine my heel. There was a clean, deep hole that seemed to reach to the bone at the back top of the heel. It was the width of a two inch lumber nail, and throbbed but did not bleed from the hole. The pain in head and heel did not stop. I looked around, but could not discover where the stone had gone. Nothing around me moved and there were no porous rocks to be seen. Farther down the slope nothing moved. I started walking again, but every step hurt. I felt warm; like I had fever. The pain began to spread, heel and knee, then my hip. I limped to the jeep. Every one was unusually quiet. They were all seated ready to go, but I could not lift my right leg to get into the driver's seat. I turned my back to the jeep front seat and slid my bottom onto the seat, using my left leg to push. I pivoted, and used my left again to push me into position holding my throbbing right leg up with my hands. I suppressed all expression and sound. No one spoke. I prayed not to faint.

With key in place I tried my happy voice. "Everyone ready to go home?" Their voices reflected relief; they were ready. I wonder how they interpreted those minutes before I got to the car. I had to use the hand-choke as throttle to accelerate the motor; my foot would not function. I tried to use my left foot to control the accelerator pedal. I pulled my right leg back and crossed my left over to the accelerator. I didn't have to use the hand-choke now. I felt faint a few times, but we were going slowly down the mountain; there were no overhangs or spots of great danger. My teacher did not know how to drive; I had to manage. We made the road and at each stop for our students, a few would leave. I forged normality. Tried to look what I should have been: tired, but happy. I went past our house, (the igloo,) and drove the teacher and last students home. I wanted no witnesses when I got out of the jeep. Victory must mean silence.

I returned to our house and drove up the slope to the front gate. It was not my practice to leave the farm manager's car out of the garage, but this was an emergency. Hazel could put it away for me later. I used my hands to move my right leg as I swiveled in the seat to get out the left hand driver's side. It ached with pain and fever. I took the weight on my left foot and clinging to the jeep worked my way around to the gate. The long hobble up our front walk was a Calvary. When I opened the door, I called for Hazel who was with the kids. "Get me hot water in a basin with Epsom salts in it, please." Her response was "What in the world?" Collapsed in the armchair, I was peeling off my sock, and looking at the red hole. The leg was stiff and felt like a fire had been planted in it; the wound was now puffy, red and purple, but not bleeding, I could feel the poison in leg and head. I explained the trip to Hazel, while my foot soaked.

"I have a week to get my walk back to normal or they will say the mountain spirit lamed me for trespassing." I said, as she looked at the wound and shuddered. We treated the wound for a week: soaking it and applying heat, liniments, ointments and sulfa. The hole closed and seemed to heal from the bottom. The band-aids showed no pus or blood. In three days I could limp at a good pace with pain. By the farewell school picnic, I could walk without a limp or grimace, but I still felt it. During the furlough I still favored that foot. I told the complete story once in a church in Saint John. The reaction was such that I never told it in all its detail again in church. Even leaving out the part about the wound the story seemed incredible. The most notable remark, the first night I told it was: "Things sure must be different there." They are.

The general population of Bolivia used witchcraft for many purposes: healing sickness; finding lost or stolen articles; telling the future; obtaining fertility; deciding the sex of future offspring; compelling love or business success. Its uses and power are constantly sought and paid for by the fearful and needy. It continues today all over the world.

After our first furlough home we returned to pick up our furniture left in the attic of the Igloo. It was November and we had my new daughter Karlene's first birthday on the grounds of the Igloo with friends present. I really wanted to make one more trip to Heapy to see if it was still in use. However, it had sleeted some days before and the mountain, even from a distance, glittered with the ice coating its slopes. It would have been difficult to get up the road, much less hike to the top. I concluded God didn't want me to go up again. One trip would have to be sufficient and it was. I never climbed it again. The work was finished. Local people, when asked, said there was no dedication of witch doctors from that place any more. Their 'sacred' egg had become a rock again.

The most evident lesson is that there are still people held in bondage by fear, superstition, and spiritual oppression. Spiritual warfare continues around the world. Prayer is part of that warfare and will be until His kingdom comes. That kingdom was started by sacrificial death; that of Jesus on the cross. It will end in time with sacrifices of His people under Antichrist. It is a blood-bought and a blood-built kingdom. Sacrifice is a constant and necessary part of the building. Our Yeshua /Yesu /Isa /Joshua /Jesus, is a good master, whatever the name, because all spiritual sacrifices for Him, of whatever kind, will be rewarded fully in this life and the next.

Look, I give you power to tread on serpents and scorpions and trample all the power of the enemy and nothing shall harm you. Luke 10:19

High mountains are often a place of spirit worship

Krystal and Maria Luisa in new aprons at Guatajata

Oruro was the historic Baptist starting point in Bolivia. We got a double dose going there early enough to start some of the work outside the mines, which were the oldest goals of evangelization. We then came back in time to see the yield in all of the areas: in the wild, dry, western Carangas, high tropical Yungas valleys, and on the short grass and thorn of high prairies.

The first time we came, the house was newly finished by Hazen & Hazel Parent and our children were small. We started Borden in kindergarten. I, Marshall, spent time after each excursion into the rural areas in our front garden. It filled up with Sweet peas, alyssum and nasturtiums clustered around two fruit trees: one on either side of the sidewalk. We tried to tame the wild tani-tani from the mountain passes and adorn our little front flower show with local plants.

The Communists had made the mines a hard area of penetration and the earlier work was consolidated under local pressure to ignore all religions. Unions were dominant and hostile to outsiders as well, yet the majority of our ministerial candidates were boys and girls from the mines and their hearty little churches. Our ministers came from there, but not our growth. The city suburbs were filling with families departing the mines and rural farms. They supplied our city growth.

There were three churches around the central Church of the Risen Lord: in the North -- Oruro Moderno, in the South -- Villa Esperanza and in the East, Norman Dabbs (the martyr.) Each was quite a distance from the center. All these churches had a number of mission points with deacons named to visit, care for and preach to them.

When I was in the city, I attended Oruro Moderno with the family. It was the nearest to our home on Velasco Galvarro Street. When I was there we could go in the car, and when I was away, they could walk. Hazel worked in the Sunday School, Vacation Bible School, attended the Monday afternoon ladies meeting, and took part in all the activities.

I was visiting the mines east of Oruro, the lowlands of Inquisivi past the mountain range, and the Carangas area in the west, and directing courses at the Bible Institute. I felt that we needed a man who could speak Aymara to serve the 33 congregations of Carangas. I would still be attending the juntas, occasional baptisms, and evangelistic campaigns. So the missions committee assigned a man to the area to try to visit each of the congregations once a month. They chose Toribio Tarque. He would go to the little village where a market was held, and since the people would come to buy, maybe he would see the deacons from more than one place. Then they would arrange for a visit to those areas. Over the years supporting Canadian Baptist Churches would send the big pictures that used to accompany the Sunday School lessons for use in Bolivia. The tiny congregations would send their deacons to these markets (they called them 'fairs') where there, in open air meetings, they would tell the Bible stories. The crowds would gather, and listen to the story, and be invited to the local church. Most of those deacons had found Jesus that way, and they reached out to bring others to Him. For long trips he would take a truck, and then go between the villages on his bicycle.

The salt water table was only a meter and a half below our patio. The water was not fit to drink, but served to flush the toilets when city water was rationed. Building the house with salt-water adobes, was a bad idea. The outside of the house was OK, but soon the walls of the inside of the house were pocked with what looked like barnacles. Arrangements were made to repaint the walls. We did the living room and kitchen, then were interrupted by the November Vacation Bible Schools, the December missionary conference, and Christmas programs. By the time we decided that we could get started again, we noticed that our newly painted rooms, were already starting to pop out with barnacles again! We never resumed the painting job. There was a resolution by the housing committee, that other measures be undertaken to provide ventilation under the house, and those renovations took the rest of our time there.

The house was built by the Parents with a legacy left specifically for building a mission house in Oruro. They lived there first, but passed it on to us when they went for their first furlough. When we left there to move to Potosi, the Frasers moved in after us. It was a one-story modern, adobe house that looked like clapboard with a red tile roof. Upon entering the gate, the imposing sand-stone fireplace immediately caught your eye. You walked straight up the sidewalk to the office door, passing the fireplace first, the living room door, and then the kitchen door. The office was independent so as to receive the visitors without being disturbed by, nor disturbing family life.

If the visitor was coming to see the family, they were ushered directly into the living/dining room by the person who answered the outside door in the 3 meters high wall that surrounded the property.

The living/dining room was only for guests and meetings. Many of the Bolivian Baptist Union's committees met there, since Oruro was situated more or less in the geographical center of Canadian Baptist work. Also, many missionary colleagues, drove from La Paz and stopped overnight before the longer lap down to Cochabamba, or the harder drive up to visit the mine churches.

If you entered by the kitchen door, you found a roomy, well appointed kitchen with lots of cabinet space. The electric stove was nice and modern, but I, Hazel, had to install a new coil in the oven while we were there. Crossing the kitchen, you entered a 'breakfast nook' that reminded one of a train dining car. The long table seated one at each end and 5 along one side; while the other side nestled up under the big picture window. The picture you saw from the window was not very pleasant, however, until we took some measures to beautify it.

At the opposite end of the breakfast nook, a door on the left opened upon the patio. The well, about 10 ft. from the door, was choked with left-over building supplies; everyone was concerned that one of the children would fall into it. It was not a good place for the children to play. Water stood in the yard until we cleaned out the well, lined the inside of it with rocks, laid a cement patio that skirted the well superstructure, and reached to the side door into the breakfast nook. We put a pretty, tile-like pattern on it, and hoped to put out a picnic table for pretty, sunny days. We also put up a bamboo gazebo like structure nearby, but it never got quite warm enough for picnics. When it was sunny and warm enough, the wind blew in the sand, fleas and mosquitoes. The children did enjoy playing there, though.

On the right, from the breakfast nook, the door opened onto the central hall mentioned above. There, a kerosene-burning space heater supplied heat for the whole house.

Once inside the hall, you could look back and see next to the breakfast nook door, another that lead to the large bath. It had all the modern fixtures in gleaming white porcelain: basin, flush toilet, *bidet*, and tile-enclosed bathtub. But since the big water heater sitting in an alcove of the kitchen did not heat, we had to find another way to enjoy a hot bath.

In Bolivia, we had already used a *'rayo flotante'* while living in La Paz. It is an encyclopedia-sized metal box with a heating coil inside. Well-insulated big wires lead to a switchbox fixed onto the wall. It looked like the main switchbox in the house where I grew up. Woe to the person who put in a finger to test the temperature without pulling down the handle! It delivered a 220 volt shock. You cover the apparatus with water, push up the switch, and in 20 minutes: behold! Hot water! The commode was flanked by two frosty glass windows in the outside wall which made it seem bright and pleasant.

If you crossed the hall, you found Borden's bedroom. Since it also served as the guest room, he slept in a big double bed. In one corner, there was a 45" beam Le Clerc loom, complete with a chest, to hold its supplies, instruction books and spare parts. Of course, when there were guests, sleeping arrangements had to be reconsidered. Depending on the number of guests, the sofa bed in the living room, or a pallet on the floor of the girls room was called into play.

Behind the space heater, the hall narrowed. The two doors on the right were for linen-closet and the girls' bedroom. The two doors on the left led to a small room where Hazen Parent had set up a dark room to develop photographs and our bedroom. We ate in the nook that had enough room to seat seven.

Oruro was the seat of a Bible Institute that was designed for short courses. Courses for deacons, youth and women, plus studies we carried out to the rural areas in the form of *juntas* (hun' tas), gatherings. These *juntas* occurred in the off seasons when rural people had time: mid-winter in June - July; the short dry season in January. The winter season was long and gatherings were held in spite of the cold. Between two rainy seasons there was a short dry spell that could last a week, two weeks and even four weeks. This was a time of high risks in both Carangas, (the wild west) and in the mountains. The mine roads were open all year, but opposition from communist-inspired activists was increasing. Fortunately, most could have a paid minister in charge.

Opposition in the wider rural farming and grazing areas was frequently violent. Believers were attacked, shunned or pressured, but never ignored. Local authorities cooperated with local sentiment to work against evangelicals. This led to fines and imprisonment in spite of legal guarantees. Fiesta-centered drunkenness was rampant everywhere. Tradition, ignorance and hopelessness was the accepted way of life, 'que sera, sera', what will be will be; all exceptions were unacceptable. That God would have something better for them never entered their minds, unaided.

Jesus said: *Come... Learn of me.* Matthew 28:11

Oruro Bible Institute youth at play.

51

Billowing clouds of choking red dust hung over the washboard road as the Volkswagen `Combi' bounced along at 50 mph. The flat pampa of the Bolivian altiplano was vaguely seen through the rising heat waves and dust of November, the hottest month of the year. From the dust ahead the bass horn of a huge diesel truck blasted as its giant hulk burst out of the haze down the middle of the dirt road. The Combi skittered toward the edge of the road, poised momentarily on the rim of the ditch and squeezed around the thundering monster, and swept into the pluming dust of it's wake.

"I hope there's no one tailgating him." Marshall decelerated and peered ahead into the cloud where sand and diesel smoke mingled. As the speed dropped, the tooth jarring bumps increased in violence and the springs squealed their protest till once again the acceleration brought the vehicle up to an even speed. It feels like you're driving on banana skins, when you have reached the velocity necessary to keep the Combi hitting the high spots of the washboard without touching the bottoms. You are in the constant danger of pitching over the edge of the road into a high-banked dry wash from the wind-created sand-drifts or piles of loose gravel, which take away your control over the steering wheel.

There is, no doubt, road equipment ahead but the road is long and there is constant traffic. It is joked that you can always get a half-decent ride going to the mines, because they are always working one half, while the other half goes to pieces. It's easy to tell which part you're on.

A large panel truck aggressively pulled up parallel, tooted vigorously and passed; leaving the slower Combi in the midst of a swirling dust storm where visibility is zero. Marshall growled and cut the speed down till the road bed appeared again and speed resumed. The trick is to look down for the edge of the ditch filled with rocks and sand at the edge of the road. On a Combi it's easier, since it has no nose to stick out in front (the motor is in the rear). By keeping parallel you can stay on your side and get up your speed again quickly.

"Just a little longer and we'll be on the graded and watered half, then we'll put down the window," he promised her.

Marshall's perspiring face was stuck with fine grit and the unventilated vehicle simmered in the heat.

Hazel nodded grimly, feeling slightly sick of the sliding motion of the back wheels with the pounding of the springs against the rough road and the yaw right and left in the effort to avoid the deeper ruts and pits in the road. She was very much aware of the grit on her teeth and lips and the hot dust in her nose and she felt a wave of home-sickness come and go. The words, "Whoever loves houses or lands more than me is not worthy of me," passed her mind, leaving peace in it's place. Then a wave of house sickness followed, the nice home she had made in that dusty desert town. It, too, passed, then came another feeling, motion sickness, it stayed.

"Pull over and stop!" Hazel urged her husband in a shaking voice, hands covering her mouth. Marshall obeyed quickly in a wide spot and she stepped out and bending double lost everything from breakfast. Marshall opened the water canteen and wet down his handkerchief which he passed to her. He looked embarrassed, not knowing what to say.

When her choking ceased, she washed out her mouth and cleaned her face, hands and some spots on her dress. She could feel the dust already adhering to the damp hands and cloth. A car roared by leaving it's plume in their faces. She shuddered and climbed back into the hot stuffiness of the car, out of the dry dusty mountain air.

`You really didn't have to come', her cranky inner voice told her. She nodded and thought back, "The Women's Crusade is meeting this weekend and I'm the counselor in the North Church, and the ladies here go by bus." It came out smoothly, she had already used it on her husband.

"Yes, I know." He looked at her worriedly, then returned to the road. She started and realized she had spoken her thoughts. `Marshall's a lamb', and always accepts her wishes although she knew he had worried about this trip. He solemnly told her "I've left this with the Lord now and we won't say more about it." There was acceptance and tranquility after that. She squeezed his arm appreciatively and he threw her a fleeting smile, she released his arm, knowing he didn't like distractions when driving. The Volkswagen made another lurching leap and then was on smooth road.

"Roll down the windows, it's been sprinkled." Marshall sighed with relief. The dust in the car stirred into a frenzy of movement and then settled or was blown out. The dry air felt cool compared to the previous stuffiness. They would soon be in Catavi (cah-tah-vee)or the traffic control building could be seen on the horizon, the heavy lift bar firmly across the road. Marshall reached for the official travel permit and stopped before the gate. Several loiterers and transport officials in slovenly uniforms nodded at the tall red faced missionary.

"Buenos dias," Marshall greeted them courteously and inside the one room building he repeated his greeting and handed his transit paper to the official seated behind the rickety table. The large ledger was open and the name, license, model and time were added to their corresponding places and the policeman carefully detached a bit of paper from a ticket stub which said, `pro-taxi'sta,' for the upkeep of the Transport Union's social program.

"Will there be more of these on the way?" It was a peso and a half, but Marshall knew the ways of the people. The officer smiled pleasantly at the 'Gringo' and scratched his stubble. In answer he brought out the stapler from a littered drawer and secured the receipt to the paper.

"Not if you keep the receipt with the permit." He tapped the two with his finger to make the point.

"*Gracias*," the missionary thanked the man,"would you like something to read to help pass the time?"

"*¿Como no*? Why not?" assented the smiling officer and the tall man reached into his shirt pocket and left a small pamphlet in the man's hand. Two other men came forward to request some of the free material.

"¡*Que le vaya bien*!" the official said. "A Dios," Marshall responded and moved out with his stamped paper. "Go well," another said as he regained the car and nodded as one of the uniformed men pulled the counter weight so that the barrier arm lifted up before the car and they moved forward. It dropped with a clang behind them.

"I always wonder if I'm supplying something for their minds and spirits or their toilet supplies." He sighed sadly to his wife.

"Perhaps both," she answered kindly. He grinned and shook his head; she often had a way of lightening his fits of cynicism.

The road abruptly disintegrated as they entered the town of Catavi. Here pot-holes and pools of dark liquid muck alternated with ruts and mounds of trash and manure at some of the ally corners. There were several potential parks where small tufts of poppies, calendula and other plants struggled for life. The poplar and willow trees were almost one story high where sheltered from the icy winds of the 12,000 foot high altiplano in the Andes range. The stray branches that had grown too high during a summer stuck up stark and bare above the green of the growing branches lower down where the houses provided the wind break against the dry winds. A few women in bowler hats, shawls and bell shaped wool skirts and petticoats walked stolidly by. Their dark chocolate brown faces averted from the wind-borne dust.

The Baptist church with its little peaked facade was closed and the pastor and wife probably gone to the Women's Crusade in Llallagua (Lya yag'wa) by bus. The road climbed through the village to the company hospital where it rose to the high banks of the river and then plunged into the fetid pools and garbage strewn gravel banks of the mountain stream. The river was only a few inches deep and in several separate currents and the ruts of trucks and cars showed clearly on the bed of the stream.

"Someday they'll have to put a road over the mountain behind the city.," Marshall observed out loud.

"I hope I live to see it," Hazel quipped wryly. A large mine truck took the broad rut, forcing the Volkswagen to pioneer another poorer rut to the side of the stream.

"I hope we make Llallagua!" was his laughing rejoinder as we climbed up the opposite bank.

We stopped at the height of land on the watershed. The stream from the right flowed to Huanuni and the salt flats south of Oruro to dry and leave their ever increasing salt deposits, marked in seasonal layers. To the left, below another zigzag hairpin road, lay another stream going to join the *Grande* River to the *Mamoré*, to the *Madeira*, which would ultimately end in the Amazon River and Atlantic Ocean.

Here, parked on the heights, about 15,000 feet, the breeze was cool at midday and the lukewarm Kool-Aid was refreshing with the little vanilla cookies. Hazel ate her fill. Marshall saved the remains for the trip back, he would eat his fill at the church.

"Almost there," Marshall said economizing, as always, with his words. Hazel glanced at her watch and asked, "Another hour to go still?"

Marshall nodded, then stood with eyes and hands lifted as if in brief supplication and lowered them to pray. It seemed an old gesture, a blessing of the land, a thanks for sky and earth. The browns of rock and soil were continued in the dry bunches of needle grass clumped out on the mountain tops and bits of dark green scrub below by the water courses. Red and yellow layers of rock were exposed on the mountain sides. A distant flock of grazing llamas were off on one hill or another, small like toys. On a high mountain trail an Indian herder moved his loaded group of animals, taking them to a market. Below near the road a tiny child guarded a flock of scrawny sheep and begged bread from passing vehicles. The dark blue sky was scarcely broken by white clouds. The solitude and quiet were overpowering. The only sound was the wind, and its motion across the sage-covered hill could be observed. God breathed a blessing on their hearts.

"It will be cold when we arrive," Hazel observed, moving first to the welcome shelter of the car. Marshall followed reluctantly. Winding mountain roads awaited them.

The shadows were longer and the evening wind was bone chilling when they reached the traffic control at the edge of town. The mine guards, stationed there to see that no minerals were smuggled out of the town, and the transit policeman were having a card game and beers; so they accepted the permit and placed it under a heavy rock of tin ore.

"Get it on your way out," they said with scant courtesy.

"But I'll be going out to the country tomorrow, towards Rio Verde," Marshall objected.

"That's okay, you won't need it there," he growled. Marshall shrugged and left, closing the door firmly on the warmth and smells. Hazel was snuggled down in sweater and coat, hugging herself and wishing the car had a heater, when Marshall got back to the microbus.

"What's wrong?" she exclaimed, seeing his frown.

"They're drinking and didn't register me; just made me leave the permit," he grumbled.

"You'll have to buy a new one for the return, anyway." She tried to look amused.

"They'll probably sell me the one I brought at five times the price because they'll say they're out of forms and need the money. The last time I came here they charged ten Pesos Bolivianos." It was a sore point with him, even with inflation reducing the value of the money. Marshall valued routine.

"God provides," she said, but he started the Combi with a roar and was in gear climbing the cobblestone street between the warren of adobe brick houses, where few had the benefit of a sidewalk and two vehicles could scarcely pass. Small groups of miners with helmet and lamp passed forming single file to avoid the vehicle. Larger groups of Indians in local country costumes ran ahead to the corners or bolted across the street unexpectedly ahead of the car. If a truck or car met the `cracker box' (as the bus was affectionately called), lengthy maneuvers or backing around corners was required .

The main plaza was more roomy with a bandstand and small garden across from the moderate sized Catholic church. The priests' car was parked by the residence. They were Canadians from Quebec and had been assigned to the areas where the Baptists worked. They had reasons to meet us occasionally, but only once had the conversation been in English, with a man from Ontario with a French surname. Normally, we spoke in Spanish, the language of the host nation. The mines were heavily Communist, both churches might have moderate sized congregations, but the fact of political preference to party members weighed heavily in the eyes of many authorities and citizens of the town.

"We need to visit the Padres this week, there is a problem about the village chapel near Rio Verde." She nodded her understanding. Chapel grounds belonged to a community, but to convert a church building seemed bad policy, though in some cases the community demanded it. Marshall preferred for them to build the Protestant church on new ground. They turned a corner to a long lane.

Occasionally groups of drunks swayed down the rough cobbles to another one of the many *chicherias*, where white flags nailed above the door announced surrender to the lure and oblivion of alcohol. Some would stare as if stupefied or be hustled by a companion or wife to one side of the road, several times it was necessary to stop and wait. Marshall sighed in frustration and Hazel shivered.

"I always know the street the church is on by the parade of flags and people," Marshall wryly quipped to Hazel. It was one of the standard jokes that when the church converted one of the bars into a meeting house, the other neighbors were so angry that theirs was not bought, that they all opened bars to drown out the sound of Christians singing. The church, however, bought a loudspeaker at the earliest opportunity and things were even. The chimes announced the meeting.

They pulled into the wide space before the church building and parked with the two right wheels upon the sidewalk so the mine trucks could still descend the one-way street. Soon a crowd of church people and visitors for the convention closed round the vehicle, swept Hazel away and energetically helped Marshall to unload the microbus.

Bibles and literature were put on display in the vestibule; many were immediately sold, especially the hymnbooks, for each must have his own, even if the owner was illiterate. Many learned to read with the hymns they loved as teacher. When this need of books was satisfied, they went to the annex.

Friendly warm talk and refreshment: hot cinnamon tea with crusty, buttered bread. There was the smell of food cooking in the kitchen for the meal after service. No one took off their coats and some of the men kept on their form-fitting knitted wool caps, complete with ear flaps tied up above the head. Women worked in their shawls in the unheated rooms.

The people on the benches in the church annex were sitting facing each other, and within the central circle of benches, clusters of people sat or stood and the talk was loud and hearty. No one in their right mind would have called them outcasts or persecuted heretics, yet that is exactly how they were regarded in the Bolivian society. They wore the same clothes, possessed the complexions, facial and body structures of those they passed on the street, but they were discernibly different, especially when together. A spirit of mutual love and family feeling prevailed. These people had high standards and values in common: they were alike, but very different from the general run of the public. They were called Evangelicals with various mixtures of contempt or admiration by the others.

"Thank God for His lovely people," Marshall said to Hazel, who was looking warm and rosy faced, clutching her hot enameled tin cup under her chin, between her hands for warmth. The buttered bread lay in a plate of similar material on her lap. Someone had brought her a special offering of jam to eat with it. Women came and sat beside her solicitously and then dashed off to attend to some duty while others came up for a few words and then drifted off to speak to another. She smiled wearily.

"It makes the long hard hours seem worthwhile and even well spent, just to be here and enjoy their company."

It was the beginning of a wonderful inspiring convention, centered on the worship and knowledge of God, through a spiritual relationship with Jesus. If heaven is like this, I'll take as much as I can get of it.

By this shall all men know that you are my disciples: That you Love one another.   John 13:35

Karlene and Maria Luisa in Oruro

59

Two months to be spent away from the high mountain altitude was the health requirement at mid-term. It was the norm when we arrived in Bolivia. In later years it was proven that this two months really took away from your acclimatization, and you had to work hard to gain it back; but then it was required.

Marshall, then pastor of the Prado church, had just recovered from the Asian flu. Though his body was inert and hurting, his mind was active. He had heard that the flu was sweeping toward North America and killing elderly people. He thought about his grandmother who had been his guide during his teenage years, and how she might not live until our furlough two years later, and might MISS seeing her beautiful great-grandchildren (our Borden and Krystal). He could not bear the thought, and announced that I would take the two of them and show them off to grandmother. That would be my two months away from the altitude (we couldn't afford for both of us to go.)

We checked the airlines, and TACA (the Honduras National Airline) was the most economical way to go. They had a regular run from Lima, Peru to Miami, Florida. They made connections with LAB the Bolivian National Airlines on our end - and we would take a bus from there to Texas where all our close family members lived. After visits with friends and family in Beaumont, Houston, Dallas, we would go to Waco, and visit Marshall's family including Great-grandmother. Our impending itinerary was announced by letter to all those people we planned to visit. In answer to my letter, my brother Elvis, and his wife Evie Bell insisted on driving to Miami to meet us. They had five children themselves, and knew better than we did how hard the trip would be.

So I got everything ready to face the challenge alone, on the human level. I believed that God would be with me. I also did a lot of praying for courage.

Marshall would be well taken care of. A Methodist family from Texas, who would board him in my absence, lived just four blocks away. I delegated my other duties and prepared for the trip.

We left Tuesday on a 45 minute flight to Lima, but the

departing stage of TACA was not until midnight the next day, Wednesday. We left home before noon, but with all the check in and out at the airport, it was supper time when we reached the hotel in Lima. I thought that rather than subject the people in the dining room to tired fussy kids, I'd just have supper in our room and put them straight to bed. I could use the rest my self. With the rush of getting ready I was spent. In Lima I called friends we had known in Costa Rica. They came the next morning to take us for a pleasant all day visit with them and other missionaries there in Peru. I was able to prepare Krystal's formula for the rest of the flight to Miami in that homey atmosphere, rather than in a hectic hotel kitchen. In the early evening they delivered me at the hotel so we could sleep for a few hours before going to the airport.

We got all ready and went down to check out, the taxi was waiting, They told me I had a bill of 53 Soles. I hadn't changed any money because the airline was paying the bill. I had very limited resources and I can't even remember how we finally resolved the problem. I probably used a few of my precious US dollars to pay it off. It was the ROOM SERVICE they were charging me for. And I thought I was saving THEM trouble. We finally got to the airport, and there everyone was very solicitous. I was accommodated and made comfortable with the two children all ready for a nice sleep. When it came time for Krystal's next bottle, I discovered that in the rush of getting out of the taxi, the one thing that didn't make it to the plane was the baby's bag. It was complete with diapers, bottles, and EVERYTHING I had prepared for her comfortable trip. That's when we found out that they had not received the notice that there would be a baby aboard. There were none of the regular provisions made for them. This was in the early days of disposable diapers and I had paid the exorbitant price they cost in Bolivia to have them for the trip. They did have evaporated milk, that was the basis for her formula, but there were no bottles for her to take it from. She was just past her first birthday and that night, taking her nourishment from a cup, was rudely introduced to her.

When she finally got to sleep, and had slept about an hour, suddenly we were in Tegucigalpa. This is the home base of TACA and you would think that they would be able to remedy not having things aboard for the baby. It was four o'clock in the morning and no businesses were open. Even if I had gone into the city I couldn't have bought bottles or diapers. We couldn't get into the waiting room, the airport was closed. We sat under a vine-covered trellis at a wooden picnic table, while a crew cleaned and readied the plane for the last lap.

In due time we boarded once again, Krystal was now hungry and got another cup of warm milk; the nightmare was repeated. She cried a lot and we all tried to get her back to sleep. When peace arrived we were only one hour from Miami.

So, on our arrival there it is five p.m. and the heat from steaming asphalt of the runway hits us in the face as we alight from the plane. The stewardess kindly carries the again-crying Krystal, I am laden with many other things and am holding Borden by the hand. When I get to the immigration window the attendant takes my passport and asks the usual questions: What is your name? Hazel Thompson. Date of birth? - Place of birth? - Etc., etc., etc.. Krysi continues to cry in the background.

Borden and Krystal are both on my passport and so they then asked the same questions about Borden: Name? Birth date? Birth place? San Jose, Costa Rica. That's where the routine is interrupted.

She got out a new form two pages long full of questions on both sides. Half way through this the stewardess excuses herself to catch her ride into town and hands me the still-crying Krysi. The lady in the wicket finishes that document and at question three on Krystal: Birth place? La Paz, Bolivia, gets out HER two page document. Twenty minutes later we are through immigration and the last ones from our plane to finish. All the other service people, porters, customs officials, and baggage checkers had seen the whole ordeal and passed us through their points as quickly as possible.

My brother and sister-in-law were beginning to wonder if we would ever arrive. They had eaten a good lunch at noon and come straight out to the airport, where they would pick us up. Our reunion was as warm as the weather. They told me the plan. It was to stop and get something we could eat on the way as he drove until supper time. Then we would stop and all eat the evening meal. The trouble was that it was already supper time. So, we started looking immediately for a restaurant, -- no, really we needed a drugstore! And I bet you can guess what the very first item on the shopping list was! That's right! It was a baby bottle! No, a WHOLE SET of baby bottles! And then at the restaurant they allowed me to prepare her formula and fill them all for the trip.

Elvis had put down a mattress in the back of his station wagon for the children to be comfortable both for sleep and for play. It was a marvelous trip. I have pictures of a picnic on some Gulf of Mexico beach near Mobile, Alabama with all of us enjoying ourselves.

Elvis' home is in Beaumont, Texas: the first on the line of visits. Our kids enjoyed themselves for about a week with the cousins. Then on to visit my Daddy in Houston. Being in my home church was such a treat, and I got to share something of our life and work in Bolivia. One evening Fritzi and Dalgus (friends from our wedding) organized a get-together to eat out with a whole bunch of my old friends. Fritzis' mother had been one of my mother's best friends, and was eager to baby-sit the kids while we were out. I gave her the change and feeding materials and went wholly trusting in what Mrs. Fisher would do.

After a lovely evening, we came back to find her in a real tizzy, seems Krysi had had a choking spell. When she got too tired, she would sometimes hold her breath, and pass out. I remember the panic that I had felt the first time I saw her do it - but it had only happened two or three times in her first year. We had blamed it on the altitude, I didn't anticipate her doing it while traveling. Mrs. Fisher was distraught, and I felt so badly for her.

Marilyn came over with her daughter Karen. I remember wondering why she wasn't in school. It was then Marilyn reminded me she was only four years old. She looked like a big six!

The next stop was Great-grandmother's house. They lived on the outskirts of Waco, Texas in a lovely, roomy old house with an outdoor 'room' of evergreens. There each morning the children went out with their great-aunt Adine, to watch a huge spider repair his web. It would occasionally catch a few flies for its breakfast, then and there, and some for snacks to be consumed later. Each was neatly wrapped in a preservative sack. They watched the goldfish in the outdoor pond, too. Of course, our university friends had mostly scattered to the four winds by then, but a few had stayed on to pursue their careers in their hometown. I saw some of them and also visited a few professors.

Marshall's dad lent us a car and we went to visit other kin-folks in Dallas. Many of Marshall's relatives I had never met before. We went into the home of one of Marshall's aunts that had been closest to his mother -- hence closest to him. Her daughter was a favorite of his. They had been playmates as children. Beverly also had a son a bit older than Borden, five or six years old. When we entered the living room I asked hastily if I could move a beautiful porcelain vase to the mantelpiece for safety's sake. Aunty launched into an hour long lecture on how to teach your children not to meddle. She recounted how she and her daughter had sat on the floor on either side of the coffee table and gently sent her grandson in some other direction each time he was attracted to the coffee table ornaments. Then, she said, "You wouldn't have to worry about your child's behavior when you were out in public, if you tried it." She never gave me an opportunity to explain that I wasn't worried about their 'meddling' with the knick-knacks. My concern was that Krysi would bump into the coffee table and with no malice whatsoever knock over that precious vase and not even notice that she had anything to do with the vase's destruction! When I left she still thought that my child was meddlesome and I didn't know how to educate it out of her.

At other family gatherings in Dallas there was iced tea, mountains of mashed potatoes drowned in cream gravy, hot rolls dripping with butter, fresh beans, peas, carrots, and corn (cooked), with salads of lettuce, radish, and tomatoes (raw), straight from the garden. Wonder of wonders, they were all safe to eat! We had leisurely visits in all these places.

Great-grandmother was gratified with what she saw, but we needn't have worried -- she was still around two years later when we came back home for furlough. Since Karlene was born on that first furlough, she even got to see our third child as well. She passed away full of years on the first anniversary of President Kennedy's death, in 1963. Marshall felt that it was well worth the trip just the same. We went back each furlough to visit with his aunt Adine and enjoyed a few restful quiet days at the old Thompson house near Waco. Borden and Krystal went back there for university and enjoyed being near Marshall's dad. By that time he had remarried and lived just off campus.

Surely I will be with you to the end of the world. Matthew 28:20

Good bye Daddy, We're off to Great Grandmother's house.

Janet Holmes and Alice Clarke were the salt and pepper of
the Bolivian missionary staff. Alice came in 1920, and Janet in
1921, and within five years of my arrival in 1955, both retired.

Years later, each was awarded THE CONDOR OF THE ANDES
by a grateful Bolivian Government for their outstanding
contribution to Bolivian education. They had worked in Reekie
College and in the Guatajata school system, in addition to their
church and community work. I was appointed to accompany
Janet (Alice was unable to attend) to the ceremonies,
banquets, teas and church services given in their honor. What
a privilege to see her as she reminisced with high government
officials or humble Indian women with the same warm interest.

Janet served many years as mission treasurer, which meant
that she was also a member of the Finance Committee of the
Bolivian Baptist Union. Back in Canada, she was an actuary --
working with a prestigious insurance agency -- when God's call
came to serve Him in Bolivia. So, it was natural for her to be
always involved with figures, keeping the accounts wherever
she was. Her quiet presence was like a rudder in whatever
group she was working with. That everyday steadiness was like
salt, preserving calm when dealing with committees
competing for funds to carry out their programs and projects.
Her teaching, before getting into administration, was often in
the math field. However, she taught everything else in the
school curriculum and in the church work, as well as HOW to
teach.

She had the ability to plod: to take care of the tedious
details with all the patience needed to do the job, despite the
multitude of interruptions she might suffer along the way.

She had the quality of being able to administer a reprimand
(to a missionary colleague, a teacher in mission employ, a
young pastor under her supervision or a maid in her kitchen)
without destroying the person's confidence. Under her
correction, you went back to the task determined to do it right,
so you wouldn't disappoint her.

One day I found her at the little church working on the
ornate old pump organ. She had her pitch pipe out and was
tuning it. It was a real asset.

Alice, on the other hand, was the peppery personality. She was enthusiastic about everything. She was a trained teacher with some experience before going overseas. She supplied the inspiration and challenged those around her to forge ahead in God's name and with His help. By the time I arrived, she was living in Cochabamba and directing and teaching in the Academy – the women's version of Seminary – the solution in those days for women who wanted to serve the Lord. When called back to be honored by the Bolivian Government, Janet graciously accepted all the accolades for both of them in the manner of a truly great lady. Between the two of them, they introduced many innovations in the field of education.

My shock came during the reading of the citation that accompanied the presentation of the medal. Besides all the above mentioned things, something important to the Government of Bolivia was the conduct of the two ladies during the Chaco War. This fiasco was a 1935 war over territory between Bolivia and Paraguay. The war has been portrayed in a movie: 'Green Hell,' telling of a struggle to fix the border to recently discovered oil lands in a waterless, but lush-looking jungle. More soldiers died because of tropical fevers, snake bites, infections, and the lack of food and water, than in battle. Seems that these two ladies organized the ladies of Oruro to supply the young men going away to war with many helpful items (like knit socks and Scripture portions) that were not standard army issue. They wrote letters themselves and news from mothers who didn't know how to write and sent packages to the young soldiers who were away. During the war years, they went to the train station every day to see off the troops leaving for the front, some of whom they had taught. For some staunch Christians that we knew, this was their first glimpse of the gospel. Many count that contact as the beginning of their journey toward a saving knowledge of the Lord Jesus.

Two or three times, Janet was called on to come back out of retirement to resume those duties when the treasurer was on furlough. From her apartment near the Southern Cross Radio Station, she dispensed wisdom, knowledge and inspiration to pastors, teachers, former students, and missionary colleagues, as well as the funds with which she had been entrusted.

Both ladies, upon retirement from Bolivia, went into

meaningful ministries: Janet in Toronto, and Alice in Hamilton, and later in Kitchener. Janet was the example that encouraged us not only to continue when we were ready to quit during our first term, but also to come back for another. Her whole personality and demeanor had a settling effect upon everyone around her. She took everything in stride, including getting lost in the eucalyptus forest. Janet had two difficulties — she had a poor sense of direction and often lost her balance.

One of the things Dr. Merrick did when he was at the farm was plant a lot of eucalyptus trees. They had grown into trunks of a foot in diameter by the time we were living in Guatajata. Most of them marked the paths between the fields, or alongside the small stream that ran through the property. The 'forest' occupied about a hundred foot square between the clinic/ladies residence and the church building. Janet, tells of a time when they were having the Christmas program. They always had their meetings in the daytime, so people could get home before dark. When the program was over, and all the other missionaries had gone home to get the festive meal ready, she stayed behind to help clean up. One by one the others left and since it was dark by that time, she lent her lantern to the last person to go. She locked up the church and started to walk home. On that moonless night, she went only a few steps before she realized that she was in trouble. She could no longer see the church. The path was only a few feet wide, and ran between the trees on the right side and a ditch on the left. On the downhill side, there was an eight foot drop-off between the path and the road. Her fear of falling caused her to go uphill to avoid the ditch. She went far enough so that she began to bump into the trees and was really getting desperate. She called out several times, but the house was made of adobe, which is a great sound deadener. Prayer was her only alternative.

Finally, the meal was ready and the ladies began to wonder why she hadn't come in yet. One went to the gate in the eight foot wall and turned on the outside light. Janet had wandered for 30 minutes and was less than 15 feet from the gate when the light came on. But, of course with the light, she entered quickly and thanked the Lord. She told it as one of her adventures and took utmost delight in laughing about it with all of her listeners.

The year and a half that we spent at Guatajata, we had no car, but we could always catch a ride with Janet or Mary Haddow when they were going into town. Janet drove a red half-ton truck, as director of schools. Mary's was identical, except that it was blue, and she used it in her capacity as the nurse, so she could attend to clinics all along the lake-side road. Actually, this road was the Pan-American Highway, that reaches all the way from the northern-most places in Alaska, and the Yukon to the southern-most tip of Chile and Argentina. Janet loved to take me along, so she didn't have to drive the whole five hours that the trip to La Paz took. Invariably, the minute she passed if over to me to drive, the road deteriorated appreciably. Then she would giggle, and say, "Isn't that something! I know just when to turn it over to you, don't I?"

In later years, we took a gift from Grace Anderson to her for her birthday and had a little visit with her in the senior citizens home where she was living. She was already downstairs in the lobby waiting for someone to take her to a party in her honor. "This is the 75th," she sighed, "and they promised that they wouldn't make a fuss like this over it again until the 80th." Her humility endeared her to everyone she met along the way.

I never got to know Alice as well as I did Janet. At one of our early conferences, though, I remember us loading up in the back of a big truck to drive out to Carachipampa where we would be living for the next week. She had ridden from the Seminary in the cab of the truck, and when they got to the depot to pick up those of us who had just arrived, she jumped down from the cab and clambered up onto the back like a teen-ager, to make way for me (the current pregnant lady in the mission) to sit in the cab. Knowing she was just a couple of years away from retirement, I was really embarrassed, but she was adamant and I got the easy ride.

They were both great mentors for all of us to emulate, and I'm sure that each of them received the Lord's hearty, "Well done, good and faithful servant!" when they came into His presence, after a full and useful life.

Well done good and faithful servant...

enter into the joy of thy lord.   Matthew 21:25

"THE LORD GAVE THE WORD, AND GREAT IS THE NUMBER OF THOSE WHO BORE GOOD TIDINGS" Psalm 68:11

The Psalm is about God's giving his people victory over their enemies. In English, 'those' is not that gender specific, but in Spanish '<u>those</u>' means 'those women.' Today we call God's giving His Son to save the world, the 'Glad Tidings.' Our Women's convention was held in Cochabamba. Our guest speaker was from the Argentine Bible Society, and in her four messages, suggested many ways of distributing the Scriptures.

Our local Bible Society representative, Jaime Goytia, was ready with a plan. When the convention was concluding, he spoke to us briefly, "I have a large envelope with 30 selections from the Scriptures. If you pledge to give one away each day, it's enough to last a whole month. Some are brightly illustrated, some in plain print; some in Spanish, some in the Aymara or Quechua language; but all geared to show someone how to find Christ as Savior.

"Hang the envelope near your entryway. When someone comes to the door, look in your envelope and try to find an appropriate Scripture Selection to give them. Think ahead of the friends and relatives who come to visit you. As you read each Selection, try to think who could profit most from that one. Be sure to give away one each day, and when the month is up, your envelope will be empty."

"The envelope is free with its first month's worth of *Selectiones.** Bible Societies is naming a person in each district who will supply you with a refill at the end of the month, when you need more, for a few cents."

*(Selection is the name of a tract that contains ONLY Scripture, but several verses put together from different Books of the Bible, to treat with one theme: Love, Grace, Salvation, God's Word, Christmas, Jesus' Baptism, the Love Chapter, the Beatitudes.)

About ten of us from the Oruro area who were present at convention signed up for the plan. So many signed up that there had not been enough envelopes prepared to go around. They supplied those who were going home to other cities first. The local people could pick theirs up the next week. Some people were skeptical, saying, "Oh, of course they will take the free ones – wait until they have to pay for it themselves." Since I was the coordinator for the Oruro area, they came to me for their refills.

I know there were some who never came for a second packet. But enthusiasm ran high, and we who went to convention convinced the other ladies to sign up as well. I had 126 people on my list before I left for furlough the following year.

It was some time before the box with 150 refills arrived in Oruro. From each of the four societies, came one person with a list. I was bombarded with requests for the envelopes. I usually accompanied the lady to her next meeting and gave those newly enrolled ones an envelope. I also took some extras along, because those who hadn't already enlisted, wanted to when we talked about the plan.

Let me tell you about a few of the 'inspirations' our local ladies had. Elena had a tiny 'hole-in-the-wall' store. She sold to her neighbors: fresh bread, candles, matches, penny candy for the kids, and maybe flour, rice, and sugar in bulk. She gave the children who came to buy at the store a Selection 'to take home to mother' each day. Of course, she ran out long before the month was up. She had to send her 11-year-old daughter to me for more and bought three refills at a time. But it was worth it. Soon the mothers began to come, and ask questions about what the *Selectiones* had to say. Elena was a fairly new Christian herself, but it fostered in her a desire to study her Bible more so she could answer their questions. She led a number of those ladies to the Lord during that year.

Petrona was faithfully giving away the Selections when she had to be rushed to the hospital with a gall bladder attack. When her little girl came to see her the next day, she said, 'Bring me the envelope.' Maria brought it, and Petrona started to read one each day after the noon meal. The other ladies being bored, asked her what she was reading and why she didn't read it out loud. Sunday, Maria came to church with the money for three more refills. By this time Petrona could be up and about, and went around the wards giving each person a *Selection*. When each had read hers, they traded around and soon everyone had read them all. After two weeks, Petrona was released, but was to go back when her blood was 'built up' enough for a gall bladder operation. We all promised to

71

pray for her as she approached surgery.

After her operation, with the co-operation of a Christian nurse, she visited other wards, and gave out, or read aloud the comforting words of the Scriptures. One Sunday, Maria told me that her mother wanted me to come and visit a terminally ill patient with her as he was ready to "deliver himself to the Lord." (local terminology for accepting Jesus as Savior.)

When she came out of the hospital, she invited us to have our regular church prayer meeting of the week at her house to praise the Lord for her recovery. She wanted to tell us all the wonderful ways the Lord had taken care of her, and about the three people who had 'delivered themselves to the Lord,' as a result of her testimony. She told us how frightened she had been when she went into the hospital: how in her concern for others, God had made her forget her own fear as she had calmed them. She recognized this as her ministry and pledged herself to go twice a week to the hospital to distribute the Scriptures and bring comfort to those in pain and anguish.

Then there was Gabriela. She had only been a Christian a short time and yearned to share the good news with everyone. Her family had made fun of her and her husband when they had been baptized. Her husband had a good job with the railroad, but shortly after they were baptized he suffered an accident that required a long healing period. The family blamed this misfortune on her conversion saying that God was punishing her for leaving the true church. However, she prayed for them and wanted to see them come to the Lord. She began making a living as a peddler -- taking fresh produce to sell in the markets of the mining communities. When she went on those trips to the mines, she always witnessed to all she sold to and gave them a tract. When she signed up, I made the mistake of taking her envelope to the wrong church (I attended more than one missionary society.) I told her that if Marshall came to pick me up after the meeting, that we would take her to the other church to get the envelope I had mistakenly left. When we left to go, she insisted that all the ladies who could spare the time come with us, and they crowded into the jeep. She said a lot of things in Quechua that I couldn't understand, and we sang all the way over, learning a new chorus that had just come out.

72

While I went to a neighbor's house to get the church key, she got everybody out and told Marshall why she had brought them all. Her aged aunt lived next door to the other church. She had witnessed to her aunt for several months, and now she was ready to 'deliver herself to the Lord,' so she had asked Marshall to come and pray the prayer of salvation with her. We went inside and sang a few hymns and choruses, and then she turned to Marshall for him to pray.

He misunderstood, and tentatively prayed for her healing. I say "tentatively" because there had been several recent unpleasant incidents. Some deacons had prayed for healing, and when it didn't happen, ended up with the pray-er being beaten up by the family. This woman looked like she might die at any moment. She was lying on a bed at one end of the room, eyes closed, terribly emaciated, barely breathing. For two months she had not been able to eat, bathe or even raise her hand or her head by herself. When he had finished, Gabriela said, "But Pastor, you didn't pray the prayer of salvation -- she wants to deliver herself to the Lord!"

So Marshall began again, praying this time for her salvation. First he asked her if she repented of her sin and committed her life to Christ. He had to strain to hear her words, even with his ear right at her mouth, because her voice was so faint. We sang the new chorus we had learned on the way over, which was all about our home in glory; rejoiced in a new sister in Christ; and said goodbye.

Gabriela and I both missed a couple of meetings, but the next time we two were there, she told the most amazing story. Two days after our visit, the Aunt's grown son and daughter, who lived with her and cared for her, heard their mother's voice from where they were working in the patio. It wasn't the weak whine of a sick, old woman, but the way they remembered it from their childhood. They hurried in and were shocked. There she was sitting up, obviously looking at something at the end of the bed that they couldn't see. She said, "The gentleman has come...He's opened the door...The Lord Jesus is there waiting to welcome me." Then she turned to them and said, "Goodbye," laid back on the pillow and breathed her last. When the family came to plan the funeral -- which in Bolivia is often a drunken brawl, the son and daughter told everyone what had happened. They said that Pastor Thompson was the gentleman who came to open the door. They refused to allow the relatives to bring in any strong drink. They asked Gabriela about Jesus instead, and several of them turned to Christ then and there! Others wanted to hear more, and she urged us to continue praying until her whole family turned to the Lord.

Then there was the man (remember, this was a 'woman's program'?) who felt discriminated against. "You mean this plan is just for WOMEN? You can't give me an envelope?" He was a deacon, and had not known about all those pretty tracts. I told him that, of course, I would sign him up, give him an envelope and sell him refills as often as he needed them! Of the 126 on my list, eight were men who heard about the good deal to be had from this 'woman's program' and wanted to participate.

What a thrill it was to take part in that plan for Scripture distribution. Being the one to give out the refills, I heard some such story several times a week when someone needed a new supply. Many like Petrona, Elena, Gabriela and the deacon, bought several refills at a time.

I think, however, that the greatest impact was made by the many faithful of the 126, who were there once a month to get their refill and lovingly, thoughtfully, prayerfully gave away one Selection each and every day. For many of those women, it was the first time they had led anyone to the Lord, and this gave them opportunities they had never seen before.

This is a page out of history. I believe it was 1971 when it happened. I'm sure it would still work today. Why don't you try it?

She who goes forth weeping, bearing precious seed will doubtless come again with rejoicing, bringing her sheaves with her.   Psalm 126:6

74

Virtuosity? I never reached it. Though my mother sacrificed to buy a piano for me when I was seven, and taught me to read music herself before engaging a teacher, it seemed a lost cause. Money was tight, and from that time until I began my missionary service overseas, I had three scattered years of lessons. It was here seven months, there three, yonder a summer; so that most of my performance was for my own private pleasure.

I learned the first movement of "The Moonlight Sonata" at fifteen by myself. For those places that were not so hard, I would place my fingers on the proper notes at the beginning, and then play it as slowly as I needed to, not going by notes, but by intervals. In the difficult passages, I would write out the names of the notes underneath them, laboriously, in order to learn them. Then, playing them in that same painfully slow manner twice, I memorized them.

When I began to work with small children in Sunday School, and later kindergarten, I learned all the songs they sang the same way. Practicing them all week, I knew them by Sunday and can still play them today. As long as I could get my fingers on the right keys, I was home free. I taught kindergarten as a home missionary in New Orleans, and could keep my eyes on the kids as I accompanied them on the piano. I really beefed up my repertoire as well.

Somewhere along the way, I got a tip from the leader of a seminar on church music which pointed out that if you read slowly, you should be able to read the top line, and just play the chords that go with it in the base. I had played enough of the little oomph-pa-pa left hand stuff in all those early exercises, that I caught on right away, although I still learned it as written when I had the time to.

When I arrived in Bolivia, I knew four hymns by heart: "Stand Up, Stand Up for Jesus," "What A Friend We Have In Jesus," "Onward, Christian Soldiers" and "Silent Night" for Christmas time. I knew many of the children's choruses - some learned by the above method, and some picked out by ear.

The first ladies missionary society meeting in La Paz, I was asked to play the piano. I protested that I really didn't play very well, and would have deferred to their regular pianist, but she wasn't there. They thought I was only being modest and insisted. I floundered through one hymn that was a familiar tune, then came one I had never heard before. I put my fingers in their proper place, and the first line ran one note with each hand going up the scale and ending in a plain C chord, then it went to four notes in harmony and totally lost me. They finally believed me and they never bothered me about it again. I did learn some of the new Spanish children's songs, and played for their Sunday School all the time we were there.

Bolivians say 'in the land of the blind, the one-eyed man is King'. While at Guatajata, with only a portable pump organ, I taught several of the young men, who were in the Institute there, to play hymns! At the Women's Convention, I was often asked to lead the singing, and I enjoyed that very much.

When we came back for our second term we sent a piano. It took seven months for our shipment to arrive, and though many things were lost (like new winter coats for the whole family) the piano made it. By this time, I was very brave because there were not as many people around who could play.

I had devised a method of writing the music out without the lines when I went to some of the meetings where they were singing new hymns, freshly composed in the Aymara or Quechua languages. The music for these had never been written down. When we went to the juntas (camp-meeting-like associational get-togethers) out in the country, we were often provided with the words of a half dozen of the new hymns. They could be in Spanish, Aymara or Quechua. They spoke of God's love for each of us, our hope for heaven, and the urgency for sharing that message with those who hadn't heard. There were usually a number of verses, and then by the second day, someone had translated them into the other two languages, so we could ALL sing them.

Of course, they also sang a number of familiar hymns as well, but they sang the new ones over and over, so they would remember them to share with their whole congregation when they got back home. I had ample opportunity to make the notation in the margin. Then when I got home, I could sit down at the piano and experiment until I found the best starting note and play off the hymn. I could draw in the lines, and put it into a book, so I could share it with my congregation!

The evening after the Ruggles joined us in Oruro, there was a musical competition planned at the Villa Esperanza Church. We asked if they would like to attend, and though they were VERY tired, they said yes. We arrived, and had to wait a while. They didn't even start until 9 o'clock. We left about half way through the program at 11 PM and were discussing it on the way home. Trying to describe it so Fay would recognize the group we were talking about, we mentioned their brightly-colored clothes, the balance of men and women, the instruments they played. She finally said,"Oh, you mean the group that sang fourteen songs with fourteen verses in each one!" By the time, they had sung three hymns, with three verses each, in three languages, it must really have seemed like that. Repetition made it easy for me to write out the music.

The instruments in their musical groups had first guitars, second charangos, and third drums. Once in a while there was an accordion, flute or pan pipes, and maybe other percussion instruments like maracas, sheep hooves strung in clusters, or a notched stick that made music when raked with another stick.

That year in Oruro, I increased my repertoire considerably. Finally, they found someone to be our partners for opening the work in Potosi, and we moved. We were six adults and five children at the start. Since no one but me played anything, that job fell to me. I demanded from the coming Sunday's preacher a list of the three hymns we would sing, practiced them all week long and played them on Sunday.

Since the Bible Institute in Oruro had lent us their electric piano, I used that until they began their next term and needed it back. For our evening meetings, it was useless anyway. The electricity was 110 volts, but our meetings began at 8PM, while the other people in the city were cooking their supper. The heavy drain on the current meant I held down the starting note a long time before there was enough air to make a noise, and it just gave them the pitch. I couldn't play any more for lack of power. Then someone dug out an old portable pump organ. When I practiced all week on the piano, and got to church, I had to remember to pump, or lack of air would defeat my purpose again. After about a year, we found another electric piano, and bought it for our own services. By that time the power in the city had changed to 220 volts, and the instrument would adjust for 110v., 175v. or 220v., so we did quite well.

When we came for furlough in 1965, I translated about ten of those hymns into English. When we visited churches as a couple or a family, I often accompanied and we sang one of them. First, we would sing one verse in whatever the original language was, and then the three or four verses in English. The haunting harmonies as we sang "Let's Sing of Jesus" were thrilling.

> Come let us sing out clear and strong,
> Sing about Jesus who righted the wrong.
> He bled and died to save my soul,
> Carried my guilt and made me whole.

Chorus:

> Let's praise the Savior, let's praise the Lord,
> Who chose to suffer torment for me.
> Let's thank the Savior, let's thank the Lord,
> Who by His death gained pardon for me.

II

> Even the sun, his face hid in shame,
> Shuddered the earth when darkness came.
> Then Jesus rose. In heaven on high
> He lives to save us, you and I.

III

> Jesus the Lord is reigning today
> And in the Bible, we hear Him say:
> "I'll go prepare a place just for you,
> And when it's ready, I'll come for you, too."

For an offertory I often played a hymn that Justino Quispe composed when the United States sent their first manned rocket mission into space. It was Christmas Eve, and a Scripture was read — not the Christmas story — but Psalm 8. It speaks of the wonder and beauty of God's creation made with His own hands. The chorus began:

> What is man that you remember him;
> You sent your only Son to die,
> to ransom us from sin.

78

Marshall says, "A small gift, even as poorly developed as Hazel's music, was very useful, both in Potosi and Sucre. Those two mission points represent at least seven years of time in our lives, when the presence of music on a small, three octave, foot-pumped organ with one deck of small keys produced joyful sounds of celebration that charmed boys and girls in the Vacation Bible Schools in Potosi. In Sucre, with the addition of a small Japanese plywood, upright, studio piano, we were able to teach harmony and music as part of the children's new life in Christ. Under the preaching and singing of the Good News, converts were taught and outsiders charmed to investigate. Small gifts make a significant difference in our lives and to those about us."

Praise the Lord...

   With the sounding trumpet...

   With the lyre and harp ...

   With strings and flute...

   With clashing cymbals.

Let everything that has breath...

      Praise the Lord!

From Psalm 150

Dr. Vallencia came to the office in La Paz where I was pastor of the Prado church. He had a problem. He came trying to arrange to retransmit some of the Gospel programs from the Southern Cross radio station on their local station. He had tried to interest the Bolivian Baptist Union in starting a mission in the mining center of Telemayu (tel le my' you) on the railroad south from Oruro to the border town of Villazon (veal ya sown). However, Marshall refused to encourage such work because of another gospel group already meeting there. He got the tapes for the radio, but not the BBU permission. He planned to do Daily Vacation Bible School for the children whose parents worked in the mine.

The railway to Argentina stretched through high prairie, mountains and valleys until it reached the border. The land frequently looked barren, but people managed to live on this varied high cold landscape. Tradition formed the basis of subsistence. The rail and its trains formed its life line.

Marshall stopped to see the Doctor in his clinic on his visits south, down the rail line. There he learned that threats and fist fights had occurred between the two elders who split the congregation and publicly anathematized each other. The Doctor felt he could not go to either meeting and had started his own; so, that year we sent him a student for holiday help and the work continued for about twenty-five years until the mine closed.

The missions committee decided to send a little, 40 year old, bald bachelor, a seminary graduate, to open work on the border. We were invited by a congregation of Bolivians living in the Argentine border city of La Quiaca (La key ah' ka). it seemed an opportune moment to preach the gospel to the many smugglers and confidence men working where many substantial, but largely illegal gains could be made. Would the people respond? A minority did and eventually meetings were held on both sides of the line. Converted smugglers either got into legitimate work or went back to reinforce home churches in the north. The church was in flux, growing and shrinking with visitors and converts. The church's power of evangelization was great, but net church growth was low, and the weak among those who remained, were often tempted into easy money.

The backbone from the beginning was a shipping agent with a large international company who yearned for a congregation where he could worship and bear witness in the community. His hospitality was warm and personal to Christian visitors.

The Pastor had been an army sergeant and was accustomed to early 'rise and shine' activity. He often started his visits to the faithful and fallen alike before breakfast. He met them in the daily market and berated those who had not been present at the last meeting. He exposed any other errors brought to his attention. After all, things are done publicly, before all the troops in the Bolivian Army.

Marshall was greeted with complaints, interspersed with laughter. Such moments usually turned into a joke session. Each person told another, yet more fabulous incident, all in indignant, yet, uproarious laughter. Most loved him, but found him hard to take. He later married Altagracia and had three girls. He called them his three Marias for they all had that name with others in long, sonorous conjunction.

The meetings tended to ping pong from the town on one side of the border to the other: according to the ever changing regulations, price of goods and border restrictions. Sometimes only one side held the church service; sometimes both had meetings. They finally, on Bolivian Baptist Union insistence, bought property on the Bolivian side. It was slightly inside the country, but not near the official border crossing, to discourage any temptation to use it illegally.

When we took films to the south we would locate a property on the Bolivian side, with a large expanse of whitewashed walls or house front (they rarely had windows on the street side to prevent robbery). When we obtained permission to borrow the use of their electricity, we would show free slides or movies projected for all to see. We sometimes had sound but if not, shouted the necessary explanations. Crowds were always big and usually orderly (unless drunk, in which case the police intervened for our protection).

I once met a 12 year old girl who responded quickly when I

asked if she knew about evangelicals. "Yes, they can't steal, rob or lie." She thought they were restricted, poor things. I responded "No, hijita, (ee he' tah = little daughter) you learned it badly. It's not necessary to steal; it's not necessary to rob; it's not necessary to lie because a loving Father God cares for you, satisfies you with all you need and Jesus takes away your sin." God frees us, not restricts us. She looked impressed. Most people on the border feel it necessary to do all those things and worse to make a living.

One lady and daughter who had come for a time to the church were persuaded by Jehovah's Witnesses and when we met on the street she wanted to know why we had not taught her God's name. I explained that the President of the Republic could be called by his true name or his title by those who respected or met him, but that was not what his daughter would call him. Within the family he was "pa pa'." It depends on the relationship. Those who are not part of God's family call Him Jehovah. We call him Father.

The guile of humanity is clearly illustrated in the stories repeated for the benefit of transients going to Argentina or to Tarija. One story has a man crossing the line early each morning with a wheelbarrow piled high with hay. The Agents poked and pierced the piles to see if any contraband was hidden within. They found nothing for a month. Then someone noted in consultation with the evening shift that he never returned with the barrow; he took a new one every day. This kind of deception is constant on the borders. Where sin abounded, grace was always apparent. The church was rich in goods and over time became rich in spirit and discipline as well.

Brother Zegara was a railroad worker. His family was one who attended church in Oruro, the rail center of the Bolivian system. His daughter tried to learn piano with Hazel as teacher. The son was interested in the ministry. They were transferred to the small town of Tupiza (Two pee' sah) a sub-center for the trains. There they found the same division and antagonism as that of the Telemayu mine. They invited us to stop and preach there. We were persuaded.

Another believing family, Fernando Diaz, living in Cochabama had a property in the town and offered the property for use. The Committee rented it and later, as growth continued, bought it. They used a series of students at first, but later a young graduate started a ministry there which prospered.

A German-Bolivian family whose father ran the city light plant, attended and one of their sons, Oscar Gossweiler was won and attended seminary. He had learned to ride a unicycle at home and produced consternation on first appearance at police controlled traffic stops in several cities. Wherever he went they noticed him immediately: Some laughed, some cursed, some tried to find a rule to stop it. "What happened to the front half of your bike?" others teased.

Like many of our graduates, Oscar later became a teacher for the state where salaries are better. The mines and small isolated towns always produced the larger number of our seminary students. Not all continued in ministry but almost all remained active in their local church wherever they worked. His home town church where his brother was a deacon, grew slowly and eventually planted a mission in the house of the original Zegara at the rail yards. All of these became a part of a circuit of churches in the south. The growth over the years was slow but steady.

The strange thing about new work is that it rarely grows as we expect it to. It spurts and drags. Sometimes it is faster, but usually slower than we hoped for at first. The problem is with people. They hear and wish to respond, but are timid or reluctant to face opposition from family and friends. We too, are like that, aren't we? Afraid to speak up, afraid of rebuke from doubters and mockers. No wonder the work is usually slow. Our faith is small and so are the results; even as Jesus warned us it would be.

Jesus said: *In the world you will have tribulation: be of good cheer; I have overcome the world.*

John 16:32

83

Brother Amos Anderson was one of those foreign field additions that people rarely hear about; the self-appointed guardian and judge of effective outreach. He could only manage the phrase `Dee yos es gran de,' (God is great) and `Hey sus es mar a vee yo so' (Jesus is marvelous) in the local language. But he managed to say a lot more to all mission and aid workers in the country. Near sixty and restless of nature, Brother Amos would turn up at surprising or awkward moments to give you his views of the failures of the humanitarian and Christian efforts in the country. He enjoyed talking about his years of atheism and complete rejection of Jesus then, after 45, his conversion.

Not content to be a good Christian, he tried to become the best kind by joining a group of proud-minded "Man child" (Rev. 12:5) followers of Brennam, a movement that was anti-church in many ways. It personalized the action of Angel associates and a confidence that all Brennam's ways were right. After years with that movement he felt that perhaps they had been too self-centered, but many of their attitudes remained.

He came to us the day we were leaving to take the children to boarding school in Cochabamba, wondering if we could put him up for a few days. We had been wondering who would stay in the house in Oruro while we were gone. High walls, guard dogs and never leaving a house unoccupied, was something we had been impressed with since our earliest days in Bolivia. Someone in La Paz had referred him to us, and there he was, a real Godsend. But we noticed on return that he had a direct way of analyzing and criticizing everything people did, especially in relation to their faith and practice of that faith. He was a bitter-sweet person full of objections and scriptural references to stir up an argument. When helping around the house he would do neglected chores and be a positive benefit, then he might disappear for a day or two only to turn up later and relate what the Lord had ordered him to do.

Once, after a trip home to the United States, he reported that he had been witnessing to his wife, who had left him after his conversion, because he wouldn't support her anymore. He was working out his faith, but still came out prickly in language and character. He challenged us.

He did not go to church most Sunday mornings. He gave out tracts occasionally, but talked to people on the street that wanted to practice English. He had a few set Spanish phrases which he would practice regularly when need arose: Dios le ama(God loves you); Jesus es el Salvador(Jesus es Savior): each good in itself, but they needed explanations. He influenced a few of the weaker sisters to get 'evangelistic' and give out tracts instead of going to church. They might have combined the two, but that was not his overall push. He managed to stay with different families in the various missions that worked in the country and enjoyed arguing theology with each. He made trips with several of them.

He once made a trip to the south of the Carangas district with me. We went south to the last village of the Chipaya language people. The Olson family had worked with Wycliffe Translators to put the Scriptures into their language.

The early Spanish priests had Catechisms written in the language, which was at that time used more widely in that area. The Chipaya language has been proved related to Mayan languages of Guatemala and Mexico. I wanted to see what remained of the church work after the departure of the Olsons. It lay between the Baptist area and another denomination.

It was my first visit to the area and we came from the west to a large wide river that formed a boundary. We lost power in the deepest part and the motor died and wouldn't start. My Indian helper and I took the electric generator we carried in the back of the jeep to the shore. We struggled to maintain the motor at shoulder level while wading through waist-deep, swift water. It was a ford in the treacherous river and a city block-wide between the low sand banks. From the river's margin we were able to start the generator and carry the wires to the stranded car. We had several men holding up the line to avoid a possible short because of the water. The car motor started, when we applied the clamps to the battery, no one got an electric shock, another miracle. With prayer I completed the passage through the river.

Some of the nationals agreed to take care of Brother Amos while we went back to one of the Baptist congregations for

Sunday. I was to return on Monday. We passed westward without trouble and had a wonderful visit. However, on our return, we again had the motor die about ten yards from the shore. We were high enough to leave the generator in the back of the jeep, start it and furnish power to the motor. This time I was sure there was a spiritual barrier there and we prayed against it. Brother Amos was holding forth and was interpreting some dreams that some of the local population had. He confessed to me later that the 'Association de Iglesias Cristianias Evangelicas' group that met in the morning had studied the Word and were spiritually healthy. The charismatic group, however, was `bound up with spirits of error and infirmity,' and a great disappointment to him.

We left Chipaya to return to Oruro, but went in quest of gas. The gauge was low but we thought that we might make it to the AICE missionary's home near Lake Poopo. We hoped to buy or get a loan of gas from him. My Indian helper decided to return home by another road, evangelizing in several villages where he had contacts. We stopped at every small store, but gas was not to be found. In a week or a few days a truck would come, we were assured by each owner. We gave several people a lift, gave tracts, and inquired for gas or news of believers. The last passenger said he was going to a fiesta. I did not want to go into a town at night where there would be drunks. When we could hear the drums and music, I asked him about a short cut around the village. He pointed it out and got out to walk on toward the music. He said our destination lay several hours south. The gas gauge had been resting on E for two hours.

I had been praying for the gas to last and the miracle seemed to be happening, but Brother Amos was in a querulous mood. It had been a hard trip and nearing seventy is not a good age for exertions. I started the short cut, but Amos kept complaining to me. I knew the Lord was doing something for us, but I too had had a long day. So I said in annoyance to myself: "I don't believe the Lord is supplying the gas." The motor sputtered and stopped that instant. I begged God's pardon and recognized what He had done. The motor would not catch and I knew that my annoyance had ended God's help.

I announced that we would stay where we were till morning. Brother Amos screeched his displeasure in no uncertain terms.

Humbled by my unbelief, I became sweet and gentle in my language with both of us. It had been an arduous adventure and it was a double failure. We both had lost our tempers. I got out to pray and could hear the drums and shouts from the village on our left. I was glad we had taken the shortcut. I walked ahead under a cold, star-covered sky and found the road doubled back from the village only half a block ahead. We slept till predawn light and I walked with our gas can until mid-morning when the sun was getting hot. Fortunately the missionary was home and I got our gas. He would have given me the gas, but I insisted on paying so he gave me a ride back to the jeep. Brother Amos may have found waiting as hard as I did walking. We made it home and he went his way to recover.

"I have wondered what some workers are doing here. But I know now what you do." He stated before departure. I wondered if it was a grudging compliment or a simple statement of fact.

The people you meet in tough situations are not always a help. They are sometimes a hindrance. But it takes all kinds to make a world where sin and righteousness live together, but are rarely open and dialoging. We need a certain measure of confrontation to discover truth and error. Then, of course, we have to choose. Sometimes our choices last a long time.

Ten years later, I met Brother Amos again. In Israel he was visiting and getting acquainted with the workers. We had a chance to talk. He was awaiting important changes in Jerusalem and his millennial views were expectant and definite. Like many self-appointed prophets, he was attracted to the state of Israel and he had a solution to the antipathy lived out there. He wanted the best for all those concerned with the need for peace and understanding between peoples. "Jews, Arabs and Christians should have God's blessings through Christ the Savior," he said. But, as one Arab Christian once observed to me, "The irony of pride and faith is that the direct physical descendants of Abraham have been the last to accept the 'messiahship' of Jesus of Nazareth."

So the first shall be last and the last first.

Matthew 20:16

We were about six months into our first term in Bolivia, where Marshall pastored the Prado church, at that time the largest in the country. We had just begun what would become a ring of missions around the sides and edges of the bowl shaped city of La Paz. A deacon, home owner, and later our Prado Missionary, Modesto Aliaga, took charge of regular weekly meetings on the street or in homes. Some of these meetings attracted others and grew. Others were eventually closed or ceased being attended to for many reasons. However, the impulse among members of the Bolivian Baptist Union was southward.

A young seminary graduate, Juan Aguila, had just passed his practice year in the Cochabamba valley. He volunteered to start a new mission in a southern town: Tarija (Tah ree' hah) or Potosi (Poe toe see'). During the Convention of the Bolivian Baptist Union, he challenged all present with his impassioned plea. Doubtless there would be many obstacles, but he had the call. Everyone voted enthusiastically for this extension of God's work. The mission committee considered the mining town of Potosi, but they feared that the young man's health and strength would not be adequate at such a high altitude and in such a hostile climate. They decided that the lower valley would be more appropriate. It was a closed, fanatical town. It lay six hundred kilometers away from our closest churches, which equaled three long days travel.

After a year of isolation and opposition he applied for a Canadian missionary to follow and join in the work. He stated that he knew from experience what a foreign missionary must feel like in an alien environment. From that time on, we would work in tandem, a national and a foreign missionary for all new towns.

Our Prado church had taken up a substantial sum for the equipping of the meeting place. Marshall went with Avelino Gonzales, a young deacon who had a deep interest in the wor, in Tarija. The Prado church paid Avelino's expenses.

We, in the Prado church, offered to finance the modification of the meeting place, the building itself. I went for a short visit while Avelino stayed the whole summer to help with the reconstruction and returned to the Seminary for study. It was money well spent and the meetings continued there for the next year. However, after the many improvements the owner raised the rent. A search started for a property to buy and build on.

We had just painted the interior of the Prado church and were still giving generously to other mission needs, besides our paying a city missionary for La Paz. A foundation had been laid for the Bolivian Baptist Union in the larger commercial cities of the north: La Paz, Oruro, Cochabamba and the mine centers of Colquiri, Catavi, Uncia, and Llallagua. Now, the third generation of Bolivian evangelicals would carry the Gospel to the end of their territory south: Tarija, Villazon and Bermejo.

Tarija turned out to be a hardship post. The dull glow of the light bulbs came on at 6pm and were cut off at 9 pm. Faucet water ran a slightly off-color brown after every rain. The flush worked feebly. Commerce trickled slowly in the city center. The municipality ruled laxly due to the dearth of tax funds for city improvement. The roads were bumpy. Only the state church sported any look of well-being. Prosperity was confined to the statues and alters of gold overlay. The city architecture was both beautiful and sad: it was decaying classic colonial. Dust overlay both town and country side. A leisurely tropical atmosphere prevailed. Poverty and unemployment were universally evident. Jobs came through relatives or politics and political loyalties frequently turned violent.

Yet the valley held a park like aspect with flat topped acacia like trees sprinkled across the landscape as if they had been intended to imitate the parklands of Africa, green and lush. Animal life prospered under the mild climate that welcomed those arrivals from the cold, high *Altiplano*. Isolated and beautiful, this land waited awakening, both spiritual and commercial. God called, men acted and it slowly became so.

One, two and three Baptist churches grew and developed, as people changed and took charge. We held youth camps there for several years on the campus of a normal school, beautifully situated, but full of fleas.

Art Wormald was the first of several Canadians to live there. On one visit he invited me, Marshall, to sample some fresh pressed sugar cane juice and we went to a mill where we ordered the juice. It held a strong alcoholic flavor and we struggled to get the pitcher-full down. When the miller returned we asked him when the juice would ferment and become the dark colored *guarapo*, (wah rah poe) a famous alcoholic drink produced there. He replied that it would be completely fermented and ready in the morning. We drove home very carefully that night.

In La Paz, I continued my ministry to the suburbs and the central church, but visited the south occasionally. After the departure of the Wormalds, I carried film or other means of evangelistic outreach. Juan stayed in the rooms above the first meeting room and ate at the restaurant of Ademar Gonzalez, a deacon of the church. Jean Pyper moved there after her retirement while they built the new church building. The older edifice had one large room below, that was sometimes used to house youth rallies. The second story contained two or three smaller rooms. That building became the living quarters for her and later for the pastors for years. The new church building that had looked too large, in time, became too small and new meetings elsewhere grew, blessed by the mother church. The youth were seeking something new.

Missionary visits brought new experiences to the local population. Once on a visit, Mary Haddow was arrested for driving her jeep in the city. When she produced her driver's license the arresting officer stared in disbelief at the *brevet* document murmuring, "Look at that! She really has one!" It was a first for him, women drivers were rare on any road there.

From Tarija eager evangelists started work in Bermejo (berr-may-hoe), a lower almost jungle border area near Argentina, where oil wells were the source of wealth. As that church prospered it too reached out into the rural areas.

A little encouragement, prayer and persistence go a long way. Jesus said:

If you ask for anything in my name, I will do it. If you love me keep my commandments, and I will pray the father

John 14:14-16

On my first arriving in La Paz to assume direction of the Prado Baptist Church I began a large change in my previous range of experiences. Especially, to take leadership in the Jail visitation program of the church. This was to enter an area of gray beyond anything I had ever known. I had never even been inside a jail before! My experience was limited to cinema roles of Humphry Bogart, Edgar G. Robinson and other films showing Mafia and bad boys behind bars. They were escorted by guards, involved in the plots and threats that make gang movies so gripping. Would reality match fiction?

We met Sunday afternoon on the Plaza San Pedro where we had permission for an outdoor presentation of music and preaching. Our maid Maria came on her afternoon off, while Hazel stayed home. After our presentation, we offered Gospel tracts and then entered into the jail. There we were not allowed to visit the political prisoners, but they could hear us and we could send them portions of Scripture to read on request. Our interaction was largely with the criminals who were currently living out their time. Everything inside was mud brick construction, but the walls were stone. The floors and passages between the cells were cobblestone and rough. The people dressed with whatever they had brought with them or what relatives had brought. Everything passed through the guards. Cells could be rented and used for safety. A woman without a cell might be victimized. Cell doors were flimsy and a few were without anything visible. It was primitive, dusty and sad. Most inmates were friendly, and some of our deacons and members had special persons that they always sought out to help. I was glad we were only allowed an hour. I soon discovered that all the city churches had jail services and did some provision of clothes, food or medicine. I was to become more intimate with the ways of jails.

Hazel and I went for the first two weeks of our mid-term vacation to Jean Pyper's home in Cochabamba. Then after a visit to Santa Cruz to meet the Brazilian Missionaries, Hazel went home to Guatajata while I took the train south to visit Tarija. I met a Danish Nazi who was avoiding jail by living in Argentina and had visited Bolivia. He challenged my faith and we talked all the way to Villa Montes. I left him with Scripture and an address. Later he wrote me a letter of thanks.

After blessings in Tarija, I was stuck in the town of Sucre at a time when we had no work or church there. I had come through from the south a day late on my schedule and the day I arrived Pope Pious died. Church bells slowly tolled for hours to announce the loss. In mourning, the legal capitol of the country suspended all traffic for a day. The Chauffeurs union stopped their drivers and I was unable to get out. But I walked to the transit office and found someone who had secured permission before the news had arrived. So I walked to the edge of town and waited until I found the truck ready to leave. It was privately owned and parked outside the traffic-gates. I agreed on a price and they departed that night for the mines of Oruro on a back road to Ravelo. There were several long night stops along the way. I had developed a fever. A kind Indian lady gave me coca tea. Sleeping on the top with the cold air in my face and mouth, I lost a filling in a molar and now had a tooth ache with the two day journey. Arriving in LLallagua I had no trouble finding a bus to Oruro, the miners were communists and did not mourn. From Oruro another bus took me to La Paz, where I spent the night in the Radio apartments. I went to the dentist's office the next day. I had missed the finance meeting, but was called to visit the Church at Villa Victoria, where the mission had acquired an adjacent property for the church. Miss Dorothy Franklin was happy, but there were problems unloading the adobes for construction in front of the church, where a market was located. Carrying the heavy bricks through the gate, connecting passage behind the Sunday school rooms to the new property was laborious. The market personnel was annoyed that the truck blocked the road before their main entrance. The money was paid and the property ours, so I ordered the wall broken in one place so a gate could be placed and the adobes taken directly in from the side street immediately. The seller had objected, but I took a pickax and broke a hole in the wall. Then the lady brought a plain clothes policeman, who insisted on escorting me to jail. I told the trucker to continue to unload and left. Miss Franklin called the lawyer who handled the purchase. I waited in jail while the lady who complained was allowed to return to her property, part of which she had sold. The policeman was called away as a new fracas developed on the purchased land. While I waited, I sang a hymn, I was angry and so my voice must have carried my feelings. 'A Mighty Fortress' is not a song of resignation! While I was so occupied, the seller robbed some of the adobes we unloaded. The policeman stopped the transfer until the lawyer arrived. By that time the annoyed police had taken me to the inner sanctum where I sat quietly in the dark and contemplated the results of defiance in song, if not in words. After a while the door was opened to admit the light and I was taken to the office from which I had been exiled. The lawyer ridiculed the actions of the policeman. He grabbed the lapels of the man, and thundered: "If you buy a coat do you get the buttons, too? Of course the street wall is a part of the purchase." He told the cowed man that the party, who gave him the job, did not favor fools. Why was my client put into the inner Jail? He replied that I had been singing. The lawyer belittled such a thin skinned-attitude, but I recognized my error and apologized then and there. Some of the listeners took it as a joke and snickered, but I was sincere.

I left after the lawyer's visit and added an afternoon in jail to my experience. I spent another night at the Radio Building. I was alive, and free although a week late getting to Guatajata.

Meanwhile back at the Ranch – Guatajata, that is. Hazel, Borden and Krystal are looking forward to the 6th. That is when Marshall was expected back. He had left with the family and Maria Luisa two months before to go on vacation. Remember? Hazel went to Grandmother's house for her two months and this time could only take one.

Jean planned to retire in the ideal climate and accordingly bought a home. Alone, she could not afford to keep a live-in maid, but by offering her home as a holiday refuge for other missionaries she could. Those who lived in the altitude welcomed the relief from La Paz, Guatajata, and Oruro. When it wasn't spoken for by our own missionaries, people from other groups were welcome. She offered lunch and dinner and there was a hot plate in the wee kitchen where breakfast or tea could be prepared. There was ample space for even big families. Maria Luisa slept in Altagracia's room, and they worked together.

The second two weeks, Borden and Krystal had stayed in the care of the two maids, with Jean Pyper taking the main responsibility. She had urged us to take a couple of weeks alone down in Santa Cruz while they took care of the children.

From there, I, Hazel, went back to Cochabamba, collected the children and Maria Luisa, and went back by bus to La Paz and truck to Guatajata. He was due back Monday, July sixth.

Accordingly, the sixth arrived, Hazel dressed the kids up and went to meet Janet. They were scheduled to return from the Finance Committee meeting together, in Janet's truck.

We greeted her and asked about Marshall. "Well, he didn't make it to the meeting." AND that was that! We had missed him so much, and he not only had not come home, he hadn't even gotten to the meeting! We went home so disappointed.

But we put on a brave face, maybe he'll come tomorrow, I said to the children. Tuesday came and went. There's no telephone to call and ask if they have heard from him in Oruro, or La Paz. Wednesday came and went. On Thursday, Fidel Cueto visited the farm on business.

"Did you see Marshall in La Paz?" we asked.

"Yes, I saw him yesterday."

"Did he say when he was coming home?"

"Oh, I didn't talk to him — I just waved at him across the street."

I could have cried.

Friday came, and sometime during the day he wandered in. When I enfolded him in my arms, I did cry. And then we settled down and he began to recount his adventures.

Some years later, one of our 'stand-up comics' (and I can't remember which one it was) on our fun night at our Missionary Conference, passed on a story that was circulating among our Bolivian colleagues. He told it in this way:

"When they brought news to St. Peter, at Heaven's gate that Dave Phillips had died and was on his way to Heaven, he said,' We must have everything exactly in order , He's always very prompt.

"When they brought news to St. Peter , at Heaven's gate that Lorne Stairs had died and was on his way to Heaven, he said, 'We'll order new papers, he'll have all his worn out.

"When they brought news to St. Peter, at Heaven's gate, that

94

Marshall Thompson had died and was on his way to Heaven, he shrugged and said, '¿CUANDO LLEGARA?', Don't worry, who knows when he'll get here?"

The North Church, called 'Oruro Moderno', was a block away from one of the larger detention centers. There I helped only occasionally between trips and teaching courses. The church had several members who had done time and one who had been converted while serving his sentence. They were regular supporters of the visits. There was competition from other denominations. The state church resented our working there and refused to help 'those who listened to Evangelicals' with CARE packages (a food program from the United States.) The Adventists had a clothing program that helped some. All tried to help ex-prisoners with re-adjustment into civilian life .

While in Oruro the nation passed several crises and it was always necessary anyway to obtain an Hoja de Ruta (oh-ha de ru-ta.) In this way any truck or car was recorded as to place, date, hours and cargo. You were traced across the nation; and time and route were important for road repairs and development, as well as political information.

The Thompsons, Habermehls and folks at Reekie School were expected to arrive in Cochabamba for the annual missionary conference. Alice Habermehl and Hazel had gone on ahead to make all the arrangements, as it was Oruro's turn to host the Conference. It was held during the rainy season while most of the children were still in boarding school, but they would be there on the weekend with us. Children from Oruro or La Paz were free to attend if able. We had the car ready to make the trip from Oruro, but we decided to pick up our Hoja de Ruta the morning of departure.

Mary was an early bird, gathered our troop of travelers and went to get the Hoja from the traffic control booth at the edge of town. She was informed that as the country was under a 'state of siege' we would have to secure the document from the central station in the middle of town. This time I went in to save her the trouble. The Jefe, (hey-fey) had evidently been there all night, or was suffering from a hang-over. When he heard me complain that we had always been able to pick them up at the edge of the city, he erupted in anger.

"Don't you think we have the right to make the rules? You

95

question our authority? You are *'faltando a la authordad'* (showing a lack respect for authority): 24 hours of detention!" I blinked, I had been talking to the man at the desk. I hadn't even seen the *jefe*. I tried to explain that I was only inquiring, but he was not prepared to listen. "No, you'll learn respect: 24 hours." I was led off without the opportunity of telling the people waiting in the car that I was detained. I got locked behind iron bars in a large room with other prisoners. I sat quietly and waited; experience was beginning to pay off. I had learned how a prisoner should behave.

After quite a while, Mary wondered what was taking so long. When she found out what had happened, she apologized and tried to see if I couldn't just pay a fine and go on. She mentioned the urgency of the trip. But the official was adamant. She got in touch with don Julio, one of the local deacons, and he came to plead the case. Then, they went by our house, alerted Maria Luisa that she needed to take me some supper, and blankets, and located my passport and brought it back to me. She surrendered my passport to the jefe, who stamped it, signed it, and found fault with it. When the man finally relented and signed my release, he called me in to give me a few tips. He said, "You see, we do have authority over those who live within our borders."

I said humbly, "If I have offended you in any way, I'm sorry. I wish to help the people of Bolivia."

At one of the stops on the way to Cochabamba, they were teasing Fred about traveling with two wives and three children. Fortunately, it was not in the presence of any harsh authorities.

A week after the conference, I was driving in downtown Oruro. Suddenly, in the middle of a light change, I saw the Jefe hurrying past my front bumper. I stopped sharply, and we made eye contact. We both knew that I could have hit him.

We moved to Potosi shortly after that, and the man who was processing our papers said, "Hey, there is a stamp in here that says that you have three months to finish your mission. Don't worry, we can fix that up for you." And they did. But, if we had stayed in Oruro, it is possible that he would have hunted us down and expelled us.

While in Potosi we started visiting the jail, but the visiting nuns threatened the men who would take our tracts or listen to our presentations, with the loss of food packages. Authorities suggested we avoid such confrontation, so we stopped the visits.

On a trip to Brazil we had our *Ferobus* stopped on the rails at the last stop before the border city of Puerto Suarez and our credentials, passports were examined meticulously.   A Japanese resident was found to lack some small technicality and they refused to allow him to continue. They bowed him toward a small room-size cell with heavy four inch bamboo bars, because he refused to pay the fine. The bunk was narrow and thin, the room dark. He decided, wisely, to pay the hefty fine rather than be detained, as they knew he would. The mistake was clerical and done by those who do the legal things, but the individual is held responsible.

I had one other experience of this kind and it is covered in the chapter: Farewells Are Never Easy. I continue to avoid such situations as carefully as experiences with the unexpected or unpleasant permit.   In the 'Ins and Outs of Jails' I prefer 'outs' and feel my education is sufficient to love freedom. Jesus promises us that the truth will make us free. Truth about ourselves and sin frees us from the illusion that we can stand alone in the world. Truth about God and his love for each human persuades us that he can be trusted to provide salvation through his Messiah Jesus of Nazareth: free from sin.

Blessed are they which are persecuted for righteousness' sake: for theirs is the kingdom of heaven. Rejoice and be glad, for great is your reward... Matthew 5:10, 12

If you are a strict materialist you should not read this section. Skip it; it is only experience, subjective at that, plus speculation and Scripture. But, if you like ghost stories and mysteries, read on. We all have ghost stories on the world mission fields and lots are going on in our home countries as well.

Most of us follow the spooky stories in magazines and newspapers for our dose of mystery to balance the extension of our knowledge of the scientific world. Certainty and mystery go together; mystery to challenge our knowledge of certainty and to cause us to investigate in new directions. We learn that there is non-molecular, gravity-obedient dark matter that does not have atoms present. I was reading in National Geographic the other day that it represents 90 percent of the mass in the world of galaxies. The visible atomic matter is only 10 percent of the same. We learn that deep in the sea under tons of pressure, life exists in thermal springs and at icy depths. If it leaves its environment, it's destroyed. Life exists under, what seems to us, impossible conditions.

Why should life or intelligence be limited to atomic creatures like humans? What people have always called the spiritual world is also full of life and intelligence of different grades and types.

At Guatajata we lived among a people who have no doubts about spirit reality. All their offerings and dealings were made with invisible beings that inhabit the world around them. They contact that world through the medicine man or brujo, (bru'- ho.) Medicine bundles for health, requests for lost or stolen items, potions for good luck in love, charms for prosperity in business, and protection in constructions and travel are all addressed to the spirit world via mediums or medicine men.

When a person engages a brujo for one of the above mentioned reasons, he/she receives a 'prescription.' They always include a bowl, alcohol, coca leaves, and perhaps a guinea pig or cat, which may be released for a scapegoat or sacrificed for the blood. There may also be fresh flowers, a small cake of lake-bottom mud, dried herbs, little colored banners, ribbons or a twist of red-dyed wool. We were cautioned, that when someone asked us for flowers from our garden, to ask what they were for. This was so we wouldn't be a party to these ceremonies.

I know you are wondering where you could get the prescription filled. I have seen such stalls in the markets in Oruro and La Paz, and they existed in all the other larger towns though I didn't know where they were located. I'm sure that all the country fairs had them as well. I have seen all the things mentioned above, and others that I couldn't identify. There are usually a couple of mummified llama fetuses at such a place. Many masons constructing a house would never dream of starting a building without first burying a llama fetus under the cornerstone. This is to protect the workers from injury while on the work site. Once I even tried to buy a small twist of the red wool. I wanted to display it with my curios during our furlough year. The seller made it clear that she wouldn't sell that or anything else she had to me. Now that I think back on it, I'm glad she wouldn't. I think of the spirit presences I might have unloosed in churches back in Canada.

The traditional place for the local brujo to work in the Guatajata area was right on the mission property. It lay between our house and the house where the mission teachers involved in the local schools and nurses who ran the clinic lived. When Dr. Merrick lived there, he found one of these séances going on up the hill between two ancient olive trees, and literally kicked the brujo off the property. By the time we were there, we could see twinkling lights just up the hill from us, beyond the property line. It was as near as they could come to that historic place of spirits. We really prayed as we put our children to bed for their safety from that evil. Their bedroom window opened onto that scene. Our little maid, Maria Luisa, said she often saw a little guinea pig running free in the morning -- one of those scapegoats -- meant to carry away some illness. (Leviticus 16:8-10)

One friend mentioned that years before, hearing that someone had engaged a brujo to cure his ailing wife, he and another youth went just to see what was going on. The brujo put the elements of the prescription into the bowl, drank from the alcohol, and pronounced his incantations. He had almost reached his trance, when he straightened up angrily: "My familiar spirit won't come! There is a Christian present!" he

99

growled. Since these things take place at midnight, the young men were able to slip away undetected, so they didn't suffer for their curiosity. Had the ceremony gone on, he would have poured the rest of the alcohol into the bowl, set fire to it, slaughtered the sacrifice (or turned it loose), and then the familiar spirit would have made his pronouncement with a voice coming from the brujo. (They tell me; I've never witnessed it myself.) Then, he would have broken the bowl and trampled the fire. They also tell me that the medium never remembers what happens. The spirit uses the medium's voice and tells the client what he/she must do to accomplish what is desired.

During one evangelistic campaign, a man came to several meetings, and finally stayed after to ask the pastor to pray for his salvation and his safety. It seems that he had earned his living as a medium for a number of years. He yearned to turn to Christ, but feared his familiar spirit. He said that the spirit came to him unbidden and said that if the man followed Jesus, he, the spirit would kill him. The pastor assured him that if he took Christ as Savior, that Christ was more powerful than the familiar spirit, and would protect him. They talked all night long, read from the Scriptures and prayed. As the day dawned, the man finally trusted Christ. He became a faithful member of the congregation in *El Alto de La Paz.*

Not all the experiences were so positive, though. Another man in the south of Bolivia came to Christ with great joy. He, too, had earned his living as a medium. He had a very large family, twelve children, I believe. We were asked to pray for this man that he might grow in the grace of the Lord Jesus and be protected from his former familiar spirit. He had never learned any other marketable skill, and needed to find a way to earn a living. Another brother in the church gave him a job, but his family began to complain that they couldn't live on what he was making. Then, his former clients complained that they had no one to hire to find lost things, tell them cures, or receive prosperity in their business ventures. How could he desert them now? They had always come to him -- now they didn't know where to turn. He tried to witness to what Christ had done for him, but they didn't want to change their lives. Always before, they had come to him, and in his séance, they had found the answers to their questions, paid him, and had gone on. We prayed for him for a long time, but between his family and his clients, they finally wore him down, and he returned to those abominable practices. We never heard whether his familiar spirit returned or if he was successful in earning a living after that. I've always been a believer in 'eternal security', and grieved to hear of this man. I'm glad that God is the judge -- He will judge righteously.

Santa Cruz was the scene of one colleague's witness to a young high school boy. Let's call him Manuel. Our colleague, John Palmquist, took him along often on trips to the villages surrounding the city. He led Manuel to the Lord, and he was getting ready to be baptized. He helped the boy find a job pumping gas. One day the boy didn't show up for work and our friend just lost track of him.

Several months passed before he saw the boy downtown. He asked what had happened to him. Didn't he like the job? The young man said that it was hard work. He'd found another way to make money!

He told of a family that recognized his possibilities as a medium. They had helped him get in touch with a familiar spirit. He made offerings and called the spirit by name for several months before making contact, and now people paid him good money for it. He wanted to show our friend how easy it was. Though John didn't really want to witness it, he thought he might be able to rescue his young friend from this life.

The boy took him to a small room and set up for his séance. A friend accompanied him. It seems he was being primed for this same occupation. There were only a couple of chairs in the room. The boy drew a circle with chalk on the floor, put on a tin can crown with brightly colored streamers, closed his eyes and spun around in a wild, lewd dance. Then, all of a sudden, the boy's mouth opened, but it was a deep, gruff voice that addressed our friend. The spirit identified himself by name, and mentioned that John had lost his jacket. John admitted that he had. The voice said helpfully, "I can tell you where it is." John interrupted him to say that if the Lord Jesus wanted him to know where it was, He would reveal it to him. John said that they talked for a while, but he did not tell us the spirit's name, nor the rest of the conversation. Then, the spirit left in a rush of air, Manuel seemed to deflate, and his friend reached out to catch him quickly as he fell. The experience left John shaken.

Shortly after that John went on furlough, and as far as I know was not in contact with the boy again. We have heard and read of new converts who reported arguments and threats from familiar spirits before conversion, but after they were converted the spirits left forever.

Spirits, Bolivians thought were both good and evil, but all demanded gifts. The most dangerous is the Cari-Siri, a man-like creature that prowls at night. It takes the fat from around the waist or kidneys from which it makes candles. The victim, paralyzed with fright, knows that he will die and wastes away despite all the doctors can do, in the days or weeks remaining to him or her. Missionaries have met people claiming to have met the creature. One Christian brother who survived showed me, Marshall, his scar. Our Bolivian friends who have met such victims assure us that they died. This is the story and the results are usually the same. Some believe that the monster could be a neighbor or someone in the community. Aymara church meetings are in the mornings or afternoons, so the people will be home before night, to avoid the Cari-Siri. St. John states that men love darkness rather than light when their deeds are evil.

Janet Holmes tells the story of Ignacio, one of the Christian teachers. Instead of elections, the office of '*alcalde*' (al-cal'de) is passed from family to family in turn. When the father in a family has served, the next time it falls to his family, his oldest son serves. When it came Ignacio's turn to serve, he came to consult with Miss Holmes. He wanted to know what to do. The duties of an *alcalde* (translated mayor) included all the village business: judging between people who had an issue over property rights, leading public meetings, and arranging for the yearly hail sacrifice. He was not sure that, as a Christian, he could serve. She pointed out that it would be a shame to the Gospel if he refused to serve, and could be an excellent way to testify that Christians should be good citizens by doing their civic duty. They prayed that God would show him what to do in each situation. She invited him to come back and pray with her again as conditions arose for which he felt he needed divine guidance.

Everything went fine for a while. One day when several of

the elders of the village were together enjoying a cup of coffee at one of their homes, one of them mentioned the hail sacrifice. He asked if Ignacio had approached any of the others to collect the contributions for that sacrifice. Had anyone heard which brujo he had engaged to do the rite? One by one they admitted that no one had heard anything about it. They wondered if he had overlooked the fact that it was almost hail season. Had he forgotten? They decided that they would go right away and ask him themselves.

They all trooped over to Ignacio's house. After all the formal greetings had passed, one of the men spoke up and asked if he had started the hail sacrifice collections yet. He said, "We are not going to have a hail sacrifice this year." What a hum started up -- everyone talking at once -- "What are we going to do?" "We can't leave ourselves unprotected." "What if we lose our crops?" "But we've always had the hail sacrifice!" and Ignacio answered, "Yes, and we've always had the hail! I have prayed to my God, and He will protect us from the hail. I have asked Jesus to keep the hail away, so that you may believe in his power."

The news traveled fast up and down the shores of Lake Titicaca. People shook their heads in amazement. When the hail came, the Alcalde would be blamed for his disregard of tradition. He and his family would be beaten. When the hail began to fall, everyone was watching Guatajata. Every other community in both directions was hit by devastating hail storms. Crops were lost in many of them. But in Guatajata, God honored Ignacio's prayers: they had a prosperous year with no hail at all.

Our skeptics will dismiss the spiritual world of tribal people as foolish superstition, but belief takes on a life controlling reality that affects practical daily habits and attitudes. Most of us are pragmatic and attempt only what we think will work. If we are sure of results, we exert ourselves to undertake an action or a plan. If convinced that there will be no results, we feel it's not worth the effort. If we believe in unseen realities that prohibit some things, but approve others, we will act in that way; even rejecting that which would most profit us. Beliefs need to be respected and studied; spirit and belief combine to make up the realities of all our lives. Under God's providence,

'Things that go bump in the night' can be understood and corrected.

Call unto me and I will answer you and show you great and mighty things that you don't know.

Jeremiah 33:3

The medicine bundle is a recipe to appease the spirits

A small, husky, red headed boy leaned out the window waving as the train pulled out of the station, "Goodbye, old cold Potosi!" he shouted and his blond sister of almost six years joined him at the window to wave and echo his refrain. Their hands were chapped, red and rough with tiny lines in crisscross patterns. Their faces, too, reflected the harsh combination of tropical sun and icy mountain winds; they were chapped over red cheeks and freckles. "Maria won't have to use lemon juice on our hands now, Krysi, plain ol' soap and water will get the dirt out." he announced wisely to his sister. After all, he was older by 18 months and was appointed protector and guide, now that they were going away to live at boarding school. Krysi, all dutch bob and hearty enthusiasm, agreed with a contagious smile. "No more lemon juice!" she sighed contentedly. Tunkie, as baby Karlene was called, sat on her mother's lap, big eyed and clinging, always apprehensive in any new situation. Though she was nearly three and had already passed years in travel, she was cautiously quiet, assessing her situation. They were off now for the warm valley town of Cochabamba, where the children's school and the Seminary were located. A two week vacation was planned for the parents now that the new church was growing and the young pastor, Avelino Gonzales had an enthusiastic group of young people to help him in the rapidly developing work.

Our first winter in the city had been difficult. We were months in setting up a heating system. In the first place the kerosene space heater had not arrived. The kitchen stove was a three burner gas camp model and the needed white gas was often out of stock in the one outlet in that city of 55,000 people.

The Kombi Volkswagen that we drove didn't have a heater either. It looked like a tin cracker box and was always cold, with it's motor at the back of the van. The rooms of adobe brick stood around a fountain and small garden casting their cold shadows over the patio. Below the equator, winter falls in May and lasts through August. At 15,000 feet altitude the sun shines weakly into the windows with a northern exposure. Walls cut down the prevailing wind, but produced more shadow.

I, Hazel, sat in the patio facing the fountain with my

105

typewriter on the cement rim and rubbed my woolen gloves with the fingers cut out for work and breathed into my cupped hands. The sun on my hands and back warmed me more than anything inside the house could do. I had frequent touches of rheumatoid-arthritis that meant that I started my writing each day with stiff fingers. I had just started editing a monthly evangelistic paper called 'REDENCION' (redemption), taking over from Miss Dorothy Francklin, who had gone on furlough. Dr. Hillyer had begun it years before for his deacons to use and distribute when they went out on Sunday afternoons to preach in the park. It had spread to other centers in Bolivia, and then to neighboring countries. There was no subscription price, but many of those who used it supported it by making contributions that would at least pay the postage. I had nothing to do with the business end; Jean Phillips took care of that. The printing was done by a printer who was a believer in Cochabamba. There was a file with some articles that had been submitted to Dorothy that I could use, at certain times of the year: Christmas, Easter, season of *Juntas,* etc. There was an exchange with several other tracts or papers, and from these I had permission to use their articles, and they mine. I did one original piece almost every month.

There was also a commission from the Board in Canada to write a book about the experiences of Bolivian converts. Someone picked the name, "Smoke from Bolivian Fires" playing on the Scripture passage in Joel 2:30. The prophet told about things that will precede the day of judgment: "I will give wonders in the heavens and in the earth, blood, and fire, and pillars of smoke." I had already done the interviews, and planned to do eight of the stories. The sun warmed my back as I sat and wondered why the dark kitchen with fire and the bright room with the glass windows were never as warm as the outdoors from 11:00 to 3:00 o'clock.

Maria, our maid, came to the door and summoned us to eat. Fernando, Maria's husband and our chauffeur, was going to leave to see to the car's repair, but she persuaded him to put it off until after lunch. We all ate together as a family, Maria had been with us from the time of our arrival in La Paz. The children had grown up with her and the family did not feel that distance had to be kept between servants and family. This was one of the things that impressed the local people.

The change to Potosi had upset the children's lives and their digestion. After a dessert of cold Jell-O, Borden had writhed in pain one Sunday afternoon. We had not found a doctor nor a hospital. After three hours Marshall put his hands on his stomach and pleaded with God to take the pain away. There was a small sound like a pop and Borden sighed, calmed and drifted off to sleep. We found a doctor and it was his opinion that the children should not eat anything cold, even fresh fruit. Everything was to be warmed or peeled and above room temperature, which was never very warm. No raw salads were permitted at 4,000 meters altitude, by Doctor's orders.

All vegetables and fruits were available in their season, but winter was poor in all those things. A few lowland items: oranges, lemons, sour grapefruit, sweet limes (which foreigners find insipid) and bananas were available. Potatoes, of all colors and sizes, stored from harvest or made into *chuño,* (chewn-yo) a black product, crushed under foot, frozen and dried in an ancient dehydrating process, were plentiful. There were the large broad bean, green pea and lima bean varieties. Carrots, onions and radishes were usually available all year.

Meat was harder to find; sometimes goat or scrawny sheep, more often beef and on rare occasions, fish or fowl. You were expected to take bone with the meat purchase to use for soup. Since Guatajata the family had become accustomed to keeping rabbits and feeding them on peelings from the kitchen with fresh or dried barley stalks as supplement. The children were allowed to feed them, but were always told that they were to be eaten, they were not pets. When older, the children helped in the skinning and preparation of the meat, but daddy always went out back, alone, to kill them.

Bolivian meals always begin with soup, all the vegetables are added here: potatoes, peas, beans, carrots, onions and usually bits of grain, rice, or bow-tie macaroni, even *chuño,* the dehydrated potatoes. Many kinds of soup are made with these ingredients. All were made spicier with the addition of green or red peppers, sometimes made into a paste with tomatoes and oil. Some of it was added while cooking, but the paste was also served in a small sauce dish, for those who liked a little added zest. The dried pepper seeds were crushed and sometimes served as well, but we had zest enough. The second course was usually potatoes and rice or spaghetti with a bit of meat and salad. Hot coffee or tea was drunk after the meal. Enormous quantities of bread are eaten along with soup, second and drink. The local breads were delicious, both round hamburger-bun type and small french loaf style which, when cut up into slices, looked like the profile of a bunny rabbit. The children couldn't resist playing with them and ended with eating them up, the fate of all the rabbits they knew. Then came the fruit.

Marshall and Avelino Gonzales had gone ahead when first appointed to Potosi, and found a place to worship. It included living quarters for the pastor and his family. They also met the owner of the property that was to be our home. Marshall wanted me to see the place, so when it was time to close the deal, I traveled with Avelino by train.

We had to deliver the money for the two years rent to the landlord's son, Humberto Flores, so he could pay off a man who held an option to buy the house. We chased around the city trying to find the man before the time ran out at midnight.

We finally did, and saved the property for the family. Humberto was only nineteen years old, but was already handling the family businesses. The *anticretico* contract that we had with him meant that he had the use of the two years worth of rent to invest, and make more, but at the end of the two years, he had to return that same sum to us. We were expected to paint and fix it up to our liking, but return it to the owner when we left, in the same condition that we found it.

We had all the requirements of a good start for preaching, but we needed a congregation. When Avelino and Marshall were doing the preliminary visits there was a series of public meetings promoted by a religious group that had captured local interest. The speaker was glib and the services skewed toward a legalistic religious system that advocated work and laws for your salvation. They were moral, but without transforming power. They attended two of the public presentations and gave out gospel tracts in the main plaza afterwards. It showed us that religious interest was high and we met young people who asked intelligent questions. Some had been exposed to Baptist preaching in northern cities. We started the church with youth meetings and young believers who wanted training. Avelino had been prepared to preach salvation messages exclusively for six months. It was unnecessary. Christian life and youth activities filled our time. Humberto Flores was among those who attended regularly even though we knew he was not yet a believer. He had been a Communist scrutineer in the last election and represented his party there to see that the election was fair. His sisters played with our children and Karlene was their favorite. They carried her around the patio and plied her with candy and cookies when we were not looking. They chatted with Maria Luisa and her new husband Fernando who, when they married in Oruro, had all our children participate in the wedding. Fernando Galindo and Maria Luisa went off to the seminary to prepare for ministry after only a year in Potosi. I did without help in the house for a while, but then Humberto's sister Feliza worked for us. We had a few disgruntled youth from the other denomination in town. They had some problems, but we taught them and some became useful in their own denomination later. Our small meeting place (15' X 26') became comfortably full most of the year. Marshall continued to make long journeys to the cities and mines of the south and was on enough committees to keep us in touch with the work in other sectors.

The Young people became interested in the Tarija work and arranged to visit them for a summer camp and hired a truck. It belonged to Humberto's father. They had help to do a piston job on the motor, but they still couldn't get it going and they left the truck behind.   Ten of them crowded into the Kombi Volkswagen bus and Fernando drove them to Tarija. The youth there waited up for them at the turn-off from the main road in the driving rain. When they got there at three a.m. the whole group came running to meet them with big pieces of plastic to protect them from the rain. Humberto's testimony was that "They greeted us like family, with 'abrazos'. (hugs)" Valley people and miners have rarely trusted each other, but those young people hit it off.   Later in the week, Humberto Flores gave his life to Jesus Christ for the forgiveness of his sins and for service. He had embraced Communism because he wanted the best for his country Bolivia. When he found Christ, he had a greater vision, and ever since has been a force for change through the power of Jesus.

In the two months following, his sisters saw in him such an improvement, that they, too, came to the Lord and all three of them were baptized in November of that year.

Later, when Associations were formed, Potosi and Tarija were so far away from the rest, that those two teamed up, and added Bermejo when it became a church. All three have small mission churches that are the result of their outreach.

After we left for furlough, Humberto decided to go to the seminary to prepare for service. God was making great changes in the old cold city of Potosi.

The Lord God . . .

will make me walk on my high places

Habakkuk 3:19

Potosi's silver mountain overlooks the city.

It was the ending of my second term of work in Bolivia. I had been called from my work in the Potosi Church to be Executive Secretary of the Bolivian Baptist Union. Many of my fellow workers felt this to be too early a step. When I was elected to the post, it was strongly suggested that I serve well, but not so well as to make the job permanent. Bolivians were used to strong Presidential leadership, so we doubted the wisdom of two strong executives. Rivalry between two national leaders would not be useful for the work at this stage of country-wide growth. I agreed, but thought it necessary to move from Potosi. My missionary colleagues felt it would be better for us not to reside in the same city – Mario Cordova, the President of the convention, was the director of Reekie school in Oruro. I didn't even consider going there. Potosi was a new work ten hours from Oruro, so that to visit any of our other churches in the more developed region would mean that extra 10 hours on top of how much time it took to reach it from there. I felt there were many advantages in choosing Cochabamba, where the work was more mature and many rural and village churches existed. I was thinking of the cost of travel, the time wasted on buses or trains, and the physical wear and tear on me, especially when I drove the car over the mountainous roads. Another advantage was that our children would be able to be home on the weekends.

I had discussed it with Mario, and thought I had obtained verbal permission to move family and house to Cochabamba. a more central position for our church work and excellent in communication and transport. After the move I found the president denied having given permission and asked that I send a letter to the executive council explaining the reasons for my 'unauthorized' move.

I listed the reasons for the move, adding that health of the family was also a consideration. Two years living at an altitude of 14,000 feet is enough. When the children were examined for admission to the missionary children's school, the doctor noted that their hearts were enlarged and pulled to one side. He explained that it happens to increase the beat necessary for circulation of the thicker blood you develop in the high places.

It guarantees enough oxygen in your blood. Air is thinner and oxygen less, above five thousand feet, but your body still needs the same amount to function as those living elsewhere. I knew they would not make me move again, but it demonstrated the president's determination to rule and keep every thing in strict order. I determined to work under the president, as a deacon works under a pastor. Rather than running a central office, I opted to visit churches helping them to solve problems. I did several tours of the new areas of south and east, as well as visit churches with problems in mines and country. Those with difficulties were counseled and given Scriptures to help in the solution. Most did not apply the lessons while I was present, but later did what Scripture teaches and were able to come to an agreement. This was the larger part of my work that year, but there were additional duties for the youth ministry and Evangelism in Depth: an international program for combined evangelism very successful in other parts of the Latin American world. Fortunately this last program had its own workers and coordinators from other countries. Since the purpose of the program was to mobilize the existing Christians, we had extra-church and inter-church meetings because of it. It was a one year program, but they chose the local workers in August, four months before the year began. This was their first few months for preparation. We had a government changed by revolution about the same time. I was due to go on our year of home assignment the next year in July, before they would have their special campaigns. They found that many of their helpers were our Baptist people because they were better prepared to take leadership. I was constantly traveling under stress in a country involved in political changes, social upheaval and highway barricades.

The building we lived in was called the Jordan Street house. It served as a stop and shopping center for families living in Chapare, the jungle region north-east of the city, and as a residence for travelers and language learners. Two Mennonite boys were there at the end of our second term, to study Spanish for three months. As conscientious objectors to army service in the USA, they were sent to aid mission or government projects. They were headed for service in experimental farms, run by the Mennonites in Santa Cruz, as agricultural workers. At a later date our personnel in the Santiago School, the Southern Cross Radio Station and Chapare were to need and use such people in their work. The boys were quiet and when I once walked with them to the main Plaza I saw young girls appear in door ways and stores where I had never seen them before. They seemed to know when the boys were passing their family business and put themselves on display. After the boys left for their agricultural assignments I went to clean up their quarters. While clearing the rooms I found a couple of Playboy magazines which I looked at before tossing them out. I found myself totally engrossed in the double page nude center piece of the slick sexy review. As I stared at the picture I found I did not want to put it down and asked myself: Why am I doing this? I'm not that kind of man. I put the Playboy magazine away in the trash, but it was with reluctance. That night, the wife of one of our colleague's, came through on a trip. They were having family problems and she hinted that she needed to talk to me about something. I was already uneasy because of some remarks she had made earlier about my blue eyes, so I said I'd try to get some time and let her know. That night was full moon and a bright still breathless night of incredible beauty. I felt the urge to get up and walk in the rose garden patio near the street gate. But the guest rooms were just across the open square and the lady would be there; perhaps also unable to sleep because of the brightness and rose scent. An inner voice spoke almost audibly. Why don't you take a walk now? If she did appear you might be able to help her. She needs someone to talk to her and comfort her. I wrestled with the idea and with the voice, but kept my self confined. When I prayed, I fell asleep and heard the voice no more, until the next day. My wife saw the lady off the next morning and I think I was late for breakfast. I discovered that the voice was still present when I passed the trash barrel and that it was trying to direct my thoughts during the day. I came to know that the word 'obsessed' could be a reality. Whatever its origins, it was with me like a stamp on a letter. It became an insistent voice in my mind. I had never experienced anything like it before.

Let me say here that I was a normal boy and found girls attractive, but I was an only child and lived with my grand parents in my teens. I took the school bus to reach high school.

I had no time for social activities. I was a book-worm. The plant nursery occupied any free time and summers. In university I stayed away from the girls' dorms. I knew I would not be financially independent for several years, and I saw the anguish of some who fell in love before they could afford marriage. I married a month short of my 27th birthday to a girl I knew in my junior year at university. But we had gone separate ways while both studied at seminaries in different places. Temporary interests and temptations had come and gone, but I was happily married now. I was discouraged about the slow progress of the work of the mission. So much effort, yet the results were not apparent. I blamed God. It was His work why was it so difficult?

I'm not sure how long the voice stayed with me; one week, or two, but it became a persistent reality. It seemed to prefer clean romantic situations, far from the present moment. It would come as day dreams at moments of delay, boredom, where one is waiting in an office or market. "You need love," the voice would insinuate, "why don't you do something about it?" By this time I knew I was becoming a battle field. I had love and sex at home why seek more? I knew I was under siege, but what could I do? Baptists don't usually practice exorcism and it would be so humiliating to confess it to the fellow missionaries. How do you get rid of an unwanted obsession?

I was due to go to Santa Cruz, a day's travel east to the low tropical lands being developed in farm lands between the Amazon and Paraguay-Parana river systems. Cotton, rice, soybeans and sugarcane were the big products. I was present at a large public meeting of Christian churches. In the audience I saw a young Bolivian girl who stared at me with large hypnotic eyes. I said to myself: she recognizes something in me that calls to her. How does she know? I concluded that some spirit held her captive also, and we would obey them as captives. I was becoming ashamed to pray aloud in church although spontaneous cries for help were increasing within me. I didn't want to go the way I was being pushed spiritually. After the meeting ended I was directed into the back of a truck to be taken to John Palmquist's home for the night. A national woman of about thirty was there also and she called to a younger woman who was talking and joking with a small group of men. One very young, clean-faced boy with Bible in hand seemed the focus of her attention. When she came running to the pickup truck, I was more astonished; she was the girl with the stare. I sat silently in the back where the lady would be between us. The truck stopped at a corner in a semi-rural situation and let the two out. However, the pickup only went about another block before we came to the missionary's house. We were too close for comfort. It was late and I went directly to the bedroom prepared for me. The voice was still active in my head. I was urged to go to the door that led outside into the warm tropical night. I resisted the incessant urging. Danger lay out in the night. I did not want to be set-up by the devil and I turned in desperation to Jesus. "I don't want to do what this voice tells me. I know you don't want me to, but if you don't help me I'll do it and please let me die if I do. I don't want to live after something like that." I meant every word, for I could see that the voice might wear me down and distract me, so I would be useless in the work of God. The sin itself would destroy my usefulness and cause me to resign and leave me with a death wish. I was desperate, hating the way I was being manipulated.

Unexpectedly, I felt someone standing beside me. I thought it must be Jesus. An order lifted something off my chest. There was a difference of some pounds weight that departed and I saw someone leave through a six inch opening in a shutter-like crank window. He smirked at me as he departed. I had the impression of a face and then it was gone. It seemed as if he thought he almost had me. The voice and the obsession were gone. I gave thanks as I fell into an exhausted sleep. I had no more of that problem through the end of the term. I felt relief with the departure of that evil spirit and my spirit was revived, as Evangelism in Depth gained momentum spiritually.

I was a disappointment to the Bolivian Baptist Union, because the Executive Secretary had been no great improvement over the old system of Presidential decrees. The repairs of the roof on the Jordan Street property had not been successful. We were being harassed by a city employee. A builder was being sent from the north to design a new center with more room for Chapare people, visitors and conferences.

This would bring new problems to the Jordan Street property and those who lived there.

I was losing faith in the impact of the gospel on the country. Changing a community's spirit, beliefs and life style is slow business. I wondered if I should return to Bolivia. The Evangelism in Depth campaign was just starting to pick up attention and get the churches caught up in its attempts to bring about spiritual changes. It would be a work of faith and obedience. What would be the results? God utterly surprised us.

Turn to me and be saved, all you ends of the earth, for I am God and there is no other.   Isaiah 45:22

Street meeting in the Garita de Lima, La Paz

"What, pray all night? I just got back this afternoon. I'm dead tired. You can go, but leave me out of it. Evangelism in depth has gone too far for me. I'm going to stay home and sleep." It was a long tirade, but Hazel was firm. No nonsense, God comes first in our house. Tired men are no match for logic and appeals to conscience. I prepared myself for sacrifice.

Evangelism in depth was a concept first tried in Central America in Costa Rica and then in the Caribbean in Santo Domingo. Bolivia was the sixth place to try the program. In the preliminary presentations there were objections because of cost. Some argued that the money rightly applied locally would have as encouraging a result. Most of us knew this was not literally true spiritually, but was true of the social and educational work.

I was personally and spiritually at the bottom of a deep dark valley. I always look for feedback and discernable results in God's work and we weren't getting any. I was discouraged and ready for anything. The idea was to mobilize all Christians for community outreach. All participating churches would entertain programs and film at the same general time explaining how each member was to help evangelize. Some leaders who had already experienced the whole program in their own countries came in August of the previous year. They organized an overall committee with a representative of each denomination. Local leaders were then chosen by that committee. These experienced foreign leaders, along with the local leaders, then adapted the program to the special conditions that they found in Bolivia. They demonstrated the use of the materials already in existence, and worked together to make them suit the local problems. The all night prayer vigils were held simultaneously in churches throughout the country.

Members of the church attended seminars to learn to visit door to door, to pray for their friends and loved ones and how to present the plan of salvation. Special city rallies were to be held throughout the country at the end of the year. The campaign's sponsors pointed to the outstanding spiritual results in other countries. Would we believe God and take the risk? With some doubt, we did sign up with other groups.

I was an executive of the Bolivian Baptist Union and attended the Calama Baptist church, three blocks from the main plaza of Cochabamba, when I was not traveling for Convention. In the months leading up to the campaign, I had watched the pastor use every gimmick and interest grabber: film, special singers, contests, and other ideas to increase the attendance at our Wednesday prayer meeting. Nothing brought the desired results at the home church. The residence where we lived needed repair, the city gave us only very circumscribed costly permission to proceed. We had paxmen, young Mennonites who did farming instead of United States Army service. This form of service lasted two years and the community where they went was grateful. The boys were not all personally Christian, in spite of their family environment. This brought problems.

I came back from visiting the new churches in the south of Bolivia. It was an exhausting trip. I was informed after Friday supper that we were having a full night's prayer service at church. The children would stay the night at boarding school. I objected strenuously. I needed sleep. However conscience prevailed. We went, but I sulked for half an hour. There were only fifteen present, a few more people than a normal prayer meeting. We prayed around the room, sang a few hymns and choruses, prayed for special places, people and for the campaign. We had a film explaining what I already knew. We had a team visit and they offered more motivation and direction on what and whom we should pray for. We continued with testimonies, songs and more prayer. It was now after two and I had gotten over my sleepiness. Some had left, but others had come to sing and pray. At 5 AM some left to open their shops or go to work on Saturday morning but we were enjoying our third tea break and more came to join us. We went home at 7AM a bigger group than at the beginning. I was quite alert and feeling peppy. I wondered what the results would be as I settled into sleep.

Sunday I was rested up, but the church had its usual attendance. Just over half full. No change here. I inquired about meetings in the other churches. Everything was as usual. Was all-out effort useless?

That afternoon marked the big push. Everyone who had

signed up for visitation had a partner and each pair was assigned one block of houses to visit. They invited people to attend their churches. If the people were already believers, they prayer together, and went on to the next house.

All the activities were being announced on the radio. On our own Christian radio station, the Cruz del Sur, there was a period each morning after the 8 o'clock news. Items for prayer were listed, and notice given of the activities coming up: prayer vigils, special musical programs, training sessions for believers, Bible studies, parades, special children's meetings and youth rallies. That Sunday afternoon visitation program that was going on all over the country had also been announced. Where there was no Christian station, time was bought for the announcements on secular stations. The enthusiasm was contagious among the believers, so that many people were prepared to receive the visit.

That evening, many reported a favorable reception from the people they had visited, with their promises to come to visit the church, but there didn't seem to be any extra people visiting THAT service.

We were a few minutes late to the Wednesday prayer meeting and the small room was full. From a usual crowd of 8 to 15 people the crowd swelled to 50. We barely found a place to sit. I was impressed.

Then came Sunday morning and I was stunned! The entire church was jammed with people. We got a seat near the back wall and watched in amazement as the deacons brought in chairs and filled the front of the church where Baptists rarely sit. Then they brought out the children's Sunday School chairs down to kindergarten size. Adults sat in them. Some of the older members went around greeting people I'd never seen nor heard of before. Many of these people had dropped out years before, but now had returned like the prodigal son! Everyone was amazed. The singing and praying was phenomenal. God was with us!

It feels great to have your faith, no matter how small, vindicated. We went early to the Sunday evening service. Those who came later filled a side auditorium that was served by loud speakers. There were a few visitors, even conversions, but most attendees were those whose faith had grown weak or stale. Those with sins and problems had dropped out. Many were reconciled that day.

We left for furlough two months later, and continued to pray for the work during that year at home. The occasional letter brought confirmation of continued blessing and movement of the Holy Spirit in Bolivia. My faith was renewed and I came back for another term's work.

Upon our return our friends said that all the churches stayed full the rest of the campaign. Many were converted and came to the Lord during the city wide rallies. Each church we visited had a number of new people who were taking places of leadership within the congregation and reaching out to their neighbors with the Gospel. Many new churches had sprung up, and the whole Christian community was affected the same way. Because we all worked together, we all were blessed. Those churches who had trained their people developed the fastest and exercised more leadership.

Problems remained and new ones arose to bother us, but the certainty of victory had changed our perspective forever. There was a new growing confidence among the Bolivian pastors and their congregations in their ability to reach out in evangelization. Through the nationals, God would increase the work that missionaries had begun. It had become their work and the victories won gave assurance of victories to come. From this time all the missions grew and national leadership and churches multiplied. National music, good and bad, proliferated. Burdens were lifted as discouragement vanished. God was doing a new thing. Bolivian evangelicals became an honored part of the national consciousness as persecution became largely verbal from a minority. Government agents and police now protected us from rural opposition. They accompanied the missionary to the areas of conflict. Several denominations received invitations to enter areas where the government had problems with unruly people, tribes or foreign settlements on the borders. We were praised by government authorities. The Catholic State Church began to institute reforms approved by the Vatican council and to evangelize. Dry bones were moving and a new day was dawning in Bolivia.

Living in the Jordan Street house in Cochabamba involved the resident missionary in many tasks because the property was old and needed constant upkeep. This meant tending to the gardens, buildings, utility systems: water, lights, telephones and appliances. Irma helped me in the house, we had a gardener once a week, and occasionally, Mary swept the patio for food and some small change.

The property was shaped like a capital B, the blank parts being two patios. It was decided to re-tile a section of the forward street side building roof which was leaking on the second floor guest rooms. The municipality denied our application for repairs and demanded a street front retreat of two meters and a rebuilding of the structure, if there were to be any changes on the facade. We stopped the work we had started on the roof keeping the old tile on the street side slope and replacing the tile only on the patio-side slope. Conformity to the city's demands would need approval from the Board and that could literally take years. No money had been committed for it, so this was all we could legally do. First the present roof had to be removed. This entailed taking the tiles off carefully, so that they could be reused. Even if we decided not to use them again ourselves, they could be sold to a salvager. The tiles, the ceiling canvas (there was no wood), the three inch thorns used in lieu of nails (to fix the edges of the canvas into the plaster to hold it up) and the antique hand-forged nails used on the beams were all recyclable. Under the tiles, there was a foot-thick layer of fine powdery earth supported by a woven cane bed that rested on the rafters. As they shoveled the dirt off the roof, it would billow up and fill the whole front patio like a mist. When those mounds began to build up, Marshall found he was allergic to it. He began to wheeze and cough every time he passed through the patio. So, having received an invitation to attend a youth conference in Cordova, Argentina, he accepted, and left the problem behind for two weeks. Though Borden and Krystal were only home from Carachipampa School for weekends during the school year (August to June), the project began in July, so they were home.

The Cserepkas, Pastor John, and Dr. Margaret, were living

on the ground floor of the front apartment, studying Spanish. They could open their windows at the front onto the street, and we lived in the second patio, so the dust didn't bother any of us too much. When it became a problem for them, they often solved it by visiting the Chapare where a residence and clinic were being constructed for them, taking their children with them. Karlene, being the tag-along was sometimes left out of Borden and Krystal's games, and made a problem by insisting on playing in the first patio with Kathy and Barney.

That back half of the roof was finally off and Marshall was still on his trip, when we were startled by loud rumblings. We were sitting at the supper table Sunday afternoon, and I wondered if it was a big truck passing by. Borden jumped up and ran to the door to look out. He reported dark clouds and thunder. We thought of the open roof. What a shock! The early rains usually came in September, the rainy season didn't begin until late November. The Cserepkas were away, so nine-year-old Borden, seven-year-old Krystal and three-year-old Karlene were all the help I had. We needed to move all the furniture from the open side of the upstairs apartment to the sheltered side. We dashed upstairs carrying all the plastic table cloths I could find quickly. Some of the furniture was so old and cumbersome that I knew we couldn't move it. We would have to cover it! We threw these cloths over the largest pieces, and began to apply main force to the smaller things. If the straw mattresses got wet, they would have to be emptied and stuffed with fresh straw. The large rain drops soon drenched us and when we had done all we could, we went back to our own apartment. We heated water and had a cup of herbal tea, praying that what we had done would be adequate.

One of the by-laws of the city of Cochabamba treated with throwing water onto the street. For many, the only exit from their house was the front door onto the street, and in the olden days, they habitually disposed of their dishwater, bath water, and night waste onto the street. I don't know how old that law was, but it was still on the books. We had already been called down a couple of times for water from our patio running onto the street. A pipe went from there under the front apartment, the sidewalk and through the stone curb. Our gardener had left the hose on to water the roses, and water had found it's way to the street. Our maid had come to me saying that a man from the municipality had come to collect 10,000 Bolivianos (about 92 cents), and I gave it to her and thought no more about it. I had not been feeling well, and had not asked her what it was for. When it happened a second time, I did ask, and at the time cautioned the gardener to watch and not let it happen again. I saw how frightened Irma was of this petty official, and told her I would deal with him in the future. To me he was an annoyance, to her a real threat of danger. Then, this 'civil servant' appeared at my door to 'fine' us when our roofers left the tap open. They had piles of sand and cement, and because the water pressure was so weak, would leave the hose to trickle into a big crater at the top of an already mixed pile. This would filter down and eventually, go into the drain, and out onto the street. I paid, and cautioned the workers: not to be confused with the gardener. At this point, I began to feel harassed. I began to pray for serenity.

Another project that I had brought with me from Potosi, was a request from the Board to write a book with the testimonies of six or eight believers. One day a week, I met with a couple of other missionaries who were already published authors. I was working on the proofs by then, and really hoped they wouldn't insist on a lot of changes to my work. This was just one more thing to disturb my peace. Marshall had received some criticism for having moved to Cochabamba. I think that a wife feels a slight to her husband even more than to herself. I pled for serenity. God was my only refuge.

Between trips Marshall had gone one day with Borden and Krysi to ride their bikes in the park. To avoid running down a child, Krysi had collided with a lamp-post causing the outside globe to fall and break. He went to the Municipality to report the damage, and assume the responsibility. He paid for a new globe, and got the relevant receipt documented. We were assured that everything was in order. Several months later, while Marshall was away traveling in the South, a different man from the municipality came. He was dressed as a gentleman: tall and stern. He really tried to bully me. He got out some official looking papers, and towering over me read a demand to see SEÑOR MARSHALL BORDEN THOMPSON, who was wanted for destroying city property. The Lord gave me strength, and calm before this storm. I said my husband was traveling and would not be back for two weeks. I asked to see the papers, and he reluctantly passed them to me. When I saw that it related to the lamp globe, I said it was not a fine, but the cost of the broken globe that we had paid for, and I had a receipt to prove it. (I did not know where to find it, but I knew we had it.) I told him that he could take it up with my husband when he returned. He went out yelling at me, back over his shoulder, that the authorities would hunt him down and see justice done. Though I faced him with dignity and spoke quietly, this was truly upsetting. On Marshall's tour, I had no way of knowing how to reach him with a warning. I prayed anew for serenity.

I consulted an ex-president of the Bolivian Baptist Union, Victor Toccocari, who also worked for the municipality, and asked how I should deal with this problem. My friend said, "The next time he comes, ask to see his credentials, and copy off the name. Do NOT pay him at the door. Ask how much the fine will be and say you will meet him at the municipal offices, taking the sum he mentions." He said, "That man has found someone he thinks he can exploit, and will look for every opportunity to do so. He is obviously in cahoots with the second man. He lives somewhere beyond you, so goes by every day to see if he can catch you on some count. You call me, and I will be there too."

One morning after a three day holiday, I had gone to the upstairs apartment to take the flag down from it's pole out the window. There had been a rain during the night, and it was soaked. I laid it across a chair to dry before folding and putting it away. Again our 'old faithful' municipality man was at the door: this time to fine me for not having my flag up on an official holiday. By this time I was able to face him calmly, and say that it wasn't up because I had just gone upstairs to take it down -- would he like to go up and see it? He declined and left saying he would be back. I was actually able to laugh about it later, saying, "If he had seen it, he would probably have fined me for letting the flag get wet!"

The next time he came to fine me about the water, when I let him in the door, he, thinking to take the advantage, passed me so it would be hard for me to shoo him out. The entrance to this large property was a pair of enormous doors large enough to drive a truck through. A smaller door was set into one side, for people traffic. The sides of the entry were windowless walls of the garage on one side and the Cserepka's apartment on the other. A large table sat on one side. The fourth side was open to the patio. When he began to rave about our careless habits, wave his fine pad, and demand his price, I asked to see his credentials. After a shocked look, he snaked his hand into his pocket, waved a card under my nose, and hid it away again very quickly. Mary (who sometimes earned a little sweeping my patio) was hovering nearby. I asked her to bring me a pencil and paper, and asked again for the document. She couldn't find anything that would write well, but he didn't know that. The man took on an absolutely terrified look as he put the card in my hand and saw me writing down that data. You could see him trying to maneuver past me to the door. I started writing on the table, but seeing his actions, held the paper in one hand, and put myself between him and the door. He threatened me saying, "Well, I would have accepted 10,000 Bolivianos, but at the office the fine will be 200,000 Bs! I returned the card, put the pencil and paper in my apron pocket, and as graciously as I could opened the door promising to meet him at the office at 2:00 P.M.! When Victor and I met at a few minutes to 2 o'clock, we waited, chatting for over an hour, near the only entrance from the street. Need I say that he did not show? As a matter of fact, we never saw him at our door again. But it was he who triggered that prayer for serenity. And that prayer for serenity, has stood me in good stead for all those intervening years. It serves to help me remember that God is in control and whatever our circumstances are, He will be present with us to guide us to do the right, no matter who our adversary is. Our serenity is in being His.

You will keep in perfect peace him whose mind is steadfast. because he trusts in You. Isaiah 26:3

"You're WHAT?" I asked incredulously.

"I'll just be away Thursday, Friday and Saturday."

"We ARE two very busy people, but didn't you remember that the missionary meeting is Friday night? I can't believe that these preparations have escaped your attention! It isn't at our house, but we are a vital part of getting ready to serve dinner to 90 people over at the Stairs' house."

"Well, you ladies always plan these things..."

"But you do usually attend. Isn't it written on your agenda? AND we count on you men to pick up extra chairs, and the fresh bread at the bakery, that sort of thing." I didn't say anymore. He was accompanying about eight deacons to visit a little rural mission spot. But that wasn't the end of the affair.

That's when I organized the 'WISTFUL WOEFUL ORDER OF WONCE IN A WHILE WIDOWS'!

If you think I lay awake nights thinking of that, you're right. I had three nights before the meeting date, and while thinking of ways to get those chores done, these other ideas kept intruding. You see, I wasn't the only one. I called Jean Phillips, and Florence Stairs, and found out that both their husbands, too, had trips to make, committees to attend, away from the city.

I thought of all those other times I had counted on Marshall to help with some project -- all equally worthy as the one at hand -- only to find out that THAT time was already booked for somewhere else. I won't say I resented them, after all those were the very things we were in Bolivia to do. Things that would spread God's kingdom on earth, give the Gospel to others, tell the Good News. And the things that I wanted him to help ME with were done with the same aim. That missionary meeting was where joint efforts with other groups were conceived, presented and planned: like evangelistic outreach, Easter sunrise services, and Christian musical presentations.   So I prayed for the Lord to help me find other helpers, and to keep my attitude sweet.

I remembered someone's advice before we married: "When you're in a seemingly un-solvable situation -- laugh -- someday you'll see the funny side." I kept thinking -- I'm not the only one

that has this problem. Every married lady who will be at that meeting sees her husband going off when she needs him desperately at home! Even the single ladies, who are counting on one of their colleagues in her mission group, experience it. We needed to organize! However, nobody had time for another meeting. Nobody had money for dues. We didn't need to organize AGAINST anything, or anybody (like a labor union calling a strike). We needed to organize to foster rapport with other women suffering from the same malady.
So I made posters:

NO meetings   NO Dues
            Just sympathetic Understanding
                  among the membership
                          join

THE WISTFUL WOEFUL ORDER
of
WONCE-IN-A-WHILE-WIDOWS

I used bright, bold colors. Not too large, but enough that they would he visible all over the place we would be meeting.

Then I made buttons: enough for all the married ladies who could possibly attend that meeting. I bought large safety pins, and attached them to the back of about a three inch disc made from recycled milk cartons that had a silvery lining. I put little W's inside big ones, and little O's inside big ones, and came up with initials for the center of the buttons, with the entire name printed around the edge.

We did get all the preparations made for the meeting, and everyone appreciated the posters, and the pins. We decided that "W" could stand for 'widower', too, and joked, that the ladies would let their husbands wear the pins, if they had to go off and leave the men caring for the kids, etc. The slogan and joke didn't end there. Once in a while, after that meeting, I would get a call for some of that "sympathetic understanding" mentioned on the poster.

Since that time I have invited many more missionary wives to be members. I haven't limited it to them, though. I've been in contact with military personnel, business people, educators, public servants, air crews, medical professionals, etc. who were left alone, or had to leave their spouses alone, while doing their job. Though I haven't always had a button to pass out, it has often lightened the moment, and helped pull someone out of depression for a little while. I've reminded them that even when your spouse is not around, GOD IS. And He is the ultimate PROBLEM SOLVER,

...a very present help in trouble.

Psalm 46:1

Seal of the Wistful Woeful Order of Wonce-in-a-While-Widows

During our missionary career, we have often been guests in the homes of others. Some homes were very luxurious, and others more middle class, and in rural Bolivia, some were very humble. But we have enjoyed many precious moments with those who have prayed for us over the years. While we were overseas, whatever our jobs were, we were often the hosts. We always sought to make our guests feel as welcome as our hosts and hostesses had made us. On one of our home assignments I made myself a guest book. I carried it with me and asked my hostess in each place to please sign it and give me a favorite Scripture passage, that would be an encouragement to me when I was feeling lonely. I read them this poem to explain:

Whether I travel to the East or the West,

I spend a whole lot of time as a guest.

So I am the guest and this is my book,

Won't you please sign it? So when I look

Back on its pages, that I can remember

My visit with you – whether June or December–

The precious moments I shared with you–

Some treasured antique – or marvelous view–

The bright colored afghan you crocheted yourself

Or the imported tea set that sits on the shelf.–

The devotional moment at the breakfast table–

The earnest prayer time when we were both able

To sense the presence of our Savior, Christ Jesus

To know that in all things that He oversees us.

And could you please write an appropriate verse,

That will give me a blessing and ward off a curse?

If it's your home, church or yearly convention,

I'll recall 'to serve Jesus', was your greatest intention!

Sometimes those who hosted us in Canada, visited us overseas. Sometimes people came from para-church organizations: Pocket New Testament League; Gideon's, World Vision, and other mission groups operating in Bolivia. We hosted parents of children who attended the same boarding school as ours did, seminary students on their way back to Cochabamba. Friends from churches in other cities stopped to see us on the way through. Often our missionary colleagues visited for a committee meeting. Highly interesting people from all over the world came: an architectural model maker from England, painting his way through South America; a Swedish medical student researching parasites; an East Indian professor, hitch-hiking across the high Andean desert; a young bicyclist trying to get into the Guinness book of records; a pair of Peace Corps girls on vacation. There too, we spent many happy hours in their company, meeting so many variations of humanity.

We saw miracles of God when someone was stranded and He made a way for them to continue their journey, or find some relative they were looking for, or gave them the job they needed. etc.

I adopted an idea I saw on a visit to Brazil. My hostess had a table cloth that doubled for a guest book! When someone dined with them, she asked them to sign her table cloth. She then laboriously embroidered the names so they wouldn't fade. Years before, I had attended Seminary with the Bumpass's, though we hadn't been acquainted at the time. She realized that we would know lots of the same people, and invited me to read the signatures, and see if I recognized any names. What a delightful evening that exercise led to. When we came to a name of someone I hadn't heard from for a while, she could often tell me where they were and what they were doing. Once in a while, I could give her some news about someone. I had already found several when I came to Frank and Polly Patterson. I exclaimed, "This time last year, they were at MY house!"

"Well, can you guess where they are now?" she asked. He had been the director of the Spanish Baptist publishing house in El Paso, Texas. She was an editor that prepared Sunday School materials for the pre-school child. They spoke Spanish, and they were going to retire at the end of their trip. I had no idea WHERE they would choose to retire. The purpose of their trip had been to visit all the places which used the literature they printed, and give them some creative hints for more efficient use of it. That was the reason they had been at our house the year before. So I was really shocked to know that they were in Rio. There was also a Baptist publishing house in the city, and they asked him to spend a year as a consultant to help them utilize some of the latest innovative practices in publishing. Though the Brazilians would be speaking and publishing in Portuguese, the practices would work in ANY language. So Frances said she would give them a call and see if they were free to join us for dessert. She found that Frank had a meeting at 8 PM, but he promised to drop Polly off for a visit. Then we sat down to a delicious meal, chatting about the mutual friends that we remembered. When we were ready for dessert, it was past 8, and still no Polly. So after another 10 minutes, Frances decided to drive over and see what had happened. She left. When the door opened for Polly, I flew into her arms for a big 'abrazo' and then we turned and started toward the table. I was shocked when the other lady said, "She's not even going to say 'Hello' to me!" Well, of course, I had presumed it was my hostess, so I turned and there was another blast from the past. Roberta had been with us in language school in Costa Rica, so she, too, spoke Spanish. I'd never have dreamed that she would be there either. She had spent most of the intervening years working for a publishing house in Mexico as a photographer. There again, they asked her to come and share her savvy in photography locally. She had dropped by the Pattersons, and when she found out we were in town, she'd suggested a surprise. She would help Polly with the dishes, and bring her over when they were done. Somehow, they had missed Frances in the process. When she asked about her room-mate, Kay Rowe (who worked in Bolivia with us) from Costa Rican days, I said that her hair was as white as mine. "But for 'Loving Care' (by Clairol) -- so would mine!" she laughed. By that time, Frances came in just mystified as to how she could explain, that Polly was gone, and the house was dark. But one look gave her enough explanation, and we all sat down to enjoy dessert and go on with our chatter.

I always said that one day, I was going to do the same thing -- make myself a table cloth that would serve as a guest book. It wasn't until I went to Turkey, and had an <u>enormous</u> table and not a single cloth that would cover it, that I finally made one. I got a Christmas print of tiny clusters of holly with its berries on white, a meter wide and a meter and a half long. Then I got the same material in a plain red, cut it in the middle, and framed the holly. That extended it another meter on the ends and the sides. The next furnished apartment had a much smaller table, so I took out the seams at the ends, and cut enough from the sides to have four inches of red on all four sides. Then at the next place we had to buy a dining room suite, and it had to be changed again. It was wide enough, but almost two meters long, so I sewed the ends I had taken off, back on and it was enough. I started writing into the four inch strip on all sides the word for "Welcome" in black lettering in every language I could get someone to write out for me. So now I have it in English, Turkish, Spanish, French, German, Dutch, Korean, Farsi (written in Arabic Script), Chinese, and Japanese(in two scripts). Since retirement, I again have a smaller table so I had to do something. I won't cut it again, though. I have tucked it back, and did a blind stitch to keep it in place, so that if I have another large table, I can stretch it out again. I used all colors in the embroider paints, and let everyone sign for themselves, so it is really bright. I got two new signers at Thanksgiving time this year. Just last week, we were looking at it with Tom and Gladys Donelon, friends with whom we worked in Turkey, and thanked the Lord for the storehouse of memories contained thereon. Some came for a meal, some stayed the night, and some came for a summer or a school term, and some stayed on and on and on...

Do not forget to entertain strangers, by so doing some people have entertained angels without knowing it. Hebrews 13:2

Messengers of Hope sing in Prado for Mission's 75th Anniversary

We had heard that Bolivia had gone through 287 revolutions since it got its independence from Spain. It was an interesting bit of trivia. So when we had been in La Paz some months, and we awoke to the sounds of explosions, our first thought was that the REVOLUTION had come. It was April 9th, and we wondered if people went out and carried on normal activities under those circumstances.

Our young helper, Maria, informed us at breakfast that they were only "greeting the dawn" with celebratory fireworks on MNR (National Revolutionary Movement) Day. It was the anniversary of the latest 'coup' in 1952 when the present government had come in. The year was 1956, and almost time for elections.

In June when they were campaigning, sometimes the youth of the different political parties were demonstrating, trying to attract others to their numbers, sometimes there would be a clash between two that resulted in a death. The next day at the funeral, the opponents would appear, and there would be another death or two. Then, the next day, at the funeral for them, there would be another death or two. The third day, they didn't announce where and when the funeral would be, to avoid more such incidents. Since we lived in the center of the city, we didn't sleep very well until the election was over because the youth continued to whoop it up every night -- and usually very late.

During the ensuing years, we saw many very bloody destructive strikes as miners, or farmers, or Unions (called *syndicates*) came to town with rifles, and dynamite caps, and demonstrated their displeasure with some government action. But it was 1964 -- about 8 years after we arrived before we saw our FIRST REAL REVOLUTION!

There had been some unrest leading up to a visit by French President Charles De Gaulle. The government had decreed that everyone clean up the city -- paint their garden walls (to cover the graffiti that said *"Viva"* (long live) to some and *"Muera"*(death) to others.) With everything in beautiful shape, about two weeks before he came, some students began to put up some new graffiti. The president sent his vice president to fire on the students if they were caught in the act. Though he refused to do that, 'Willie' was caught, and imprisoned. The vice president then led a revolt -- offering the president safe conduct to the airport/exile -- if he would go before noon the next day.

We lived in Cochabamba where all this was happening. Our older children lived at a boarding school 45 minutes away during the week, and came home for weekends. Karlene went to kindergarten in the city. Marshall was away in La Paz for a committee meeting.

On Monday November 4th there had been a women's retreat at a lovely campsite outside the city. When Mildred Goulding, a colleague, and I came home everything seemed so still. We stopped to have ice cream in the plaza, and commented that it felt like the quiet before a storm. That night we heard shots, and the radio told us that students had erected barriers around the University, and were throwing rocks at the policemen, who were responding with gunfire. Karlene was justifiably afraid, and I played down the gravity of the situation, just repeating what they said on the radio.

The next morning the radio suggested that we should go to the market and stock up on food, in case it was a long drawn-out disturbance. I sent Irma, our maid at that time, off to get what we needed, but she hurried back when the radios at the market had announced that the schools were being closed, and the children being sent home. She had two children herself, and had to leave me to be there when they got home, as they didn't have a key. The lady who came to sweep the patio, also had to leave for her two little girls. We went to the front of the building where we could look down on the street. A friend was there on his motor scooter to pick up his little girl from the school across the street. He had another going to a school near where Karlene was, and offered me a ride over there. The first girl stood on the foot board, and I climbed on behind. I thanked my friend and said goodbye as his second daughter took my place. Most of the kids and teachers had gone by the time I got to the kindergarten. I took Karlene by the hand and we hurried down the street. Two blocks away, coming fast, was a crowd of students with signs stating their protest, shouting and singing.

134

"Can't we take a taxi, Mommy?" Karlene asked anxiously.

"If we can find one." The truth is, that at the hint of riot, all the taxis disappeared from the streets. Tire-slitting, tipping over and fire-setting were activities practiced in this sort of situation, so they played it safe. They pulled into their own patios -- or a friends', if they were far from home -- and waited out the trouble. We finally got home out of breath and worried.

In an upstairs apartment, two young Paxmen, David and Daniel, were staying. They were 'conscientious objectors' from the United States, who were there to do their 'military service' working on a Mennonite farm in the lowlands. They would need some Spanish, though, and were acquiring that at a local language school before going into that work. They shared a living room, and wee kitchen and each had a bedroom to himself   On the way from school, they had seen what the students had done to the house of the local police chief (who had conveniently disappeared) sacking and burning over the loud protests and flood of tears of his wife and daughters. They were wide-eyed and excited, pouring out the story. In case it did last, I decided to organize. I told them that we would cook together, while we had electricity, using my stove unless/until the electricity was cut off. Then we would use their kerosene stove. I left Karlene with them and went to the market to get the things that I had sent Irma for earlier.

On the way home with supplies for a couple of weeks, I found that the two heavy bags were really hard to handle, after I had bought a couple of loaves of bread as well. Still several blocks from home, two ladies came up behind me and offered to help. Each of them took the other handle of one of my bags, and we set a loaf of that bread on top of each, and they walked me on home. Though I had never met, or noticed either of them before, they knew who I was. They lived a little further down the street and were kind enough to help me in the emergency.

We had our lunch and kept tabs on things with the radio on. I was sitting in the patio, praying and really wondering what I could do. I was not worried about Borden and Krystal, they were safer in their school dorm and walled grounds in Carachi-pampa school, 45 minutes outside the city.

I had just been reading TIME magazine about a Christian

doctor in Africa who was captured and tortured to death. They had found him hiding in a store room in his hospital, dragged him out, cut him cruelly, and then threw him on the ground and went round and round the circle doing their war dance on his back until he was dead. I didn't want to be caught and treated like that here. We did have lots of storage places, but I tried to think of where we could hide and not be found. At one part of the second patio, visible from my lawn chair, was a bed of snap dragons. The seed package promised plants 18 inches high, and these were even taller. The patch was about 10 ft. square. I remembered that when the children had been playing hide and seek the week before, they had stepped into that flower bed, lay down among the colorful blossoms, and were really instantly invisible. They could only be seen when the person who was 'it', climbed up several walls and things that finally took them to the roof. Then, they could look down into that bed and spot them. I called Karlene and suggested that if anyone hostile came to the door, that WE could play that little game. I stressed that we would have to be VERY, VERY QUIET.

We had it all planned when the doorbell rang. I went to the door and asked timidly, "Who's there?" It was the man who noticed my keys in the door, and knew that I'd want to bring them inside. I expressed my gratitude.

That evening, after we had finished our meal, we decided that it would be better not to show a light at the front, so David and Daniel moved their things to other rooms that opened only onto the first patio. We kept the radio on, listening for significant news. Suddenly, the doorbell rang. David was quite tall, and felt that he should go to the door, in case there was danger, so I wouldn't have to. He was gone a LONG time, so I decided that I'd better go see what was happening. But, Daniel too, turned chivalrous, and said, no, that he would go. More time passed and I finally had to go, anyway. When I got there David tried to explain that this lady wanted them to help her move her car. But all three of them were talking at the same time. I finally quieted them down, and asked the lady what the trouble was. "You must get your car off the street," she said." The students are coming and every time they see a car, they turn it over and set fire to it." So I explained to her in Spanish and them in English, that it wasn't our car. We decided that it probably belonged to someone in the cantina across the street. Then Daniel and David COULD help. The lady couldn't properly go into the cantina alone, but they couldn't go without her, because they couldn't explain in Spanish and find the owner. We laughed about that. They did find the owner, and he came out and drove his car away when the students were still lacked about a half block. At this point everyone hurried home and barred their doors.

This was my (Hazel's) experience. Now, Marshall takes up the narrative in La Paz. There, I am the guest of Mission treasurer, Janet Holmes, retired but returned to her duty because the current treasurer was on home assignment.

I had parked the jeep I drove up from Cochabamba at Villa Victoria Church in a poorer suburb on the road to 'El Alto' where the Airport is located. The city of La Paz is in a bowl and the rim must be passed over to escape from it. The road to the remainder of the country passes through 'El Alto de La Paz'(The Heights). There it emerges on the high prairie with roads to Lake Titicaca, where the ancient indigenous civilizations first developed. From the Alto other roads lead to the Pacific coast westward or down to the temperate valleys, jungle hills and lowlands of the Amazon to the east. This strategic city became the seat of power. The Spanish empire conquered the cold windy high prairie and then sought the protected site of the valley they named for "Our Lady of Peace" (La Paz). I visited the Cruz del Sur, Southern Cross Radio station where I had a guestroom for the night. I had my permission to travel issued by the police the day before. The mission committee would meet in the morning. The atmosphere in the city was tense and I wondered if the Lady of peace would be disturbed by politics again. Army guards were posted at the radio. It had been captured and used on other occasions of protests. I walked to the meeting at Janet's house and discovered that the meeting was canceled. But the Señoritas insisted I stay for lunch. It was safer than being at the radio and the restaurants were all closed today. We talked over the situation and Janet insisted that the salary of the teachers and pastors needed to be in the hands of the local treasurer for the first of the month. She had visited the bank the day before and the money was in the house. I was appointed to take the several thousand dollars in local money up out of the city to deliver it. I agreed and then went out on the front porch to watch one airplane, an American surplus war model, dive into the bowl of the city to strafe the football stadium four blocks away, where the miners and political militia had gathered. Janet spoiled my view to order me into the house. By that time shooting had broken the earlier calm and we listened to the radio to try to get the latest city by city developments. By late afternoon it was obvious that the defenders of the Socialist President were exhausted and the conservative Vice-President's revolution had carried the day. We would be under curfew that night and if I were to leave the city it would be necessary to move now. The stacks of money, were tied in ten folds of ten thousand bills equaling 100,000Bs,(*Bolivianos*) in each bundle. These bundles formed a block of bills that were eighteen inches long and too bulky to hide. I wrapped it in newspaper and doubled two magazines around it and tied it securely. After a moment of short but earnest prayers; they sent me on my way out of the house into the turmoil. I carried the money under my arm like an umbrella or a roll of housing plans through the armed posts and the center of the city.

With all the patrols abroad, and no buses or taxis available I knew I would be forced to walk several kilometers uphill. A formidable task at 4000 meters altitude. Taxis seek the privacy of their patios and garages at the first sign of trouble. It is a sensible precaution to avoid confiscation or roving patrols of patriots wishing to display their revolutionary zeal by joy riding through the city, shouting and shooting. Having lived in downtown La Paz, I knew it quite well, so was able to choose the easy routes, and avoid the worst of the trouble zones where fire fights sprang up. Their quarrel was not with the foreigners, but their own local political enemies.

I could see snipers atop the walls along the street, and could hear them call to one another—revealing their judgment as to how dangerous the current passerby was. I hardly even captured their attention. A group was crying near a devastated building. "We warned the old man to run away but he delayed and they caught him." one said. "He had enemies." said another. "God wanted it this way." A woman mourned. All nodded in agreement.

I occupied my mind in theology for the next few miles. Did God will it this way? If a child is killed by a car they say: *"Dios lo queria asi."* It seemed a terrible insult to God. When things go wrong or people make a bad decision it's God's fault. It's the lie we use to deny human responsibility. It's the mentality in much of the world I've worked in. It says, "I've done nothing wrong. It's God's fault." Others will say: "Those people got into it, it would have been fine if they hadn't interfered. It's not my fault." Denial, as well as guilt dwell in us all. No one likes the reality that exposes our true selves to the world. The theme was good for the climb as I carefully walked to my destination in Villa Victoria. I drove to the Alto Police control center on the lip of the plateau just before dark. The airport was closed down. A few trucks were on the road but traffic was scanty. I was in Cochabamba in the morning with the money for Mildred to pay salaries. With the dawn peace returned as rapidly as it had departed.

You shall not be afraid of the terror of night
... A thousand may fall at your side ...
But it will not come to you.

Psalm91:5,7

Snow capped Illimani guardian of La Paz

While in my first year of seminary I had come to the point of examining the doctrine concerning the baptism of he Holy Spirit. Many charismatic groups were making much of the experience as something new, but I reasoned that leaders in Christian History must have had the same experience without necessarily being accompanied by the manifestation of tongues which every one seemed to expect with its presence. St. Paul spoke in tongues, but did not exalt the experience unduly. (1 Cor. 14:19) Therefore, it was necessary to be filled with the Spirit, but not be demanding of specific gifts with the experience. The Spirit would equip His servants with the necessary tools of His work. One evening I decided to seek the spirit's filling alone in my bedroom. I read the key passages of the baptism of the 120 gathered in the upper room in Acts 2:1-4 in a modern translation and asked God to fill me and give me the necessary gifts for a missionary. I waited, but nothing seemed to happen. I read it again and again. No feelings, nothing visible, so how do you know you have it? I decided that it had to be like the gift of salvation -- something you receive by faith. You couldn't work yourself up into it or earn it by hours of prayer. It was a gift. I asked for it and the eager Giver would comply. I decided that He had heard me and I had it. I felt rather warm and happy. God is not scanty in giving to His children. A voice seemed to come from the foot of my bed. "So, I guess you'll be perfect from now on." There seemed to be a sneer in the expression. I looked at the empty area for a moment, decided it was the enemy and said out loud. "No, not perfect, but more effective and blessed." Nothing more happened and after a time of happy prayer I went to bed.

There followed a number of interesting experiences the next weeks. Let me tell you one of them. A young Jewish man I had met on the Berkeley University campus and I were walking down the street together. He was explaining that his sister had converted and was helping a Quaker ambulance service. But in spite of her joy, he expressed doubts: "You can't really be sure of these things ... there is no way to know." I protested vigorously: "Oh, but you can be sure... God can confirm it to you!" He glanced at me as I started talking and ducked his head. He hurried to the corner to cross the street, saying he had to leave. I glanced at myself in a store window supporting a column of six inch wide mirror glass. My face was shining! It was like the *shekinah* glory that Moses wore coming down Mount Sinai from his meeting with God (Exodus 34: 29-35; Matt. 17:2; Acts 6:15). Moses hid it behind a veil, so no one would see it depart (2 Cor. 3:13,18). Mine was gone by the time I got home, but I thought that it was Jesus' way of confirmation to a man He was witnessing to. I was a link in that witness. I never saw the man again.

My experiences at Guatajata were of spiritual opposition and oppression. My early experiences were with the Holy Spirit, all of which were of a building, positive nature. Until I met the ruling spirit at Heapy mountain I had had no direct confrontation with the enemy. That is, I knew of temptations, I experienced them, but not direct conflict with spirits. This was at the end of my first term in Bolivia. By the end of my second term I had experienced direct oppression of a spiritual obsession and presence. I had seen the effects of vigils and mass prayer groups during Evangelism in Depth. I decided to investigate exorcism and discernment of spirits, which are mentioned as gifts of the Holy Spirit by St. Paul in the New Testament. (I Corinthians 12:7-11) Would God give me such discernment? I decided to research the topic and request the mentioned gift of spirit discernment. I seemed to become more aware of such activity in Canada and the U. S. as well as in other countries. The film <u>The Exorcist,</u> came out about the same time and presented new angles to the question of spiritual phenomena. From our second home assignment or furlough through our third period of service, I earnestly studied and experimented with the detection of spirits and other phenomena. It was in this period that I met brother Amos in Bolivia, several times, several years running. He proved interesting to watch because of his faith in dreams and his sensitivity to some things. (See Chapter #15)

On a trip with him, I faced opposition by a territorial spirit in Carangas, the far west of Bolivia where our work was growing rapidly. We had the motor of the jeep die halfway through a wide river each time we tried to cross. We had verbal invitations by Bolivian government men because the

Pentecostals from Chile were crossing the border to plant churches, and authorities wanted the village people's allegiance to a Bolivian-based entity like the Bolivian Baptist Union. We already had work north and east of that area so most of the communities knew and welcomed us.

The upshot of our continual expansion west was the steady growth of our membership in rural areas. Special funds spent by the newly formed Oruro Baptist Association encouraged local churches to reach out in evangelism. We discovered that group prayer at certain river crossings and mountain passes made for a smooth visit while neglect in these matters could lead to problems. Going through the mountains east of Oruro to visit an area not evangelized, we once had three flats in one hour. That was my yearly average! I felt it was to keep us out.

Statisticians told us that our membership doubled in about three years during this time. Dr. Daniel in Canada was trying to get the Union on self-support, and it caused much turmoil among the pastors, who felt we were taking away their job assurance. Yet we were growing in numbers and extent by God's power at the same time in areas away from the fear and arguments. About that time the Campaign of the Americas, an evangelistic effort among Baptists, simultaneously in all Latin America, stimulated church growth in our cities. My third home assignment came after this successful campaign.

In Canada during this time, I got indications of spirit presences in various homes I visited. One of the most notable was with an old friend whom I had met in his single days when he was a great youth worker. Later when I returned, he was married, and I discovered his house was an abode of a spirit of irritation. His wife showed the presence of this spirit by her annoyance at my arrival as she called her husband who was bathing to say, "Your preacher has arrived," and left me in the hall to await his towel-wrapped appearance. Later I had the hair on my arms rise and skin tingle passing a room on the second floor. I asked the pastor who lived in that room. It was an empty room located over the kitchen. I told my friend what I had found and that I had sent it away. He said that he wondered if a hostile spirit indwelled his wife. I didn't detect anything like that, but he told me of several happenings, accidents his son suffered that made us wonder. Some years later, after she was widowed, all reports say that she became a very faithful, quiet, loving church worker who visited the sick and needy at her home church. In other words her behavior changed after his death. I found these experiences upsetting, because I was sure that these spirits are drawn to fights and quarrels, just as flies are drawn to rotting meat. They are attracted to and stimulate their environment by their presence.

One of my friends, Hedley Hopkins, in La Paz had a frightful dream. A giant hand reached out to claw at him in anger. He had the dream several times. He lived in an area where militia went to guard the ridge between the main city of La Paz and Miraflores, the valley where the radio and other of our rented properties existed. It is an area where men were killed in every revolution and some riots. Our prayers seemed to make a difference there. Years later he had an experience in Santa Cruz, the tropical city of eastern Bolivia where a man with false doctrine had come to the church to argue some theological points. After spending time with the Bible to search for answers, the pastor asked to pray with him, and as he did so, he saw a dark cloud fill the space between himself and the inquirer which suddenly vanished with a slight wind sound and was gone. The man became humble and grateful as he told the pastor he would come to service. The pastor went singing into his house with a feeling of triumph he couldn't explain.

I have discovered several kinds of spiritual personalities. Let me list them for you and compare them with scripture.

First, there are the territorial spirits, which demand worship or at least sacrifice and submission. These are like the Baal of Scripture. Their authority is over a district and they are worshipped on the mountain top. Sacrifices of animals, (Judges 6:25)and in times of crisis, persons were offered to them. (Judges 11:30-40) These Baal had priests or practitioners who were dedicated to the service of these beings (I Kings 18:17-ff.) On Heapy mountain our teacher said that according to his father there were many youth in training for service as brujos. That day when we met the spirit, there was only one young man to be consecrated by its authority -- the last of an old tradition.

Second, there are other spirits that will advise people through a brujo or medium of some kind. They, too, demand offerings and payment to the medium. (Acts 16:16-19). They give instructions, which they expect to be obeyed. The person whom the spirit favors must call and seek its help. Familiar spirits are recorded in Scripture as in the story of the witch of Endor (I Samuel 28:8-ff.) Medieval history is full of encounters with people in such relationships. The séance and fortune teller is the modern version of spiritism. The popularity of Screwtape Letters by C.S. Lewis shows that the workings of devils, junior or senior, is still intriguing and challenging to modern minds.

Thirdly, there are also controlling spirits that obsess their victims until they obey their insistent demands and sin in some way (Luke 8:2.) The Scriptures also show multiple occupation by imps or demonic spirits (Mark 5:1-13.) People with various bodily afflictions are described as being bound by Satan (Luke 13:16), which is not the same as being possessed, occupied or obsessed. These three words describe various conditions of demonic power and of the spirits' actions. Possession is the complete domination by the spirit personality (Matt. 17:18-21.)

Occupation may be part-time or occasional dominance of the personality. Obsession is a form of attack that is less than possession or occupation, but seeks to strengthen itself into one of the latter states. It is an attempt at invasion. The number of personalities or invading spirits can be great, as in Christ's encounter with the maniac at Gadara. (Luke 8:26-30.) When Jesus asked the evil spirit what his name was, 'Legion, because we are many.' I looked 'legion' up in the dictionary, it said a legion of Roman soldiers was six to eight thousand! That's a formidable army, enough to panic a herd of pigs.

People who have been bound by spirits need help to break bonds and gain freedom. People occupied must be vacated by the spirit before freedom is attained. Freedom must be maintained, also. Jesus describes the state of a man, who after freedom, leaves himself empty and open. The expelled spirit returns, bringing other helpers to keep his prey subdued. (Luke 11:24-26) The last state of the man is worse than the first.

Scripture, however, does not explain spirits. It simply affirms their existence and activity. Most theologians maintain they are the angels that followed Satan in rebellion against God. The best teachings we have state their reality and unity, as well as how to deal with them. (Matt. 12:22-30) We don't know if they die, reproduce or have environmental limitations. We have no way to know if they are increasing or decreasing in numbers and activity. Do evil men become demons after death? Are the living haunted by the dead? Does knowing their name give power over the spirit? Opinions are many and varied. In Genesis 2:7; 3:19, man is created of the dust of the ground. In 3:14 the serpent is cursed to eat dust all the days of its life. Does this mean that they consume the energy or soul of people? Does this early declaration signify a spiritual reality as does the *proto-evangelium* (first good news) in Genesis 3:15. The seed of the woman will crush the serpent's head, and it, his heel. If this Scripture is true, why not all of it? Spirits seem to both avoid recognition and yet to seek human contact. Naturally, if they need people to get energy and strength, they will find those on whom they may feed. The high energy of hatred or despair would seem to be the best sources of emotional states of mind: a banquet for beings that consume or live on such products.

Do peoples' fears take physical form and visit on them the feared results? Do we create our vampires and *cari-siris* or do we create a state of fear where they can operate freely to produce more fear? Faith, like love, is a powerful force in the world. Can our beliefs make reality in its own image? Does materialism destroy spirits by refusing to believe in them? Or does it blind us to an interacting reality which all our ancestors understood and people labeled primitive are still in touch with? Is it a reality we refuse to study or recognize? Do our friends and neighbors become victims of malignant spirits we have chosen to ignore? These are questions about which we can only speculate. We lack research and extension of our knowledge toward things difficult to detect. Every nation and people have believed in spirit reality, but we presume that we are wiser and more discerning in ways that they were not.

In the study of atoms, we have arrived at a point where researchers can't see the object of their studies. Atomic and chemical contaminants are also an invisible presence, and we need special instruments to detect them. When we suffer warfare that utilizes invisible realities to destroy humans, with viral, biological, chemical or atomic weapons, we will have made full circle, to fear again the invisible threats to our lives. Perhaps now, we will be more willing to study other spiritual realities that are invisible, yet real, that threaten human well-being. It's all a question of spirit: bold inquiry or fearful denial.

When an evil spirit comes out of a man,

It goes through the arid places of the earth

Seeking rest, and does not find it.

Then it says,

'I will return to the house that I left."

When it arrives,

it finds that the house is swept clean,

and set in order.

Then it goes and takes seven other spirits,

More wicked than itself,

and they go in and live there.

And the final condition of the man

Is worse than the first! Luke 11:24- 26

Troops of devil dancers perform at Carnival in Oruro.

For a good part of our time in Bolivia, we didn't have the use of a car. While in La Paz, we could use buses or taxis. We lived in the center of town, so both these modes were readily available and reasonable. When we wanted to go out of town, as Marshall did occasionally to visit country churches, we had to borrow the "Blue Beetle," a pickup truck that belonged to the Radio La Cruz del Sur, or take a bus or truck.

On one of those visits with deacons, Marshall sent me to pick up the Blue Beetle, and bring it back, while he made other preparations for the trip. I arrived, got the truck out to the street, and to the Triangular Park a block away, before the motor died. It was the first time I had tried to drive that vehicle. Two twelve-year-old boys, stepped up and offered to help. Actually, they insisted on it, and wouldn't take 'no' for an answer! They didn't even wait for an answer. They began to push. At the next corner, I should have turned up the hill and driven up to the Prado. They began yelling that I should turn downhill, or we couldn't get it started. The motor caught and then choked out before we got to the corner. I had no choice, I had to turn down hill! Each time the boys would jump off, push, jump back up on the fender, and scramble into the back until it choked out again. The General Acha Avenue plunged straight down for several blocks, and then went into a zigzag until it got to the main road again. Here was another opportunity to head uphill.
Right at the corner it died once more, and I missed it.

The road was serpentine for a while, and I'm sure the fits and starts lasted another couple of kilometers (making at least three in all), before it was almost level. In one of those stops, a man in a suit came running up. He asked me what I thought I was doing! Why had I forced these little boys to push my truck all the way down there. By now I knew that the kids had wanted to go swimming just about where we were at that moment. The man whipped out a little pad and filled it out, making a citizen arrest. He told me that I should be in the traffic police office at 11am the next day. Fortunately, he didn't take me straight to jail. I'm not sure how I got back to town; I'm not sure how the car got back to the radio building. I don't know if Marshall made his trip or not. Sometime later in the day, I remember recounting my story with all my indignation to Art Wormald, the Radio's director, and when I showed him the ticket, we realized that man had made out the ticket at 1pm, and cited me to appear at 11am, and then dated it THAT DAY, instead of the next! Those boys had really gotten me into trouble.

The next day, Art picked me up at home, and instructed me to stay at the counter while he talked to someone in the back. I was not to open my mouth. If I noticed that they were looking at me, I could bat my eyelids at them as though I might cry. It was just one BIG office with a long counter right across the whole length of the room with lots of desks, each with an officer working away at it, on the other side. Everybody could see everybody else. I stood there and looked as pitiful as possible, and I never knew what was said. After a few moments, Art came back, and said everything was alright. I suppose that he must have excused me for not knowing enough Spanish, or being new in the country, or maybe just being a woman driver!

Then there was the time when Marshall was invited to spend Easter at Santiago de Chiquitos High School. There was to be a youth retreat, and Matilda Findley wanted him to come. His duty at Easter, however, was to drive the preachers, leaders, and any special guests to the "Junta" (associational meeting) out in Carangas — the Wild West of Bolivia. I could see that he really wanted to go, so offered to drive them out myself, if he would be sure that I had a good guide to tell me where to turn. In Carangas, the roads were mere tracks here and there made by the trucks that carried on commerce with Chile. You sort of sighted on a landmark in the distance and picked your way through the scrub growth.

So, he made all the arrangements: Dona Juana would be my guide. He gave me a list of the others who would accompany me and flew away to the high school retreat.

Came the day to go, there were a few hitches. Dona Juana had a toothache. She wasn't ready to go at 2 p.m. -- the appointed hour of departure. I arrived at her house to find she hadn't returned from the dentist's office. When she did come, he hadn't pulled the tooth--as she had hoped he would. It seems the tooth was abscessed, and only after the abscess had burst and drained would he extract it. But she still wanted to go. Though none of the guests were from Carangas, Pastor Francisco had visited there. He sat in the front seat with me, while she sat in the back and nursed that painful tooth. Dona Juana did speak Spanish, but she explained to Francisco in Aymara – their mutual mother-tongue – the general things that he should know, and she promised she would prompt him at the places that we should turn and sight on another landmark.

We went along very well for some hours, but one place the ruts over one stretch of the road became so deep that even though we tried to straddle them, we slipped off into the rut and ran aground. We found that we had left the shovel (standard equipment when we packed the car for any trip) and all we had to dig out with was a skinny, double jointed, jack handle. Any time we exerted a little too much pressure, it folded. We took somebody's tin plate to take out the earth that they broke loose until we finally got free. By that time, darkness had fallen, and we knew that we were supposed to be looking for a road on the right. So every time there was a break in the scrub brush and stiff desert grass, I would stop and Francisco would jump out and investigate. Each time, Juana would assure us that wasn't it. We prayed, sang, encouraged each other, trying to keep our spirits up. We hadn't eaten since noon and were all feeling the chill.

Finally, we saw a light. We followed the light, and abruptly found ourselves plunging down a steep bank into a dry stream bed and up the other side. We were in a village and the first house we stopped at we found Bineranda—our little maid. Since I wasn't going to be home, she had left before I did, and caught a truck out to her village. She planned to come to the Junta with a group going from there. We talked to several people and finally her uncle said he knew the way and would guide us the rest of the trip. We were already very crowded, but they snuggled a little closer together in the back, and made room for him AND a spade!

It was midnight before we arrived, but someone fired up a little one-burner kerosene-fuelled pump stove and gave us some hot coffee and cold bread before we fell into our sleeping bags, exhausted. Juntas begin early and the camp was alive before seven. Every one came by to see how we were and to welcome us. Breakfast was a treat. The junta was joyful and, after all, well worth the struggle. God seems to recompense extra effort with nice rewards.

However, when we lived in Sucre, a new vehicle was acquired, and assigned to us. It was purchased in La Paz, and needed to be driven for 500 km. before it got a checkup and was released to us. Kay Rowe, who lived in Guatajata, did the driving, and saw to the checkup, and radioed us that it was ready. Since Marshall was busy with other things, I was asked to go to La Paz, and bring it back. We're talking about the 20 hours or so driving time necessary to bring it home.

By this time, Borden had left for University, and Krystal was passing her time, trying several jobs, before she left to join him after Christmas. She was living in a little apartment in back of the Radio building and working there at whatever they assigned her to do. I was more than happy to stay with her and help her get comfortable.

We stocked her kitchen. Since I needed flour in Sucre I bought a big bag, and just left her a large full canister there. I got in on several meetings, and things that I enjoyed before starting back shortly after noon on Friday. That way I could make it to Oruro in time for supper, and a good night's sleep before the next lap which would take 10 hours.

I got my travel permit in town and stopped at all the checkpoints along the way without incident. It was just about 5:00 O'clock when I arrived at Eucalyptus, less than an hour from my destination. I noticed as I was getting out of the car that there was a swarm of students from Cochabamba and rightly guessed that they would all want a ride into town. They had probably spent the day on a truck that was on it's way to La Paz, when they really were going to Oruro. Then they would take whatever came along from this fork in the road for that last little bit.

I was in a hurry to get there for supper, which would be at 5:30. I didn't want the bother of driving around for twenty or thirty minutes delivering them to their homes.

So I jumped out of the car with papers in hand, and slammed the door, and ran in. They registered the car license, my driver's license, the time, my point of origin, and destination. I ran out again, and lo and behold, my keys were not in my pocket. There was a spare set in my purse – but I hadn't taken it inside – and there the others were, dangling from the ignition! So much for being selfish...

So I humbly go back in and ask if the traffic policemen have any ideas. Fortunately for me, one of them keeps a box of keys. It was about shoe box size and brimming with keys. He only had to try 10 or 15 before finding one that would work. I gave him a tip, and many thanks. By that time the students had all caught rides with somebody else.

Muriel Harrington and Cathy McGorman had already eaten when I arrived, but they had saved my meal, and heard my tale of woe while it was warming. Then they had another cup of tea, and accompanied me while I ate my supper.

The next morning, I started on the long haul to Potosi. The girls had prepared me some sandwiches and a thermos to take along, so that I could eat as I drove.

At the checkpoint at the outskirts of Oruro, I was faced with a request from the traffic police to take a couple of passengers. In this sort of arrangement a lot of local drivers collected the going rate for a bus, but we never asked for money. Usually the person offered something. However, I didn't mind taking these ladies who were going to places along the way.

They were good company and we chatted pleasantly. Each got out when we reached the point on the road nearest to their village. Usually, some family member was waiting to help carry home the purchases she had made in the town.

Up until noon, the gravel road was straight as an arrow and relatively smooth. There was an occasional stream to be forded, and that usually had a bed of rocks set in cement to make it easier. But from there to Potosi, there were several sets of zig-zags going up higher and higher into the mountains.

Again, at the checkpoint, there was someone looking for a ride. It was an old man. I wasn't afraid of him, but I didn't think it would look right to take him along. Besides, I didn't want to take the time to eat there, I didn't have enough to share with him, and I wanted to eat while I was driving. So I said no.

After the first set of zigzags, I drove along enjoying my lunch and the dramatic scenery. The beauty of Bolivia is in its wide expanses and earth colors. The plain with its sparse desert-like plant life, showed a herd of llamas once in a while, and the backdrop of snow capped mountains in the distance was breathtaking. On the other side a little further along was a drop-off that looked like pictures of the Grand Canyon. I didn't run across more than a half dozen vehicles all day long. About 4 PM. I'm suddenly startled by the sound of a tire blowing out. I struggle to maintain control of the car and bring it to a stop. I get out to look at the left rear tire. It has an 18" to 20" tear in it. Here I am, all alone, and have to change a tire.

I locate the jack under the driver's seat. It is held solidly between two points, obviously so it won't rattle. But, how do I get it out? It takes me 45 minutes, standing outside the Jeep, in the freezing wind off the afore-mentioned snowcap, to figure out how to extract it! I also have tools to get out of the bins under the side seats at the back. My suitcases, are there and all the supplies I had bought to share with Krystal. Remember the flour? Well, it was not in a fabric bag -- but in a paper bag with several layers. I had obviously not closed it tightly enough -- because everything is covered with a fine dusting of flour. It takes a little time to get the things moved, so I can get out the tools -- and night is coming on. Having assembled everything, I jack up the car and loosen the bolts. Then I go to take the tire off the back. By this time I am chilled through, and I never had noticed before how your efficiency is impaired when you're cold. The jacket I was wearing was comfortable inside the car. I notice as I work how sharp the rocks are in the road -- that was the reason for the blown tire. I can actually feel them through my shoes! So everything takes longer. It is VERY difficult to get the tire down. I wonder why I hadn't taken it off before I jacked the car up.

"Finally, I get the bad tire off and the good tire on. I roll the bad one around to put it on its holder at the back. Even though I had taken down the jack, and the tire weighed less without any air in it, it is further to lift it up to those bolts since the air-filled tire is in place. It's doubly difficult to get it up there. The tears that came from just the effort of getting it on, did not freeze, but I am sure they would have if I had stayed out there just a few minutes longer!

I really wondered if my hands would be able to operate the car, I was so cold. There was no heat in any of our vehicles, so you can imagine what the rest of the trip was like. I was still hours away from Potosi. About an hour later, I arrived at a small cluster of houses, one of which was a restaurant. It did not have that lovely Canadian comfort of thermostat controlled heat, but it was certainly warmer than the open plain or the unheated car. There was hot soup, and hot tea, and people to hear my tale of woe.

A fellow diner was a young teacher in the rural school who was hoping to catch a ride into Potosi for the weekend. Needless to say, I was happy to take him along -- in case of another difficulty. And would you believe we DID have another flat before we got there. He was able to fix it, and I was so thankful I had found him.

When we arrived in Potosi, the teacher said, "I know the people at the local Jeep dealership. Let's go there first." Sure enough, the front door was closed, but he went around to the back door, caught one of the men coming out, and tried to see what could be done. They did have some more 4 ply tires, but all of our other vehicles had eight-ply, and that was what I wanted to replace what I had. I knew I was authorized to pay the difference. I really wanted to continue my journey that night. Marshall was leaving the next morning about 9 AM to fly off to a meeting, and I did want to see him before he left.

We had some friends who lived in Potosi and drove a Jeep. So after delivering my benefactor to his home, I went to see if they might have a spare that they could lend me. They were not expecting me, but quickly brought out a meal for me. They tried to talk me into staying the night, but I felt I couldn't afford to. They didn't have a spare tire, and they were really afraid for me to go with one tire shredded and one already patched. We prayed after supper, and they saw me off, at a little after 9:00 PM. I drove about half the remaining five hours, then pulled over to the side and slept for a while.

Fortunately, I had no more trouble, and arrived at home in the wee small hours of the morning. I talked to Marshall for a while before finally drifting off to sleep. We woke for the 7 AM news and found that he couldn't travel anyway. There was some kind of strike, and the plane didn't come or go. When we went to the dealer in Sucre, they tried to order four 8 ply tires, but there were none in the country. We finally had to settle for

6 ply. And happily didn't have any more trouble with the ones we had before they were replaced.

In my youth, I enjoyed driving, I crossed the North American continent twice before Marshall and I married. The three experiences that I relate here, at the start, middle and end of our missionary time, are probably the most dramatic that have happened to me. We could have filled a whole book with other driving events: a wheel coming off and frightening the coming traffic or carrying a Canadian youth group from waterhole to waterhole with a rope serving as a fan belt, or a flat in a desolate place with only three matches in the night wind to get a hot patch started, etc., but we don't enjoy them like we used to. There is usually unpleasantness in any long range goal that has to be borne. Driving in mountains was one of those things.

What we have learned in it all is that wherever we go, whatever we are doing, whenever we call upon Him, the Lord can be depended to give us strength, stamina and will to bring us through.

"*The joy of the Lord is my strength!*"

Nehemiah 8:10

Talk about WHOOSHES! Look how it has eaten into the road!

154

A triangle of land remains to Bolivia south of our work in the Tarija valley. It reached into an oil town in Bermejo, (Bayer may ho) where it was separated from Argentina by a neck-deep river. I know the depth by watching smugglers, carrying large bundles of goods on top their heads, pass from one side to the other, where there were no guards stationed. In flood season this traffic almost stopped. I say almost because drowned bodies did appear from time to time.

This new work was definitely jungle in climate, much warmer than the valleys of Tupiza or Tarija, and a contrast to Villazon or Telemayu. Rushing rivers plunged down the mountain sides through green tunnels of bamboo and climbing vines. Here again workers spent their earnings on wine, women and song. Or in Bolivian parlance: *chicha, chicas y cueca* (coo way' ka) with *charango* (cha ran' go) to play the music.

The work there began after we had started in Potosi (Po toe see') to fill in the gap between north and far south. I lived poised there in between: in Potosi first, and later in Sucre (Sue' kray), while making frequent trips in both directions.

My most vivid memory of Bermejo was a visit with a number of pastors, local deacons and students from the Cochabamba seminary. The work had grown remarkably in spite of a flood-destroyed house-church the year before, and other problems inherent in this new work. The Gospel was spreading among the farmers and sugar cane cutters in the rural sector. We finished our program, but an all-night rain cut the road of return to Tarija. It also flooded all the lower parts of the town. Most buildings are made of dried mud bricks which easily melt when immersed in water. The water had risen precipitously and many had escaped with only their clothes and little else. The city authorities were desperate to feed these victims of natural disaster. We had brought a speaker system for our evangelistic program and offered to use our equipment to announce the needs of the city. They granted permission to receive goods and money for those '*damnificados*' (dam nee fee cah dos – victims) using our audio equipment. They sent a man with us to collect the money and we took the clothes and foods directly back to the mayor, after spending the morning going around the higher parts of the town with speaker blaring and collecting for flood victims.

When we returned, the authorities sent us to a public restaurant, where they served us and a few of the important men and women a deluxe chicken dinner. I made sure our pastors sat next to these people. Everyone knows that foreigners are different, but when one of your own acts with a different motivation that helps people, they want to know why and how. It was their chance to witness to the power of Christ to change lives.

Local reports of road crews indicated miles of highway damage and wash outs. They predicted weeks of isolation. There were two other roads out: both undamaged, passing through Argentine territory. One paved road went down hill to the Chaco, (Cha ko) the other, a gravel road, went up the mountains to Villazon (Veal ya sown). We chose down/warm, over up/cold. One of our group had forgotten his identity card. Should we leave him? He hadn't enough money to live there, even with believers' hospitality. There was no Bolivian road open. His church would be waiting for him. We prayed and left the next day via the local bridge to Argentina. We felt that to take a man across the border was no sin, unless we left him there. That would be illegal. It was good motives vs. the letter of the law.

Our jeep was crowded, three in front and four (or was it more?) in back. We filled the tank and drove the jeep over the bridge to the regional office across the river and piled out to get our 'right of passage' documents. Guards were everywhere. The man without identity card waited at the office door and as two of the men emerged he accompanied them back to the jeep and got in. When the rest of us followed we left. We drove south and then east to follow the road to Yacuiba (Yah kwee bah) on the border of the Bolivian *Chaco*, (Cha ko) a region of great tropical heat. After a day of travel we came to the border again. There were lots of people walking back and forth across the line, only flashing their IDs, going to the stores which sold produce. As we went to check out of Argentina, I told our pastor to join the crowded pathway and we would meet him on the other side. When our car papers along with our identities were processed the rest of us drove across, got our friend, and went to the market center for supper. We had not eaten since breakfast: having no foreign or Argentine currency. I had not brought extra money for more than one gas fill up and we had eaten with friends and made purchases as all visitors to the Bermejo area did. We had to pool our money to buy supper and gas. The pastors began some good-natured badgering on one of their number, when they discovered he was holding back some funds. He finally came across with some money so they could eat. I promised to pay them the gas money back when we returned to Tarija, where much of our luggage had remained. We did not have enough cash to fill the gas tank. We decided to drive all night, and if and when we ran out, we could find a truck passing, promise them money in Tarija, if they would give us gas. But the Lord had another plan.

When we went for coffee before the departure, we met a believer I had known in Potosi. He had been left with a bill to collect for me regarding the house reimbursement. We had lost contact after our home assignment because he had left the city. He recognized me and came over to talk. He worked with border police and was doing well. When he knew of our short fall he offered to pay the sum owed me. I was happy to receive it even though it was in Argentine money. I gave him a receipt and took it to the money changers (who are active at all hours) before we left Yacuiba. It was with great relief that we drove all night to Tarija. We agreed to pray for a church to be planted in Yacuiba. Sheila Buchannan, our treasurer, was delighted to finally get the money and settle the account outstanding on the Potosi house.

The Czerepkas moved to Yacuiba to open a successful work at a later date. Dr. Margaret Czerepka worked in a local clinic and they found all the many elements that border cities attract to themselves. Transient believers and people in trouble, soon made themselves known. The church grew apace. Professional elements responded to the Czerepka's zeal and high status in the community.

John Czerepka, who participated in the evangelization of the Yurah (You'rah) tribe of Chapare (Cha pah' ray), the jungle area north of Cochabamba, made contacts with the Toba (Toe' bah) tribe and other tribal people of the Gran Chaco eastward and north up the rail line. Eventually, outpost churches were formed in Villa Montes (Veal' ya Mown' tes) and up the railroad line to Santa Cruz (san' ta cruise). There both Canadian and Brazilian Baptists worked in the Bolivian colonies and along the rail line to Brazil. Mennonites, Latvians, Okinawans, and other foreign colonists were entering and clearing the jungle.

Between Sucre and Tarija there were fruit growing villages that produced grapes, figs and stone fruit (apricots, peaches and plums) that they dried for export along with wines and liquors. They occur along the north-south trucking road from Potosi and Sucre to Tarija, in dry parallel valleys just below the higher Altiplano where the railroad runs. These areas were much slower to respond to the gospel. I know that there are congregations planted there now, but in my time we only gave out tracts or sold books, when passing through. Several times we had car problems along the way providing new chances to meet people. River travel provides the same opportunities and half the borders of Bolivia are tropical rivers.

We all guard our own business so zealously that we fail to take advantage of these human encounters, for whatever reason, and miss the rewards of witness and faithfulness.

It is required of a person that he be found faithful.   I Corinthians 4:2

Argentine smugglers wade Bermejo's River to waiting trucks

We started the Fifth Chapel or *'Quinta Capilla'* in the corner building of the institute. The youth helped, laughing at the name, which signifies the same liquid fire-water that the English fifth implies. The *Quinta Capilla* was the place where our fifth congregation was to be founded. It remained small for much of our time in the city, first as a children's meeting and later as a church. The neighborhood was prosperous, middle class, Spanish of old Creole stock and mestizo, all very conservative, proud, secure people. We lived on the edge of this neighborhood at the bottom of the avenue. It was a flat *pampa*, but near the railroad and grist mill; therefore it was considered the bottom. However, the children who came were not rural transplants and all the meetings were in Spanish only. Vacation Bible Schools were a large attraction.

Oruro is a city surrounded by tin mines on one side, and the wild west of Bolivian desert on the other. The city is a rail head with lines that reach through La Paz, to the highest navigable lake in the world to the north; the Chilean port of Arica; to Guaqui on Lake Titicaca, (almost 13,000 ft. above sea level);It reaches to the pleasant valley of Cochabamba (only 8000ft.) to the east. The rails go South, branching to another Pacific port, Antofagasta, and into Argentina as well. It's on a border line between two Amerindian languages: Quechua and Aymara. These mix freely with Spanish in the city, along with the distinctive accents of all the neighboring countries.

The Catholic Church was in the midst of reforms and I, Marshall, was able to attend some inter-faith meetings and get to know the local clergy and teaching sisters.

I'm not sure how Ruth came to us, but one day she appeared at our door wanting to buy Bibles. We always kept Bibles to distribute, though we were not officially 'colporteurs'. She was a Victory Knoll Sister who had 17 years of teaching religion classes in the slums of Chicago. She had come to Bolivia to do the same. She was teaching in one of the public schools in a poorer district in which the pupils could not afford to buy the New Testament that she used as a text for her classes. In the more affluent schools, it was in the list for the parents to buy at the beginning of the school year. She felt she

159

couldn't put that kind of economic burden on the families of these children, so she came to buy one set of books that could be put away in a cupboard at that school, and be used in turn for all the students to read from in class, and then be put away for the next group when that class was over.

She was taken care of as far as quarters were concerned, and also had her meals with other religious workers at one of the local Catholic churches. She had a modest allowance that equaled $15 a month. This group did have a habit, but she was not required to wear it in the classroom, and preferred to dress modestly and not wear the habit. Her allowance had to cover clothes, shampoo, toothpaste, etc. She had saved her allowance for several months, and wanted to buy 40 New Testaments so that each child would be able to read from his or her text.

During that initial conversation, she talked to us about her experience in the classroom. There was a provision that evangelical pupils going to public schools could opt out of the religion classes. When Marshall was in La Paz, parents in the congregation would come at the beginning of each school year to get a letter asking for this exemption, which Marshall had to sign. We got on to the subject, and she begged us to talk to parents that were in our churches, and convince them not to take their children out of the classes. She said when she asked questions of the kids, it was the evangelicals who knew the stories of the Bible and could answer her questions. They were the only ones that she got any feedback from. This was shortly after the permission to read the Bible had been granted to Catholics.

We became friends and we saw her from time to time on the street , and greeted each other cordially. Some time later she came to our house again, this time in tears. At that school she had access to a locked cabinet in the hallway where she kept the Bibles she had bought. In each class where the Scriptures were used, there was one monitor authorized to get the key from the office, and get out the Bibles and have them all passed out to the pupils before she got there. This gave her more time for teaching, and taught responsibility to those charged with that duty.

One week she was sent to another school for some all day

affair and they sent a Franciscan Father to take her place. When he came into the classroom, they were all sitting there ready to begin the class, with their New Testaments open to the lesson for the day. The young girl approached to tell the substitute teacher that they were all ready with their texts. He was used to lecturing, and he responded haughtily and asked what text she was talking about. When she told him it was the New Testament, he flew into a rage, demanded that she gather them all up, and bring them to him. She was bewildered, but did as she was told. As he stuffed them into his satchel, he told them that they couldn't expect to understand these books. They should never have been exposed to them, and that he was taking them to burn them. When Ruth came to class again, the little girl greeted her sadly, feeling badly about having been the one responsible for losing their precious New Testaments.

Ruth was distraught, but had come bringing her whole allowance for that month, and asking if she could take all forty and pay for the rest when she got her next month's allowance. We were happy to give her the books without charge; and we prayed together that the priest might find Jesus for his Savior.

The film of Martin Luther was made available and I, Marshall carried it to all the mines and to the rural areas and the new work in the south of Bolivia. It was obvious that the gospel was taking root and producing changes.

At the time when the *Reina /Valera* version of the Bible was revised in 1960, Don Jaime Goytia, Secretary of the Bible Society in Bolivia, coordinated a contest on Biblical knowledge. This would be open to all the Christian churches in the country. There would be studies throughout the year. Then, near the end of the year, a contest would be held first in each local church, the winners of which would then compete in some central church in each region. There would be a run-off in which each region would send it's winners to the national competition. The grand prize was a trip for two to Israel.

The Archbishop of La Paz was asked to inaugurate the contest. By asking this authority of the Catholic Church, Bible Societies felt that greater participation would be stimulated. The archbishop commissioned all the priests, nuns, and catechists to begin Bible Studies.

A priest we knew started a Bible Study in a small village in Carangas. These were evening meetings, and they went from one family's home to another, week by week. They started with Genesis, and the studies were going fine until they got to the Ten Commandments. When he came the week after he had assigned them to read Exodus 20, they were all very nervous when they had read in the Bible (rather than the Catechism) about not having 'graven images'. They asked the priest if it really meant that, as they cast sidelong, furtive glances at the images on the small shrine in the house where they were meeting. He told them it did. They asked what they could do. They had prayed to these images all their lives, and felt that they could not do away with them. Father Joseph said that he hadn't brought anything to carry them in, but if they could hold onto them another week, they should all bring theirs to the study the next week, and he would take them all away. The next week, they did as he asked, and he took them away and buried them in the garden of the church where he lived. Burial rather than the breaking of images had always been my policy, as well.

The problem of disposal of images was constant. One couple, who had just come to the Lord, had a saint's image given to them at their wedding several years before by the husband's aunt. In their study of the Ten Commandments, the lady became convinced that she should destroy the image. When the man came home from work and found that she had smashed it, he was very angry. He feared that the aunt would take it as a personal affront, and scolded his wife severely. He felt that it would have been best to return it to the giver. They came to the missionary to arbitrate, and patched up their differences. They had been married for several years and had never had any children. Soon after destroying the image, she realized she was pregnant, and attributed it to the fact that she had obeyed the promptings of the Lord in that act.

Local officials required community labor on religious buildings. The evangelicals affected were preoccupied as to what they should do when it was demanded. The community was supposed to work together on building or repairing the local state church. I suggested that the promise of work time spent on school or administrative edifices might be a suitable substitute. It was a community project where they could participate. This seemed to help smooth matters with local authorities.

I offered small gospel portions at the government schools I saw from the road going to and from visits to churches, or families of believers in the rural setting. There, a visit created an event in an otherwise monotonous life. I was welcomed by pupils and teachers alike. I was often invited to say a word. While morality was an acceptable topic, religion was not. I had a 'God and Country' speech that most teachers delighted in hearing. I explained that Jesus was a Savior willing to help them in their growing up and would relieve them of their sins if they would seek him sincerely. God would love them and give them opportunity to serve their country and people.

About the same time there was an attempt to substitute reading courses for seminary classes. It was called 'Theological Education by Extension'. The theory was that more could be accomplished in one's hometown by meeting with a supervisor to review the material studied and getting pointers on the next lessons. One of the missions, in enthusiastic support, even closed their Bible school to initiate the new program. David Hillen became our local supervisor. I had concluded that since the population was not highly literate and bookish, it was an unprofitable way to go. Several men completed some of the studies, but none to my knowledge became pastors. Most of the students were mature men: deacons, preaching in their own church's mission points. Not having to uproot their families, look for housing, change the children's schools, and being able to retain their jobs proved a help. They were able to raise their level of Biblical knowledge, in turn instructing the country people, who in turn witnessed to their neighbors about the Lord and His power to save them.

Our short term Bible school (a month or less) continued to sponsor courses that demanded daily meetings and much discussion over texts and biblical ideas. The spoken word was the basis of learning in our situation, even with the presence of three local languages: Spanish, Aymara, and Quechua. Communication had to be largely from person to person: not book to person.

I, Hazel, taught at Reekie School while we were there:

English for grades one through five. Marshall was asked to fill in from time to time. Then, late in the school year, Dave Hillen contracted hepatitis. They kept him in the hospital for a month, and then he moved in with us because Janet had returned to Canada to have her second baby. Fortunately, the children were away at school, and I had help in the kitchen, so I could continue with my teaching. Marshall had to suspend some of his trips to the country and do the classroom work teaching Psychology and History of Philosophy classes. Dave was very well disciplined and carefully prepared the material, and written exercises to be brought back to him to grade. He adhered to a very rigid regimen recommended by the doctor. He strictly followed food restrictions and rest periods. They told him he was lucky to have it there in Oruro, because people recovered more quickly in the altitude. Mary Haddow, our resident nurse, visited him every day.

His hepatitis meant that everyone in the house had to take gamma-globulin shots, for safety's sake. I didn't mind seeing to it that he got his medicines, meals, and other needs, but I sure did hate those shots!

We were in Oruro for five years that term. Borden, Krystal and Karlene were all studying at Carachipampa during most of that time. It was situated just outside Cochabamba, a school run by the Bolivian Indian Mission. It went up to eighth grade. Actually, it added grade nine the year Borden was to leave and start at Tambo, and he was upset with his father for insisting that he stay at Carachipampa, when he wanted to go with all his friends. The next year he and Krystal were both studying in Tambo. After one year there, we went on furlough.

But what I really wanted to tell you about Oruro was the way we celebrated Christmas. Marshall wanted to have all our local pastors and their families over for an open house. I had a little gift for each child. I made a pretty apron for each of the wives. Marshall gave a theological book to the pastors. We all worked at decorating, and making the sandwiches and sweets. Our girls helped to serve while Borden washed the dishes. We sang Christmas carols, and chatted, sharing our plans, or resolutions for the new year. We timed it for the 26th, so the children's Christmas concerts, young people's dramas, and family celebrations were all over and we could relax, though not for long.

The New Year's Watch-night service, less than a week away, was just that: you stayed up until mid-night. Whether there were ten people or 300, upon arrival at the church, you had to *abrazar* each person present. As others came in, they embraced you. At 10 minutes to midnight, we began a prayer time to pray in the New Year. Then, there was another round of *abrazos* to wish everyone a Happy New Year. Next we sat down to the first meal of the New Year. Before parting, we owed each person one more *abrazo.* When we first arrived, Marshall was pastor at the Prado Church in La Paz and there had been 300 people present. Sucre had about 20 in our last year in the country.

In the Christian Education field, I initiated what we called a Comet Course. We would call the Sunday School teachers interested from the four churches, to one big all day meeting on Saturday, when the children were starting back to school. The General methods for teaching different age groups were presented. Then, subsequent Saturdays, we got together for about an hour, when they would go over what they would be teaching the next day. Some found it useful, but it was not the most successful program I tried there.

Our children also accompanied us to the Juntas during the winter there (June-August) and helped us sell Bibles, Scripture portions, gospels, and hymn books. When we first came back from furlough to Oruro, there was a new hymn book of all those Aymara hymns that had been composed during our year away. Justino Quispe was translating the Casa Bautista Sunday School materials into Aymara, which was distributed in and around La Paz and Oruro each month. They decided to print a new hymn on the back cover. He also led a women's choir on his 6 am radio broadcast. He and other teachers, and pastors were composing the words and music for new hymns. During our home assignment, we, Marshall and I both had worked toward another degree and had been away two years. So they had taken all those hymns and quite a few others, and made a hymn book. Everyone heard Justino Quispe leading his women's choir in singing them over the Radio, and those that hadn't already bought them wanted a copy. The publisher couldn't keep up with the orders. For this particular junta we had ordered 100 copies, but they only had 50 to send. We picked them up at the bus station on the way out. We had gotten lost on the way and had arrived in the wee hours of the morning. So. when the people rose for the devotional and breakfast, they besieged the car.

The hymn books were being passed down from the box on top of the car by Marshall who stood on the hood, to Borden who was standing by the back bumper. When Borden asked if Marshall had change, Marshall said give them to the people who have change, and you'll soon have change to give. In ten minutes they were all gone – and he didn't sell more than one copy to a person. Krystal was selling Bibles from inside the car sitting in the driver's seat; Karlene had her bag of gospel portions: in a different color for each Gospel. She had her own little following of children with their 50 centavos to pay for it. We did have a few books left. We came with 5 or 6 boxes full of books and went home with one.

Work continued to grow in the Yungas to the east, a region of jungle hills, and was expanding in Carangas in the west. Trucks rather than buses were the main means of transport there. It was slow and erratic at times. Sometimes a truck was hired by villagers just to go to the junta. Some came by bicycle, but others walked incredible distances, taking two or three days to arrive. They stopped to rest: sitting or leaning on a big boulder, from which they may have had to brush the snow away first, it was so cold. They carried bundles on their backs, done up in brightly-striped *awayos (woolen squares* of homespun, hand-woven material.) Inside the bundle was probably a Bible and hymn book, in either the Aymara or Quechua language, their good shoes, their Sunday-best clothes, some food for the trip, a plastic or metal plate, mug, and cutlery, and bedding for the whole family. Some of them came with a burro that would carry the bedding. Some came on bicycles, motor bikes, jeeps, trucks or buses.

Once at the Junta, meals: morning, noon and night, were provided by the hosting church. No matter how small the church, they were expected to feed those who came for two or three days. There could be anywhere from a hundred to five hundred in attendance. In preparation, they chose a place near their water source, and dug a long trench. The men

166

brought in three 50 gallon drums, which they installed to straddle the trench. They bought the wood, gathered the *tola* bushes that they used for kindling, built and tended the fires and filled all three drums with water. They usually butchered the meat from their own flocks of sheep or llamas. All the ladies chopped the vegetables, peeled the potatoes, and further cut the meat as we would for stew. One of the barrels was for the beverage. They often chose sultana for the drink. Although, It is made from the shells of the coffee bean, it doesn't have the same flavor. It tastes more like tea. The other two could include peas, fava beans (like a large lima bean), carrots, onions, corn, some form of pasta, rice, potato and small cubes of meat. They served both soup and second plate: the difference being that one was served in the water it was cooked in, and the other drained.

To the North, on the La Paz side, Aymara was prevalent, while Quechua was spoken more in the South. In the city, there was an overlap, mixed marriages, and children who spoke both equally well, and Spanish, too.

Within Bolivia the constitution guaranteed all religions freedom to meet without interference. Our Baptist churches outreach continued in spite of harassment. The fact of celebrating marriages, births, funerals and other religious ceremonies locally, without waiting for an annual or biennial visit by a priest, appealed to isolated communities. These wanted to know more about God. Literacy, health care and co-operatives offered a door to community development unknown in the past. God showed love to the rural Indian peasant, for God bestows dignity and acceptance on those who know and follow him. Jesus said in Matthew 11:28:

Come to me all you who labor and are laden ...

The Thompson Train of Thought was our messenger

During our third term, the ladies in Oruro formed the executive for the *Cruzada Femenil Bautista Boliviana*. Lidia de Rivas was the president, Mercedes de Herbas, recording secretary, both were pastor's wives. Marcela de Diaz, Vice President, was a pastor and the wife of a pastor. She pastored the Norman Dabbs (East) Church. Muriel Harrington, corresponding secretary, lived in Cochabamba, so was not in on all we did as a group. I was named as counselor. Lidia, Marcela, Mercedes and I made a number of visits during the year to societies in Potosi, Tarija, Santa Cruz, Cochabamba, La Paz, Guatajata, and all the Oruro Societies. The executive of the *Cruzada* decided to hold a Women's course.

We invited the ladies from the 33 churches in the area. We used the facilities of the Institute. Let me tell you about that Women's Course. There were 24 ladies, present, and all the languages mentioned were represented in the group. There were three, each, of both Aymara and Quechua, who spoke no Spanish at all! They stuck close to the ones who knew both Spanish and their own language, and got a lot out of the course as well.

The country ladies usually bathed their babies down at the local stream. In that cold country, it's a wonder that more babies don't die of pneumonia. One of our single lady missionaries had been given flannelette diapers, baby clothes, and some other baby supplies, to give out when there was a need. When she heard that we were having a women's course, she sent them to us saying we could give them away at that time. When Lidia brought her 7 month old daughter along, to show them how to bathe the baby; she also showed them how to use diapers. We decided this would be the ideal time to distribute them. Each lady was given one of the diapers. Even though some of the ladies were grandmothers, we figured they could use them on their grandchildren.

Actually, one of our ladies was just ready to deliver her baby. She was the wife of one of our rural pastors, and didn't want to miss the course. So, she had brought her midwife with her, in case her baby came while she was there. The big room with about a dozen beds in it, was where the rural ladies were billeted. Sure enough, Thursday morning, our little maid hurried in to tell us at breakfast, that the baby had come during the night. We finished breakfast, but then went to call on the new arrival. My girls got out the gifts we had ready for the baby, and were so excited to see him. She had a perfect, healthy baby! We were happy to see that she had used the diaper, though not for it's original purpose. She had quite a headache after the birth process, and had tied it around her own head to ward off the chill.

Quinoa is the name of a local grain that is very high in protein. When Marshall had the men in for courses, he usually invited a local man from the experimental farm to show them the better, larger varieties they had developed. He would then offer them the improved seeds to plant. Most bought a pound or two. At the women's course, we taught them some new recipes to make with that grain. I sometimes take a casserole using it, when we have pot luck dinner at the church here in Canada.

The USIS (United States Information Service) offered us films on Hygiene, Inflation and Economy. The ladies got their own breakfast (coffee and bread from the nearby store.) We had our time of singing and devotional, and then a Bible class. We all cooked together at noon. We tried some new things with Quinoa, Peanut soup (common in the lowlands, was new to our ladies), then they expressed a desire to learn to bake bread, and cake! We had brought a camp oven from Canada. It could be set over any burner and would work. We didn't use our electric stove, because we wanted to use something that these ladies had access to. All of them had an *enafe*. It looks like a Hershey's chocolate kiss, was made of brass, and was powered by kerosene. Another lady brought her oven which was made locally. She took the tin-smith three five-gallon lard tins. He made her a two-*enafe* oven: with hinged door, two racks, and two rectangular pans that just barely fit in. Taking out one tray, you could use the big oven, for something as large as a turkey. We made a two layer sheet cake in her oven, and an eight inch round two layer cake in my oven on Thursday. Then on Friday, we iced them. At the closing they were served with the tea, when they had received their certificates with some of their families present.

169

After our regular meetings, we worked on our plans for the Women's Convention and practiced a cantata called <u>The Marvelous Story That Has Never Been Told,</u> to sing there. Janet Hillen, a nurse serving in Oruro with the Baptist Youth Team, played the piano for us. It was written for a whole choir, but there were only five of us singing. Since we were all women, and another could sing alto, I sang the tenor.

Later, during the Campaign of the Americas, Jaime Goytia organized a choir with people from all the Baptist churches in Cochabamba to sing that Cantata. They had uniforms made: long rose colored dresses with white blouses for the women, and rose ties for the men to be worn with white shirts and dark trousers. Though Marshall and I lived somewhere else by then, he ordered them of us as well. They traveled to other places, singing it many times. When we were visiting in Cochabamba, he always invited us to take part, and I still have my dress and Marshall his tie.

The virtuous woman rises early to give food to her household, & portions to her servant girls. Her lamp does not go out by night. Her children arise and call her blessed, and her husband also praises her.Let her works praise her.The woman who fears the Lord is to be praised.

From Proverbs.31

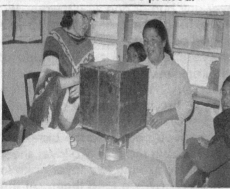

Learning to bake bread in a locally-made oven.

Marshall never had enough baptismal certificates and he had already decided not to count baptisms. He didn't want to move toward a zeal for numbers. For this reason he doesn't know how many people he has baptized. The importance rests in the individual's life and motive for leading a new life under God's power. Any mention of numbers in this article are out of Hazel's memory bank.

Marshall's first baptism was in his first pastorate in New Brunswick. It marked the end of a very successful evangelistic campaign in Upper Blackville, New Zion, and Underhill churches there. God provided the baptistry in the Miramichi River when one 12 year old girl plus 21 men and boys were baptized: 22 made the occasion memorable. After that we stopped counting. Marshall had agreed with God that he needed the proof of an effective ministry in English before he would learn another language and serve overseas. The baptism and the construction of a basement Sunday School rooms/social center in the New Zion church gave him the confidence to venture further. So he pursued taking up work in India where he felt called to serve. As it turned out, we never got to work in India. Apart from two grandchildren he never baptized anyone else in North America, again.

In South America it was a different matter. There, many came to know the Lord in a personal way, and obeyed His command to be baptized. Romans 6:4 tells us that "We were therefore buried with him through baptism into death in order that, just as Christ was raised from the dead, through the glory of the Father; we too may live a new life." A few were personal converts, but most came to a saving knowledge of the Lord through the witness of a neighbor, a family member, a pastor, a local church, or evangelists scattered over the wide and varied topography and social environment found in that beautiful nation.

Marshall's first baptisms in Bolivia were at the Prado church. There was a baptistry at one end of the platform in the sanctuary. When it was filled with water, a *'rayo flotante'* with a long electric cord controlled by a master switch on the wall, lay on the bottom and was turned on all the night before the baptismal services were scheduled to heat the water. While some other city churches had baptistries, even those that did, often went to some river nearby and made a day of it when they had baptisms. They invited their friends, and took this opportunity to show the world that they now belonged to Jesus.

Living in Guatajata meant baptizing several times in Lake Titicaca. At one such gathering hundreds of people lined the lake shore to see the event. An Aymara choir from the Southern Cross Radio was present and Justino Quispe directed the singing. A square of four blankets was hung for the candidates to dress behind. The Aymara New Testament was read by one of the deacons and several of our Aymara speaking pastors were on hand to preach and baptize the people. I had the joy of being a spectator rather than a participant this time. But there were times when no other pastor was present. At Guatajata, Lake Titicaca was shallow for fifty feet out from the shore. It was a long trek through the totora reeds to deep water. But also, there was an irrigation tank. Marshall had memorized the words of the ceremony in Aymara. He asked his fellow teacher at the Bible High School, Remigio Gutierrez, to write it all out for him on the inside cover of his Aymara New Testament. Remigio also corrected his pronunciation as he practiced saying it. As we gathered in a circle around the tank, he went down the steps into the water. The shock of the cold water made him forget everything. He said to me in English, "Open the Bible so I can read it off," I drew closer, opened it, and held it where he could see it, and he went on without another hitch.

Once we were about an hour from Guatajata baptizing in the melt waters from the icecap of Illampu, the tallest mountain in Bolivia. Marshall baptized 15, and Justino baptized 22. As he waded into the water far enough to immerse them, waist deep, he began to lose the feeling in his feet, and it hurt like needles in his brain. He hoarsely asked me to send in the Spanish speakers first. Fortunately, some of the deacons stood like a bucket brigade at a fire, to assist the candidates out to the pastors and back. Marshall needed their help to get back to the shore as well. Justino Quispe then waded into the freezing water to baptize a group from another community who had been converted by his preaching in Aymara over the radio.

Our first baptism in Potosi was in November: seven short months after our arrival there. Many churches in Bolivia had baptismal robes, some white and some black. It was decided by the church that we would buy a whole bolt of material, and make our own. They didn't have either of those colors where I went to shop, so I looked at the colors that they did have in cotton drill, and decided on maroon. We cut out a 'one size fits all' pattern and went to work. We got them done on time for the big day. This took place in the irrigation tank in the field behind the house we rented for our residence. We stood in a semi-circle as the seven candidates lined up to take their turn. Each gave testimony to his/her faith in the Lord Jesus, and was baptized. Like many new materials in the first wash, the robes had 'bled'. Feliza told us later how she came up out of the water reddened by those new robes and felt that she had really been 'washed in the blood of the lamb.'

A couple of years later we went to a small lake created by a volcanic vent. It was too dangerous to baptize or stand at the edge of the vent itself. The steep sides were too slippery. People who had drowned there before were drawn down into the vent and did not surface for a week or more it was said. They had sounded with three kilometers of rope, and never hit the bottom. However, there was a small overflow pool with a cement bottom, about 15 ft. by 20 ft. where we were able to do baptisms.

As field missionary over one of the three older sectors of Bolivian work: Oruro, La Paz and Cochabamba; I also had influence in the south and eastern mission areas of the Bolivian Baptist Union. The lack of trained pastors in the poor rural areas caused the area minister to assume many responsibilities that are handled by the church pastor in North America. The regular preaching was usually done by the first deacon, Sunday school by the second deacon. The treasurer is usually the third deacon and if they have a fourth deacon he is the missionary, who spends two Sundays away in other villages visiting or preaching. Baptism depended on the area minister who interviewed and baptized candidates recommended by the local churches. Many preferred the area minister to bring the communion as well. This happened at the *juntas* or

173

occasional mass meetings held by the believers seasonally. There, they would enjoy several days of teaching, preaching and singing, ending up with baptism and the Lord's Supper.

The rainy season came in the summer when the sun is at its highest and hottest. We could only travel in the low sun period when the pampas were dry and cold. The rutted trails were most passable then. That meant that water had to be collected to obey God's command for the new believers, but it was rarely heated. This required a measure of ingenuity and planning. The collecting could be done by damming a stream, collecting in a sheep dip, diverting a village water supply or hot springs, utilizing a public swimming pool, or an irrigation tank. Lakes or rivers of any size were the easy way out. You can baptize in six inches of water by a bit of excavation by laying the candidate out flat to be covered, 'scarcely' might be the qualifying adjective. But it was once used near Telemayu in the southern mining area.

One lady, just as she was going into the blanket cubicle to put on the baptismal robe, saw a truck coming with a big barrel of water in it. Since they had broken the ice that had formed at the edge of the pond earlier, she thought that it was coming to dump it's hot water in, so offered to be the first into the water, before all the heat dissipated. What a shock she got! The water was going to the kitchen, and was cold anyway!

The next Sunday she came to me very worried: one lady on the trip back to the city, told her she wasn't really baptized, because the pastor hadn't gotten her whole face into the water. I reassured her that the Lord knew her heart, and would accept her obedience.

One community prepared a way to beat the winter chill. Large rocks were built into a loose, semi-circular wall so that the wind would blow through it. Fast burning 'tola' (a kind of sage brush) was set afire inside the semi-circle, and heated them. The resulting hot boulders, were rolled into the icy pond to mitigate the temperature. You could touch one with your foot to feel the heat; but you didn't dare to stand on it or you'd burn your foot. In other places fifty gallon metal barrels of boiling water are poured into the ice covered pools, but countless times the ice was broken for a cold plunge into 'death to the old life and resurrection to walk in newness of life.'

In one community in Carangas, the authorities refused us the privilege of baptizing in the reservoir. The brothers were resourceful, however, and said "Pastor, never mind, we'll just use the sheep dip chute." The ramp, built for one sheep at a time, started down gradually, and then plunged the sheep into the dip solution, intended to disinfect them from ticks and lice. After the brothers scrubbed the walls of the chute they filled it with a water pump. In order to baptize the believers, Marshall had to stand outside the chute beside the deepest point, and reach over the side to dip them under the water. Marshall said, "As I was baptizing, I noticed a little girl walk out into the reservoir leading her calf, which promptly relieved itself. I thought how fortunate we were that they had refused us the use of it. Our deacons thought that it was very appropriate that Jesus, the Good Shepherd, should wash His sheep clean in the sheep dip chute."

When Pastor Modesto Aliaga was baptized, his still unbelieving wife had timidly asked the officiating pastor what his name would be now. To her 'baptism' meant naming the baby! The pastor assured her that she could still call him Modesto! There were several individuals who took the opportunity to change their name and everyone understood and approved. It heralds a new life.

We managed to bury in water many, many people, but every one of them had made a personal decision to follow Christ, who will live in and through each of their lives. Gradually towns and villages held men and women, boys and girls, who were living a different life, by different principles, to please a God the majority of the people did not know. It slowly began to change the society and its customs and attitudes. The leaven of the gospel worked in the local population. But each person's story, like each baptism, is different and distinct.

Go into all the world and make disciples

baptizing them in the name of

the Father and the Son and the Holy Spirit

and look, I'm with you to the end of the world.

Matthew 28:19,20

In the book of the Revelation 2:17, Jesus promises to those who have an ear to hear his message a white stone with a new name on it. We have to wait for that one till we get to heaven, but I got a new name just seven years into our Bolivian experience.

That was the year we moved to Potosi. In Spanish my name is 'Hazel Fay Vincent de Thompson,' since Vincent was my maiden name. You don't lose your identity when you marry in Spanish-speaking countries. The 'de' means 'wife of'. For those first seven years I was called Hazel. They could make the sound, but if they read it off, it would sound like 'ay-ee-sell'. If you spelled it so they would give it the English pronunciation, it would be 'Jeisel'.

One of the disadvantages of living in Potosi was a trip of at least 10 hours to visit any of our missionary colleagues. To take our children to their boarding school, we would leave before first light, and arrive after dark in Oruro. Cathy McGorman would take us in for the night, and we would rise early the next morning, and again ride until late afternoon.

Our first trip with them was by train, but thereafter, we went by bus. In order to ride the inter-city buses, you went beforehand to reserve a seat and buy your ticket. Of course, I was used to this procedure, and it didn't bother me. However, Marshall went to reserve a seat for ME, this particular time. He told them my name, and they wanted to know how to spell it. The person could not understand how you could spell H-a-z-e-l with an 'H' so he gave up and said, "Well, I'll just give you her other name then: Fay!"

There was another problem. She spelled it 'Fe', and asked, "Oh, short for Feliza?" He had to laugh in spite of himself. I didn't really mind, The word 'fe' means faith, 'feliza' means happy. She thought that faith was short for happy. He guessed that the one did lead to the other and accepted it. I thought it was quite fitting for a missionary that was completely dependent upon God to receive this designation. When he came home, he said, "Well, you have a new name. From this day forward you will be Fe." If they had seen it written, 'Fay', they would have pronounced it 'Fie'.

When we first arrived in Bolivia, Hazel Merritt was already there, so among our colleagues, they teasingly wondered if they should call me Hazel Nut, or Witch Hazel. Given my lack of solemnity, they decided to call me Hazel Nut. There was no question of Hazel Merritt giving up using her name: her middle name was Jean, and we already had Jean Pyper and Jean Phillips!

Then, just a couple of years later, Hazel and Hazen Parent came. They teased her and said she was stuck with the Witch Hazel, but I don't think anyone ever did REALLY call her that. She informed us that she called her husband Hazen, Honey, and expected everyone else to do the same. While she was there, I could do that, but when she wasn't, I could not bring myself to call him "Honey"!

Thus, for the last 16 years of our Bolivian service, I was known as Fé de Thompson, or Señora Fé. A real irony was that Fay Ruggles came just after the change. I'm not sure if she had had it legally changed or not, but hers WAS short for Feliza. Then, when Phyllis Brunton came, they translated her name to Feliza, as well.

Once I was introduced by Marina de Goytia as the wife of the ideal missionary. Why ideal? Because he had come with his faith (Fe) visible for all to see.

When we went to live in Cochabamba, Regina de Oropeza was the district secretary for the Cruzada Femenil Bautista Boliviana. She called the local society presidents and lady missionaries together, and made a plan to visit all the groups in the district at least once during the year. She looked at dates, and assigned each one a date acceptable to them, to bring the devotionals. She said that she knew that as busy people we might not make all the meetings. She hoped that everyone would come as often as possible, because she wanted us to serve as a choir as well. She asked if they couldn't come, to please let her know ahead of time, and she would understand. Then, she turned to me and said anyone could be excused for missing a meeting except me! Everyone was quite shocked, until she delivered her punch line: "Without faith (Fe) we can do nothing!"

To the one who overcomes..
I will give a white stone with
a new name written on it...

Revelation 2:17

Krystal Thompson's & Dorothy Winstanley's Birthday 'party in the patio' on Jordan Street with Borden T., Susan & Bruce Amy

We didn't know anything about 'Third 'Culture Kids' (TCK). This acronym was compiled later as sociology continued to affect public interest and research. It treats with children whose parents grew up in one culture, taking them to grow up in another culture. So the children find that their parents have some rules for them to observe at home. But when visiting with a family belonging to the local culture, the rules may be quite different. This affects their language learning, behavior, eating habits, manners, etc. What happens is that the children accept behavior patterns from their parents in some areas, and from the local cultures in others, ending up with a 'third culture'. This new culture is unique to the individual.

We knew Scripture, and we came from a tradition of no nonsense, but lots of love for kids. Limits were set: "You can't put the needle on the phonograph record until you are five." "You can't pick up records until you are five." "You choose and daddy will put it on for you." As teenagers, the objects changed, but the system didn't. "When you are 16, I expect you to choose and buy your own clothes." This produced consternation on first view, but sisters, brother, uncles, aunts and grandparents all started giving clothes or money on birthdays and Christmases. That meant money earned could be spent for more personal items.

At home anything in reach was unbreakable or expendable. If it was in the living room, it was for the benefit of guests and could be lost or given away. We chose to live simply and with basics that Bolivian nationals could afford. Only in essentials like books and some electronic gear, needed for our ministry, did we exceed this rule. Travel gear was strong and durable. Pressure cookers were a necessity in the kitchen because of the problems of cooking at altitudes of above two miles high. All missionaries and most middle class nationals had maids.

We, too, found it necessary in a culture where most foods were purchased daily, raw and ripe in the market. Canned or boxed goods were very expensive. Imported foods were highly taxed and few could afford them on a daily basis.

We had a small washing machine with a crank wringer on the side. When we lived behind the Prado Church in La Paz, a

179

room upstairs with large glass-less windows on most of two sides served as a drying room.   We also had a clothes line downstairs in the patio where we could dry things when there was sunshine. In Oruro, as in other cities, we had an enclosed patio.

In order for the wife to have any time for ministry at all, she had to have help in the house. There was a wee room at the back of the kitchen for a live-in maid, and Maria Luisa came to live with us.

She helped with everything! She helped me with the cooking, shopping at the market, cleaning house, washing clothes, and taking care of our children. Borden was about eight months old when she began. She loved to take him with her when she went to the market.

I took him with me to the market only once. He loved the bustle and was awed with all he saw. I was busy bargaining over something, and all of a sudden he wasn't there! I looked around and found him sitting on the lap of one of the cholas, who was sitting on the ground behind her display of vegetables. I asked if he had found a friend and we chatted with the lady. I think I even bought something she was offering. Then, I told Borden to come along, it was time to go home. He wouldn't come. Everyone had a good laugh over that! After a while he gave up and came along.

Sunday afternoon after the morning service, we all went for a walk on the Prado. The name means pasture, and that is what it was originally. When the church tried to build their sanctuary across from the municipality, many years ago, they were thwarted at every turn. Powerful religious forces teamed with the mayor, and refused to grant a building permit.   The municipality finally indemnified the church for that property, giving them a piece of land on the extreme outskirts of the city. That was in the 1920's.

When we arrived in 1955, the church was on the principal avenue that led from the lip of the Altiplano (13,050' altitude), down through the center of the city (12,800' alt,) and another thousand feet to luxurious new suburbs (11,800') that developed lower down in order to escape the rarefied air at the top.

This marvelous avenue with two lanes of traffic on either

side, separated by gardens, and wide promenades on the *esplanade*, was the scene of everything of importance. On Sunday afternoon, those who came to worship with us, often had a little walk on the Prado; so we did too. At first Borden loved this *paseo*, but after a little while, he didn't want to go anymore. He had flaming red hair, and that's quite rare in La Paz. When we went anywhere, everyone wanted to touch his hair. When Marshall's mother heard how cold it always was in La Paz, she sent him a little cap with furry earflaps on it. From then on he was willing to go out with the earflaps down – that way no one would notice his hair .

With red hair, there is a delicate skin that burns easily. Even though Marshall's hair wasn't red, his beard was, when he grew one; and he too, had that easily-burnt skin. Hazel had dark hair, but her fair skin made her vulnerable, as well. She had suffered heat stroke on an eight block walk to the library one summer day, in her childhood. Being that much nearer the sun and feeling the cold just being in the shade, made you seek the sunshine to keep warm. This was in contrast to the habit of staying in the shade to avoid the damaging effects of the sun, that both Marshall and Hazel had to overcome. They had spent a lifetime of dodging that blazing sun as children born and bred in Texas! A blistered skin and soreness was the pay for failure to stay out of the sun. It was a built in automatic behavior to seek the shade.

When you're waiting for a baby, doctors, nurses and literature prepare you for a red shriveled-skinned baby at birth. But Borden, however, had a Gerber-baby, peaches-and-cream complexion. Just to prove that each one is different, Krysi had a purple cast to her skin; Karlene's was orange. She joined the rest of the family with her sensitive skin, while Krystal took a beautiful even tan from day one.

On a visit to Guatajata, two-year-old Borden was wearing his new orange, hand-woven poncho and little cap, but they hampered his play. So he took off his hat. We had covered his face and hands with a cream so he wouldn't burn in the altiplano sun. That day he played around a place where someone had dumped the ashes from a fire, outdoors. The ashes and soot clung to the cream and his clothes, and when we stripped him and plunged him into the water where I was doing the wash; all these elements combined with the strong detergent to give him a bad burn on both face and hands. He cried and cried.

Somewhere in those early years he decided not to wear a hat, and has resisted ever since. As a teen-ager his back was so badly burned while swimming, that he has permanent freckles all over it. Karlene had very sensitive skin as well. Her hair and skin were lovely and fair. Each child lost the hair they had at birth and the girls went through a period of having white hair. The first time we visited Sucre with Karlene about two years old, we walked through the market, and all the vendors called out to her, 'Abuelita' (little grandmother)! She enjoyed the attention and, therefore, wanted a 'bleach' for her fourteenth birthday since if had begun to darken. With that birthday gift It turned honey- colored. When we left Bolivia she was content to let it go to her natural rich brown. She was seventeen by then.

Krystal, on the other hand, rarely suffered from the sun. She had lots of hair, but it was so fine that it would never take a curl. We would do it up on Saturday night, and not take the curlers out until the very last minute before leaving to go to church. It would look so nice, but by the time we were half way to church, she would have 'bounced out' all the curl. I think she still fights with it to this day. Until a few years ago, she wore it long – half-way to her waist! Then she cut it short, and works on it every morning, to look her best.

We were fortunate, our children were good, obedient and learned the rules. Each step in life was a matter of arriving at the permissible age. Everything eventually came to those who waited, watching and learning till the acceptable day when they were old enough to do: this or that. Training in patience must start early. We expected and got cheerful compliance. They cleaned up everything on their plate, normally; there were some exceptions when traveling. The youngest, however, was a slow poke, grudgingly giving up playtime to eat.

When we lived in Oruro, Marshall was invited to some event at one of the mines and took Borden with him. They stopped at a restaurant just before arriving, and ate, thinking to save the hosts trouble. For miners, the restaurant served generous portions of soup, the main course, lots of fresh bread, and coffee, so it was a big meal! Imagine their dismay when they arrived to a veritable feast at the church. It would have been an insult not to eat. So they had to sit down to eat another entire meal. Borden still felt stuffed when they got home late that night!

Education is very important in any culture. After much prayer we sent for the New Brunswick Correspondence Course for Borden to do first grade. We didn't want to send him away to boarding school, but we didn't want him to lose the classroom experience, either. He went to Kindergarten in Spanish in the morning, and I worked with him in the afternoons with the course. We thought the two might be the answer. However, it didn't work out that way. His perfectionist personality made him take forever to do anything; which in turn drove me up the wall. It was like wading mud to teach him! The next year, when Krysi was the right age, we sent them both to Carachi-pampa, a school that reached to the eighth grade which used a curriculum from the State of Nebraska School System.

It is wrenching for all concerned to send your children away. When we were in Potosi, they went off to Boarding school in Cochabamba, when Borden was seven and Krystal almost six. When there was a free weekend at Carachipampa, it was too far for our children to come home. Borden went to Maria's (where Fernando was studying at the Seminary.) Krysi went home with the Habermehl's three girls. She was such a hearty eater and Alice was really impressed because she and all her family were 'picky eaters' (her words). She wrote me a note to tell me how satisfying it was to cook for someone who enjoyed the food so much. Seems that when they were all through, Krystal finished off everything left on the table.

Health care is one thing that was always a concern. In La Paz, we found a doctor that spoke English very well, and we were happy with the care he gave us. He was recommended by some of our fellow missionaries. When we went to other places, though, we had to find someone on our own. In the physical exam required with the application for the school in Carachipampa, we found out that in the four months since we had arrived in Potosi, both Borden's and Krystal's hearts had shifted to the left in their chests. The doctor attributed it to the extra effort needed to pump the blood in that rarefied air at

14,000 ft. altitude. When we went for the blood work to a local lab, we had to rise very early and walk nine blocks to get there, and of course they hadn't eaten. When he had taken the blood, the doctor sent out his nurse 'post haste' to bring coffee. Borden's face had turned paper-white under the freckles, and he thought the child might faint!

I think that knowing that, confirmed our decision to send them away, since the altitude in Cochabamba was only 8,000 ft. and there was usually a nurse among the teachers at their school.

The first year they were away at school, there was an outbreak of scarlet fever at the school, and several staff members were ill. They had to pull staff from other works to teach, and care for those who caught the fever. Though the weekly letters they were required to write to their parents continued to come, there was no mention of scarlet fever. We only learned of it when we went to pick them up when the term ended in June. I know that they probably didn't want to worry us, but I do wish they had at least mentioned it. We could have prayed for them (the sick ones), or perhaps, one of us could have come to help relieve the shortage of workers.

While still in Potosi, at the Christmas break, Borden began to run a fever. It was just as our Vacation Bible School was ending. Two days later Krysi came down with it as well.

Before all of us parents came to pick up the children at school, one child had been sent home with chicken pox. They were hoping to avoid an outbreak at the school. And by the time we were to take them back to school, Karlene's rash began. I don't think that any of the local children caught it, fortunately.

It still caused a few very difficult days. Marshall was away in the South, and should arrive back by 5 o'clock that afternoon. I had to take the children on the ferro-bus to the airport at Sucre. Feliza was willing to give Karlene her meals, and keep an eye on her until Marshall got there. One of the parents from Tarija was bringing her children from there and would be on the plane. She agreed to take responsibility for Borden and Krystal as well. I entrusted them to her care.

I had hoped to go back on the return trip of the ferro-bus, but the plane was late, and I had to go to the truck departure area, and find a truck home. Since we were a little late leaving Sucre, we arrived at the bridge which crossed the Rio Grande at dusk. This bridge had been out of service for 2 years, and when they finally did something about it, is was only a stop-gap repair. Everyone was required to unload all their bundles and carry them across the bridge. Some had several bundles to unload, so had to take more than one trip. Then the driver would cross the bridge at a creeping pace. To make a long story short we were too late to get across before dark. So the driver announced that we would go to sleep now, and cross at first light.

I had been riding in the cab with the driver and his wife. They had a rolled-up-pallet that they carried for just such an occasion. They set this up underneath their truck, so it would shelter them. That left the cabin for me. I could curl up just fine and cover myself with my coat. When it began to rain, they didn't get rained on, but the stream of water, that came running down the incline toward the bridge, passed right under the truck and right under their bed! When it had soaked through until they felt it, they came and climbed back up into the cab, making it uncomfortable for all of us for the rest of the night.

We all woke up feeling stiff the next morning, but made the trip across without too much more trouble. You will understand that I did a lot of praying that night, and the next day until we arrived.

Both Feliza and Julia pampered Karlene and she hardly missed us. All during that illness, she had been allowed to spend the day 'enthroned' in our bed, and was only required to go back to her own at night. There was more room there, and the other kids could come and play with her there. She does remember that she spent one whole night alone in our bed, when neither of us was there during her bout with chicken pox.

During the June to August vacation period in 1971, we were planning to go as a family with some local deacons on a visit to the Yungas of Inquisivi, the lowland northeast of Oruro. However, Karlene wasn't feeling well, and I stayed home to take her to the doctor. She ended up being operated on for appendicitis, while the family had exciting adventures, and hair-raising close calls on the trip. Then in September, Karlene broke her right arm. That meant that she spent about six weeks in which she could not turn any written work in. No one took the time to give her an oral exam. Toward the end of that period, she did start to write with her left hand, and one teacher commented that her handwriting was better with her left hand than it had been with her right. She insisted that this helped her to start trying to improve her writing with her right hand, when the cast came off.

Just after Christmas we were staying with the Stairs when we went to put the children in school after the holidays. They had had compassion on a wee kitten, and all of them and our girls broke out with ringworm. The school administration decided they would have to be quarantined. The Stairs children came on the bus each day, and all of theirs were under their clothing, so they didn't miss much. Krystal and Karlene were both put in a room apart. Then, it was noticed that Krystal's were also covered, so she was allowed to go back to her own room, and classes as well. The others had only a few ringworms, but they kept popping out all over Karlene. She was covered from head to foot. At the last count, she had 33! She was not allowed to go to class, she might shed germs around, or come into physical contact with the others. She was not allowed to handle the books, because, some other child might get ringworm later because she had touched them. There went another six weeks!

Then, Typhoid hit the school. She lost 2 weeks when she was very ill with high fevers. They did mention that she had ringworm, but nobody told us that she was not allowed to go to class, or to do her lessons, or to study. The other children were all afraid to go near her, afraid they would get ringworm, too. All but one, that is. She remembers that Carol Wormald would sit in the hall and they would play word games. Someone gave her a super-ball, too. She got pretty good at managing it.

When we went to the closing of school in June, they talked to us about Karlene's possibly not passing. They didn't say it was already determined. In all the discussions, they NEVER mentioned that it was because she had been kept out of the classroom for more than 3 months. It sounded like they would decide when she came back in the fall. Marshall went through a lot of things that she had studied, and when we went back, looked for an opportunity to speak with the staff. We wanted to tell them how much they had studied during the summer, but couldn't arrange it, and they didn't mention it again. So we figured they had let her go on. At Christmas, when we went to pick them up, we found that she was repeating the fifth grade work. We were upset, but there seemed to be nothing we could do about it.

Then came furlough. We were back in Canada. She went into sixth grade. We found out well into the year that Karlene was studying the same texts in sixth grade that she had studied twice in 5th grade at Carachipampa! So when we got back to Bolivia, she had had the same material three years in a row, and had missed what they had studied in 6th grade, because they were using texts a year ahead of those used in Canada.

She went to Tambo for 8th grade in spite of everything. But had been branded a dummy for so long that she began to believe it herself. She asked to be able to study at home for ninth grade. So we wrote to the New Brunswick system again, and got their Correspondence Course. They sent three courses. She did fine in the English, and the history courses. However, the French book for the course, had already been used for eighth grade, and her lessons began with Chapter 22. So we wrote that we would have to hire a tutor to take her through the first chapters, and when she had done that she would begin sending in those lessons. So, that took the fall months, but for the oral portion of the study, we went to the *Alliance Frances* (actually we all three went for classes) and she was speaking French by the time we went on furlough the next year. When they tested her she went into different grades for all her subjects. When she entered the French Class, she spoke to the French Professor, and she came out with very good grades at the end of the year. She had a little chat with the professor every day when she came in. I'm sure part of her success with French was due to the fact that she already spoke fluent Spanish.

When on our last furlough from Bolivia, we went to take some studies in Montreal, she asked if she could work that year instead of studying. It was the year that Bill 101 went into effect. We were told that she could not go to school in English, unless at least one of her parents had gone to English schools in

Quebec. We were plunged immediately into classes ourselves, and did not have the time to research on how we could get her into school, so we allowed her to find a job.

I think that she was afraid we would go back overseas, and she would be all alone. Before we went away again, both our daughters got married.

Two husbands and four children later, Karlene went to Community College and took a course in Architectural Drafting. She started with 32 others in September, and marveled that by Christmas 18 had given up. She persevered, found that she was a whiz at math. She enjoyed her studies, and dared to decide that she wasn't such a dummy after all. She found a good job, and worked at it for six years, before she had to leave it to care for her disabled husband.

Our son Borden graduated from Baylor University with a BA in Political Science and a BS in microbiology. He finished off the requirements in Ben Taub Hospital in Houston Texas. He has remained in that city working in several hospitals in the huge medical center there, as a medical technologist.

We thought of our children as normal North American kids, but our Bolivian neighbors thought of them as the children of rich foreigners. They adapted to local customs and courtesies, and yet, they *were* the children of foreigners. At home in the north they were missionaries' kids and just a bit different for that and other indefinable reasons. They were not totally confident in either culture, but fell between in a third, intermediate position. People with children overseas, whether as business people, teachers, military or diplomatic corps, technicians, or missionaries have children who will display the third culture traits. Some will adopt totally the surrounding culture; others will resist it totally, but most will range between the two extremes. These children are forced to adapt to and look critically at the habits and ideas of two self-centered cultures and pick and choose between them. Just as Christians choose some factors of secular culture to follow and yet maintain others based on Christ's teachings: we are a mix -- not completely one or the other. Are we third culture Christians? To be holy means to will one thing. Could we become wholly His?

These commandments that
I give you today
are to be upon your hearts.
Impress them on your children.
Talk about them when you sit at home and
when you walk along the road,
When you lie down and when you get up.

Deuteronomy 6:4-7

**Margaret Habermehl plays teacher to
Borden Thompson, Cathy H., Debbie H., Karlene T. and Krystal T**

During our second furlough Borden and Krystal were baptized. They had each made a decision when they were seven years old, but their being away at school made it awkward to find the right time to be baptized in Bolivia.

Rev. Austin MacPherson, while we were on home assignment offered classes, and both started, but the first year only Borden finished and was baptized. The next year Krystal did the same, and Karlene began to want to be baptized, too. She had just made her decision, and I had studied a little book with her and felt she was ready. However, she kept talking to me about it, asking me to speak to her dad about it. He didn't take me seriously -- kept saying she would have to speak to him -- that I shouldn't be pushing her, etc. So it just didn't happen for her. That urgency hit her again every time she saw a baptism, but not hard enough to talk to daddy.

Several years passed. One *Junta,* as we watched some baptisms take place -- leaves, slivers of ice and twigs floated on the not too clean, chill water. Then Karlene asked if she would have to be baptized in that dirty water. I explained again that she hadn't said anything to her dad so, no, she wouldn't. That triggered the talk with him. They agreed that if she would talk to a deacon at our church, that the next time there was a baptismal service, it would be her turn.

Finally, a gentleman from a rural congregation, way out in the country, came and asked Marshall and some of our deacons to come to baptize some people of their little church. It, like most, was too small to have a pastor all to itself. He came into town and went back with us to show us the way, because none of us had ever been there before and it was a long way on many very primitive roads. Karlene's hopes soared.

So on the trip, the deacon talked with her and decided that she was ready. The roads were terrible, and about half way there we had a flat tire. This threw us a bit late, so the people were already in their service when we arrived. The church was in a little hollow, and a little rill had been dammed up so that there would be enough water to baptize in. It, too, had twigs and leaves tumbling downhill with the waters, but that wasn't important this time.

We had brought black robes that our church used for baptisms: enough for the eight people who were to take part that day. All of them were for adults. Karlene was a small child's size ten. I checked my purse, and found a measuring-tape we could use for a belt, and pulled it up to blouse out so she wouldn't step on the hem, and fall down. She was so excited she hardly noticed. Most church baptistries are as big – or bigger than – this tiny, dammed-up pond. As they stepped out of the water 'to walk in newness of life', one little man passed a precious blossom that he had picked on the way to church, as something each one could press and keep as a memento of the occasion. Though each of those baptized was vitally important to the little church, they made much of the fact that the missionary's daughter had chosen to be baptized with them in their humble little congregation.

After the sermon, there was a picnic lunch, and a time of fellowship. Then we all started home. Most of the local people were walking, and all wanted to get home before dark. Some of those who came with us stayed, or went in another vehicle, which meant that it was only the family in the jeep for the return trip. This happened during the Christmas holidays so besides conversation about the beauties of the countryside, we sang Christmas carols. It was a lovely trip.

Night was just falling when the second flat occurred and the jeep swerved to the side of the road. Marshall worked under heavy clouds, with lightening strikes, peals of thunder, and between splashes of rain and hail. The risk had been calculated and after the first flat, nine hours before, we hadn't attempted to mend it. We had decided to take the short way home instead of the longer road, which would have taken us to a tire repair shop at the cross roads north of the city. There were lots of repair places in the city itself only a half hour west of where we sat.

Marshall had not packed the tire patching kit he normally carried when touring in the country areas. The room was needed for the extra people who went for the baptisms. Now, whatever regrets one might feel, we were stuck. "Let's pray" he said, and we did with fervor, especially for some vehicle which could take Marshall and the two tires into Oruro.

He then got out and took the tires off, and leaned them both against the side of the car. He was really sopping by the time he finally got this done. He then was forced back inside by the intensity of the weather.

The storm increased in fury and bright white bolts of lightning struck from dark blue-black clouds and the rain and sometimes a sprinkling of hail stones pinged off the top and hood of the Jeep. Marshall looked out at the storm, searched the hills for shelter, but there was none. There was a little one room adobe hut that passed for the Golf Course utility room about 200 yards distant. The jeep was safer even if metallic in parts. The golf course was all sand and rock without greens or trees, so logic said wait out the storm. Was it God who spoke through Logic? So we sang hymns and choruses for about half-an-hour while the lightning continued to strike around us.

During a short lull, the rumble of an approaching truck came clearly through the twilight. Marshall jumped out of the car and waving vigorously he waited hopefully for the truck to stop. A friendly face appeared at the window and the man motioned Marshall to the back of the truck. The cabin was full, so he heaved his tires and himself on to the back. He was glad he had a sweater and leather jacket on to cut the force of the wind and cold.

Marshall continues the story. The lights of the city were immediately apparent as they passed the hot springs where the pool and baths were frequented throughout the year. We passed the flats, with their sand dunes and brick kilns, crossed the drainage ditch with its waste products and entered the town. I pounded my fist on the cabin roof as we neared the street where the tire repairers kept shop. I went to a friend there, left the tires with full instructions and then went to seek out some transportation to go back for the family. Matilda Findlay was home and gave me a warm meal. With her Jeep we went back to pick up the repaired tires and the family.

Meanwhile, the children had finished the sandwiches, cookies,& all the fruit and drink. When Marshall left, we knew we had at least two hours to wait, and we had just about exhausted the Christmas carols, as well as a lot of other hymns. So someone proposed that the children would give a repeat performance of the Christmas Concert they had done at school when we went to pick them up. Of course, not all the participants were with us, but it seems that all the kids had learned all the roles. If it was a choir number, they sang three part harmony! So as God handled the special effects of the chorus line of many lightning bolts simultaneously dancing back and forth across the sky, playing up and down between the horizon and the upper reaches of heaven, we listened to the entire performance again. What with the comments between numbers treating with the quality of performance (i.e. better or worse than the original), the time passed pleasantly while Marshall was gone.

We weren't afraid of the lightening -- it had moved away some distance by this time -- and we took it as essentially just a great fabulous display: God's contribution to the staging of something meant to celebrate Jesus birthday! Remember, He sent the angels to announce the original event!

I must report that Marshall did finally get back with Matilda in her jeep. We left him to put on the tires and replace the spare and drive the car home alone, while we zoomed off to a hot supper at Matilda's. It was ready on our return. He arrived in time to join the festivities and later took us all home to our warm beds. But Karlene will never forget the day she was baptized. It all added up to a very eventful 20 hour trip. God had given us a very special Christmas Eve to remember.

Breaking the ice to baptize believers in the mountains

We believe Christ is the answer, our church believes Christ is the answer. But does every one in ALL the Americas believe that? Some people believe there are other answers: Communism was a popular candidate for the Americas' greatest need. Many countries passed through this experiment in Communism and Socialism in South, Central and Caribbean America. It produced much turmoil, but little light. It generated strikes, riots, shortages, injustice and lots of death and despair. Our people in the churches they attended believed <u>Christ is the answer,</u> That is the slogan they used in English-speaking countries. The Latin countries went a step further, they used the slogan <u>Cristo la unica esperanza,</u> this means <u>Christ the only hope.</u> It was painted on walls, boulders, buildings and advertised in dozens of cardboard, wooden and paper signs of different sizes in every town and village. Thousands of tracts and study pamphlets were distributed by the faithful on this theme.

Nelson Fanini, a pastor in Brazil and the President of the Baptist World Alliance promoted his ideas for an America wide, year long, simultaneous evangelistic campaign. First, he had already held it in Brazil before proposing it to the Spanish-speaking countries of America in 1970. It was five years after Evangelism in Depth. Our people in the churches were now more prepared for directing and participating in something of that magnitude.

Since we had largely passed the persecution stage of spreading the gospel message, we began new, steady growth in church numbers and sizes. The state church had begun a process of dialogue with evangelicals and the Pope had declared Bolivia a Catholic mission field. Among evangelicals, national pastors were replacing foreigners in most strategic and prestigious public positions as pastors, teachers, and administrators. Prejudice against the gringo's leadership could not be valid against evangelicals anymore. The work that had first started among the middle class artisans and people of independent means, and then spread to the indigenous people after the agrarian reforms, now reached to other social classes. Instead of being heretics, they were being seen as moral and progressive. Now, in the Campaign of the Americas, closer contact between the public and the believing community was established. The public in general came to know more about what Baptists believe. Interest grew, we became a social force on the national scene. One of the signs of these times was the evangelical character in a TV soap opera. He was always portrayed as upright, honest and honorable in all the dealings touched by his small business. The proof is in the pudding we like to say. Society women started looking for maids who were evangelical because they were known to be more honest and dutiful than the others.

Being a believer was a recommendation in business. One of the newer members of a La Paz church lost his job. They were going to turn him out on the street when they heard he had been baptized. He came to prayer meeting asking us to pray that he would be able to find a job and a place to stay. Someone mentioned that a downtown bank was looking for a janitor. We prayed and the pastor said he should mention that he was an evangelical if he got an interview, so there wouldn't be trouble later.

He went early the next day. The manager was favorably impressed. He mentioned in the course of the interview, as his pastor had recommended, that he was a Protestant. The manager said, "They have a name for being honest," and they hired him on the spot. Then the manager asked when he could move in. He didn't understand, so the manager explained that he was expected to live in the back patio of the bank as part of the job. He would be responsible for security any time the bank was not open for business. Thus the Lord had provided an apartment for him and his family as well as the job. He could hardly wait to go by on the way home to see the pastor and tell him the good news!

There was a rash of choruses on the theme, 'Christ is the answer.' During the years we were in Bolivia, I recognized many hymn tunes that had been translated from English, or French, or German, but now the reverse was occurring. Every little Evangelical musical combo had its own version of that theme set to its own music. Some of those flowed back to North America -- the United States and Canada. Like:

Christ is the Answer to all your need!
Christ is the Answer, so let Him lead.
He is the only one who saves from sin,
Christ is the answer, A-men.

Another thing that impressed you was that many persons who were Catholics had had a personal salvation experience during Evangelism in Depth. Though some left their church and joined an evangelical church, where they had heard the Gospel and responded to the Lord Jesus, others had chosen to stay in the Catholic Church. They had begun Bible studies and prayer meetings. These exercises in faith blessed the Catholic Church and sparked a real revival of interest in spiritual things within their own congregations. These Catholics had been blessed in evangelistic meetings so they brought their friends to hear the preaching during the Campaña de las Americas. Again both groups were blessed! Instead of a competition, there was an interest in witnessing to what Jesus had done for each of them, and the Holy Spirit blessed us all!

La Radio La Cruz del Sur (The Southern Cross Radio Station), begun by Canadian Baptist Dr. Sid Hillyer in 1949, had been a great help in the Evangelism in Depth campaign, and again for the Campaign of the Americas. There were prayer bulletins directly after the world news, weather and sports. Rallies, prayer meetings, parades, special musical programs, visitation campaigns, and preaching campaigns were all announced well ahead of time, so you could plan to participate. Their technicians were there to tape many of the activities, and then play them afterwards on the air.

Evangelical emphasis on education changed the social caste system that had existed in colonial Latin America. The open, friendly, cost-effective clinics run by churches, treated people on the basis of need and not social position. It impressed people in contrast to the government hospital which sometimes showed racial or social bias in their treatment of individuals. Among the younger generation the children of church members were graduating as doctors, lawyers and other professionals. The public perception was being reversed. The Campaign of the Americas confirmed to all the churches that a change of attitude existed among the population.

Evangelicals were okay.

The Catholic hierarchy started to advertise the fact that Protestants were 'separated brethren' and an attitude of reconciliation became evident among them. We were welcome at public meetings of their workers and catechists. As one North American priest jokingly comforted an uneasy co-worker, at an inter-faith conference, who asked: "Is this the only way?"

"Well, we tried the inquisition and that didn't work!" One of the leaders of a neighboring denomination resisted the invitations until I said "Well, the Methodists are going. Would you want Catholics to think they hold the typical Protestant position on doctrine?" He answered, "You've almost persuaded me." At any rate, inter-faith cordiality began to appear at this time. Persecution still occurred in isolated places or by individuals in city settings, especially by the drunk, but it was spontaneous and no longer organized. We had truly entered a new era in the outreach toward the needy. Catholic co-operatives and make-work projects began to appear in city and country. Bible reading was being promoted in the public and Catholic schools. A new day of liberty has dawned over the Bolivian hills.

If the Son make you free, you will be free indeed.
John 8:36

Campaign of the Americas parade

A junta (whom' ta) is a gathering. After a military takeover of a government, a junta of three officers as rulers is often put into power. It can also be of a group of like-minded people who have a determined purpose. In our case, to learn more of the Bible and about God and His will for us.

The evangelicals, especially the Baptists, were always strong on juntas in a rural setting to serve and educate people of a certain district or area of the country. Timing as well as place were of vital importance to the success of a junta. Best times were when the agricultural or grazing year allowed rest and time between duties or needed work. Rainy seasons were always hard to move around in because of the dirt roads. Holidays were appropriate times if there were no problems with roads or venue. The meeting place could be by election or in central locations or especially, a new or frontier work for encouragement.

Networking the area allows people to get to know each other. This has great value. It decreases isolation if other nearby believers get to know each other. It always decreases opposition, if those opposed know that nearby communities will object to how they treat their evangelical outcasts. Study of Scripture in a large group always increases faith and practice. They learn from each other. Some communities will arrange for part of their congregation to come at the start and others, caring for the flocks, goods and homes, will come for the last part. The early birds go home midway through to take over their duties. These forms of mutual help and co-operation arm communities to progress socially, economically, and spiritually. Within a few years small improvements and optimism make a significant difference even when only a minority believe. Villages where the gospel had entered were noted for combed hair and washed faces. The majority of people didn't want to look unkempt if the heretics were doing it, dirt made you look bad in comparison.

I would go to villages and speak in the schools about serving God and country. The communist and socialist teachers did not object if we talked about virtue or ethics, but religion was a forbidden topic. We never attacked the state church. We simply taught the Bible and sold Scripture portions at prices the children could afford. I told them how to ask Jesus into their hearts to forgive their sins. They learned how to read and obey God's word. Teaching is a lonesome occupation out on the rural plains and mountains and teachers are happy to have visitors to talk to and share news and experiences.

The state church learned of our outreach and soon started their own social programs and even assigned catechists to work in the western districts. It was too little and too late. Once we succeeded in passing the persecution stage we grew.

The training of deacons and leaders soon brought spiritual authority and order to the group of believers. We knew that no rural congregation would be able to pay a city trained man for leadership. We established the first Deacon as preacher, he was sometimes the first convert in the village who had resisted the pressures of persecution. The second was usually a Sunday school teacher and often reader of scripture in the meetings. Many of the older men were illiterate, while many of the younger knew Spanish as well as Aymara (I mah' rah) or Quechua (ketch' oo ah) languages. The third deacon was often the treasurer and richest man of the congregation. I think the theory was that he would know how to handle money and would be less tempted than a poor man. It didn't always work out that way. If they were large enough for a fourth deacon he was their missionary. He was expected to spend one or two Sundays away at a preaching point, as well as do open air preaching at some of the fairs and open markets.

The converts sometimes were members of the extended family of a city believer. City people often kept touch with rural relatives and traveled back to visit and to persuade. I always took interested deacons and city people when I went to the country. I would contact the teachers or other local authorities. Our large number of city people visiting was impressive and our talk conciliatory. First contact was always the most crucial for our enemies always gave us a bad press. We knew that they had always heard terrible things about us and would be happy to discover we were human and cordial.

When I was in Oruro in charge of rural work, we planned a junta on the northern border of our county with La Paz county, where the gospel had just arrived. It was to occur during All

Saints, November first, an important state holiday. The custom there demands a visit to the cemetery and graves of relatives, where flowers, drinks and food are placed. The spirits of the dead need only the essence. The meal can be enjoyed by the celebrants and strong drinks are imbibed freely, resulting in inebriation.

For our junta, permission had been granted by our Oruro county government and the local village authorities were also contacted for permission to hold the gathering. We arranged for David Hillen, a teacher in Reekie College, to go with his wife, Janet, a nurse and their baby. They carried Dr. Coates, an MD and Spanish language student in Cochabamba, with the clinic medicine in one jeep.

I was to carry preachers, deacons and people who had made the arrangements. I also had the projector and books; I enjoyed the work of colporteur. It took most of the day, eight hours, by dirt road and ferry across the *Desaguadero* (des ah gwa deh' row) River to arrive in the mid-afternoon.

The Hillens, however had a late start. When they reached the ferry, it was near enough dark that the ferry operator did not wish to make another trip. They had no place to spend the night on that side of the river, and so showing him the baby, convinced him to come across for them. San Jose, where they were expected, was so near. Half way across, the cable snapped. Both Dave and Jan jumped into the cold arm-pit deep water to help push the ferry, jeep and all. The ferry man poled, but they could not go back upstream to the ramp to disembark. They had to improvise their own ramp. They arrived chilled to the bone. Happily, someone served them with bowls of hot soup and loaned them blankets.

The Baptist church was a half mile south of the village square. We went to the square because we had permission. The women had prepared the supper meal there in the community center. The late comers were still eating supper. We were starting to prepare for an open air meeting in the square.

Nearby there was the beat of a tom-tom from the cemetery. We were far enough from the drinking to feel confident. It was misplaced. Suddenly there erupted a shouting, cursing mob bent on trouble. Stones and adobe fragments were hurled

200

through the air. I ran with several leaders to close the distance between the two groups. It would have been worse if we had run away. They would have chased us all the way to our building. Face to face we could ask what was wrong. "Why the anger?" "We have permission." "Your neighbors invited us." "The Pope has declared that the Protestants are separated brothers." "We come in peace." We became a line of people pushing and pleading; few blows were traded. Most of us kept our arms down and our hands spread. On the other side, I saw one man with an open short-bladed pocket knife, his arm would move up a few inches and then fall again convulsively. He never struck a blow. God was protecting us!

Suddenly one of their leaders called out to the attacking group: "We'll meet at our church and talk there." He pointed at our trucks. "You people get out of town."

We did. By this time the trucks were piled high. People had gathered helter-skelter: women and children with bundles of personal goods. Confusion reigned. They went to the Baptist church. I ran after the leader up the rise, where his men were trying to stone the medical jeep. It was turning the corner away from the square to depart by road. I yelled to get their attention and objected again. He turned his back on me and proceeded up the hill with his men. I ended up walking to the church.

I stopped to rest on the way and noticed a blind man hurrying toward me across the flats, guided only by a walking stick. Suddenly, about ten yards away, he threw up his arms and cried out as he fell forward. There was a ditch invisible from where I was resting. He fell into it, but others on the road sprang to help him. I thought of the blind leading the blind; a parable of Jesus. How a church can mislead men in what they hate and how they show their love.

At the church, in the growing darkness, families, which had been lost from each other while scrambling to pick up belongings and children, were still in the process of getting together again. We set up the generator which helped with the reunions.

Needless to say the medical team was busy with bruised and emotionally wrought-up patients. Sedatives & methiolate were applied generously. Our lady doctor had a bright colorful bruise on her own leg from a rock. After a rousing night meeting outside the church building, we slept on the floor inside the different rooms and main floor of the sanctuary. All slept in their clothes. We wondered if the group would launch a night attack on us, at the same time they were worried about a retaliatory attack by us. Neither side slept well that night.

Word got out that we had a doctor. In the morning first the women, and later the men of the center, came to the doctor to get the same medicines our group had enjoyed the night before. In addition, our Dr. Coates said she felt like a quack, only handing out patent medicine for their hangovers. Chronic complaints and illness showed up on the third day after news had spread that the doctor was friendly.

Authorities offered explanations and excuses. They were in a face-saving mode. Politics reared it's ugly head. Some said that we were trying to change the village from belonging to La Paz county to Oruro county where we had come from. I left the squabbles to the men of the congregation located in Oruro, and the authorities of the village in La Paz to settle.

Each junta had something special to impress it upon the memory, the stoning was the item at San Jose. As Dr. Coates was leaving from the airport, she raised her pant-leg to show us her fading bruise. She quipped that she might have to touch it up a little or people would never believe it.

A few years later when the church at San Jose applied to enter the Bolivian Baptist Union, some of those same municipal authorities signed the minutes of the meeting constituting it as a church. This was a long way from the drunken mob that threw the junta out of their town.

I believe that our move to conciliate was prompted by God, and saved us from difficulties in that place. Eventually it drew many to the saving knowledge of God, and established their place in the community. Many times the State church wished to 'tax' everyone in the area to contribute money and labor in the construction of their church building. Negotiating with the authorities often led to their contributing to a community center, school, square, market place or park which would be available to the whole population, in lieu of that kind of arrangement. We were amenable. Later local authorities invited us to enter a frontier area to evangelize because some villagers who were converted while visiting in Chile, were establishing church relations to a foreign denomination from that country. They wanted any loyalty to go to a Bolivian based denomination such as the Bolivian Baptist Union. The government had by this time recognized our usefulness because of the positive changes made in the villages where the gospel was proclaimed. They saw that our continued growth was not politically motivated. Our kingdom is not of this world.

He who wins souls is wise.. Proverbs 11:30

Bible portions on sale are displayed everywhere

In my first year in La Paz I was called upon to go to a church in a high mining town and hold a heresy trial of some brothers who were making innovations in the gospel they preached. My Seminary had not prepared me for such an eventuality. At the meeting we asked the brother, a man in his late forties, about the doctrine he was teaching publicly. Did he believe that those things given up for the sake of Christ: houses, lands, goods, family members and wife, (Matt. 19:29) would receive them all, now in this life, Luke 18:29. Wives is not mentioned in the receiving category in Mark 10:29-30. (In Western tradition multiple wives are not acceptable.) Was it true that they were marrying younger ladies to replace those left? Were there other doctrines in contention with the congregation? There were many doctrines, with which he was not willing to part, especially the young wives. I, according to apostolic mandate, committed his body to the enemy for destruction and his soul to God for judgment - 1st Tim. 1:19-20. We closed the meeting and he went his way and I never heard more about him or his movement ... except his death later.

Relationships are supreme in the work of Christian evangelism. We believe God has called us into a relationship with Jesus, the Messiah and Christ. As we come to know Him we are met in love and respect to learn to lean on His strength and guidance. We form a bond so strong, as this friendship develops, that we know His mind on many matters. We talk to Him in prayers and we learn more by the study of Scripture and by experience with the Holy Spirit and life situations. This bond also develops between believers who meet together and become His body; His brothers and sisters in worship and obedience. Business meetings, associations, and conventions arise from this mutual need to consult and act together. For the missionary this activity can have its hard moments: so many people, so many needs and actions to evaluate and decide upon.

Evaluation of men's efforts for God's Kingdom calls for judgment and responsibility for the use of time and money. It also implies approval of teaching and the things taught. This brings you into trial, in case of mistakes, and critical thinking in planning future activity. None of this excludes the guidance of the Holy Spirit, although, some feel that any thing that is not spontaneous is not of God. I disagree on this point and so support group activity and planned action.

For most missionaries this involves us in local, regional, national and sometimes international meetings. Each with more and more new faces and names to learn and new situations to deal with, decide about or support.

The regional meetings I loved. I knew many of the delegates and knew where they were from. The musical pastors would meet with instruments in hand to exchange newest songs and tell of new or old singers and their performance at one or another meeting. The evangelists would meet at lunch or in spare time also, to exchange stories of experiences, opposition, souls gained, baptisms and new advances. The politically active would meet to complain of rules, structures, key opposition figures and allies; and to plot new motions and candidates for the election. I tended to rotate between the three groups and get a bit of each. Lady delegates exchanged news of children, and caught up on personal situations. Teachers and institutional directors tended to group and exchange experiences and problems. All were there to contribute to the whole body of Christ's work in their country.

Associational meetings, once they were started, were as intimate as church meetings. We got church and congregation reports, triumph and despair in the local situations, additions and losses and prayer items.

It was there that we learned about and faced the problem of the *Profeticos*, who were invading our congregations. They were very legalistic: prohibiting photographs of people, claiming that they were idolatrous. They banned private Bible reading because only the teachers are authorized to interpret Scripture. Soccer? I never learned what was wrong with ball games. And you were required to go to Argentina to their headquarters to be baptized. We found a place to meet them and after searching Scripture and confrontation, condemned them and warned our church people against them. Their influence, too, waned.

We also had to deal with local splits, dictatorial pastors or deacons, denominational divisions and independent minded individuals who tried to acquire property as well as people for themselves. We were reminded again that people are like sheep and there are wolves active, whatever they may look like outside. Local responsibility dealt with such important problems.

The National Convention's meetings were always another matter altogether. At our first convention we heard Juan Aguila offer to expand the work by going to Tarija or Potosi to open new work. The young man looked delicate and for that reason was sent to Tarija. The convention not only looked forward to national work, it looked northward to the source of missionaries, vehicles and money. Church reports were heard, but as the years passed they were accorded less time until necessity called forth the regional meetings. Proposals to the north and counter offers from that source plus committee reports of progress and problems occupied our time at the national level.

This was where the slow work of empowering started. An apt person was elected by friends and fellow workers to a position of importance on a committee or was approached as a possible worker for the Missions Committee or the Ministerial committee. A church with a problem or of larger size sought responsible and charismatic pastors to invite. We had a small and competent group of lady pastors who served brilliantly, but were frequently married off in the process. Although among missionaries the opposite was true. Ladies held the majority in mission conference meetings; they were a versatile and able group with whom it was a pleasure to work. In relation to national participation in decision making we started small and grew. This was a process of including outstanding nationals as consultants on mission committees and then when the committee was passed over to the National Convention of the Bolivian Baptist Union, such persons already were habituated to seek the biblical and modern solutions to maintain its function. The nationals also elected a few foreign workers on such committees for help.

One year my friend Hedley Hopkins noticed that no missionaries were elected. All were replaced by national workers. He called Marshall's attention to the fact. "Well, it's where we want them to go, isn't it? Lets hope they can do it alone," I answered. Hedley agreed. As some Bolivians dropped out or resigned; missionaries were named by committee presidents as appointees to serve until the next convention. Leadership among national figures continued to grow as the work expanded. Experienced workers were requested by the elected members to fill them in on historic practices and to do some of the leg work that employed Bolivians had difficulties in finding time for. It worked out well in the long run, but there were resignations, insistent demands that it be thus, and not so, and accusations when mistakes occurred or results differed from that expected. It was a learning process, but sometimes emotionally jarring, as one person said:" Jesus walked on water; missionaries learn to walk on eggs." Growth and improvements in the work of committees continued. Social and religious programs aided community life.

I had the privilege of representing Bolivia on its first invitation to the international meeting of the Baptist World Alliance one year, at my expense, until money was found to send a national representative to later meetings. It was in London that year I went and I got to visit Paris as well; for, after all, the rewards for drudgery on the mission fields are the moments of travel that take us to exotic places where we can only afford to stay a few days. My flight to London was routed through France, an unsought bonus from the Lord. There are other rewards, but travel is the most obvious. Meeting people is another reward, but it can also be a heavy burden. On our furloughs the pastors at convention had largely changed fields of service and perhaps moved far away from their previous charges. Children had grown almost unrecognizably and new faces were always added. I used to dread conventions in the north. Everyone expected you to remember them and would often ask, "Don't you remember me ... ?" I found it hopeless to keep up with everybody. I was simply a living exhibit while in the north, bearing the label MISSIONARY and expected to speak of one thing only: my field of work. Some found this difficult, but I enjoyed it. Home assignment or furlough was usually fun. True satisfaction, however, does not come from situations, but from accomplishment. This I had in abundance as national believers increasingly demonstrated the ability and responsibility of directing the work of God in the congregations of their country and in relations with the world of Baptist believers elsewhere.

Discipleship conducts to leadership and to empowerment.

Each new addition to our national outreach: the Book depot and distribution agency, the printing press, the Canadian Baptist Institute in La Paz were pioneered by nationals helped by missionary efforts and sometimes money. Old mission schools like Reekie Elementary and High school and the Guatajata schools and clinic systems were placed under national direction. Even the Radio *La Cruz del Sur* eventually became national in personnel, administrator and technicians. We continued to work ourselves out of jobs to help create new outreach or institutions and to repeat the process of growth and nationalization.

The transfer of properties from the name of the *Corporacion Bautista Canadiense* to the name of the *Union Bautista Boliviana* was presented as a change of name rather than the transfer of properties: which would have cost a large sum in taxes. It was accepted by the government and the change of name was done over several years. The *Corporacion* held an annual meeting in Spanish to register the acquisition of properties and vehicles. When this phase of missions ended, so did the meetings of that legal entity.

After his first year of experience as a national missionary alone in Tarija, Juan Aguila requested missionary help. Art Wormald volunteered to join him. Outreach to Provincial capital cities after that was always a joint venture by a pair: a missionary and a national. The pastor was always the national and the deacon was the foreigner. In every case it worked well. I tried it twice in Potosi and Sucre. Santa Cruz was a more difficult matter. Brazilian Baptists worked there, but we had to place a buyer and link with the city of Robore where a school in the hills of Santiago de Chiquitos was sponsored and developed for a decade by our mission. John Palmquist was the first agent and missionary there. After a time the Brazilian missionaries invited us to occupy an unchurched part of the growing city of Santa Cruz, now the second largest in Bolivia. We were able to contact migrants from the highlands who started congregations in the jungle and wanted to be related to our Union. Our work there increased rapidly.

Total nationalization never occurred. Experts continued to be sent from the north and new projects opened. After the project developed nationals assumed management. Local leadership continued the work and it grew. Canadian Baptist Volunteers visit to aid in projects of the local churches. The communities are blessed with foreign visitors who come as friends. They help in building church facilities or other services: medical, or social that make local improvements. Pleasant memories are shared. God is glorified as brothers work together.

Behold, how good and how pleasant it is for brethren to dwell together in unity!

Psalm 133:1

Pastors Heredia and Cueto with Potosi young people.

With about a month to go before leaving Oruro for furlough, there was a regional convention held on the Institute property, which was so revealing.   Each church brought a report of the years activities that was read aloud.   Local churches wanted to find the encouragement and blessing that everyone felt on hearing reports of their trials and triumphs in 1972.

We had been impressed with the way the work had grown since that first young man, Toribio Tarque, went out ten years before trying to visit all 33 rural churches in Carangas each month.   Marshall came home to have lunch with the family after a session in which he had heard, and noted down numbers from those reports of the new churches, congregations, and preaching points.   He said I think that these would add up to a total of at least 80. I challenged him to name them. It wasn't that I didn't believe him, I just wanted him to add them up: one by one, so that we could see for ourselves that there really were that many. He didn't take time to add them up then because he didn't want to miss a minute of the session.   When convention was over, we could sit down and calculate. We would look at a report with its number of 'daughter' churches, or congregations or preaching points. I don't have the figures at hand, but we often recounted, as we spoke in churches during that furlough, that there were 26 new churches, 119 congregations, and 19 preaching points.

On my last visit to the border area, I was making a promised last turn around to farewell those congregations because I was not coming back to that job after furlough. I was going for baptisms to the last large administrative center on the border. I had sent my passport in to the La Paz Department of Emigration with papers to get permission for myself, my wife and three children to leave the country in two weeks time. I'd noticed that there had been a problem of revolutionaries connected to Che Gevarra's fall in Bolivia. I did not realize that it was precisely in the area I was to visit that there had been an armed attempt to escape from the country and into Allende's Chile where they would be allowed temporary refuge.   Hazel and our colleague Matilda Findlay made me promise that I would go by when I got my *hoja de ruta* (permit to travel) and ask them to give me a letter telling them that I had business with the churches in Carangas. In the rush of picking up all the local brethren that were going to accompany me on the trip, I forgot to do it. I was supposed to return in time to preach at the East Church (Norman Dabbs) on that Sunday evening, but reminded Hazel that if I didn't make it, I had told the Deacons that she would speak instead. So she was preparing in case it was necessary.

Several of the places along the way we stopped for a night and took part in evangelistic efforts, and left one brother to help them in the rest of their campaign, with a promise that we would pick them up, on the return trip. It was so encouraging to see the growth in spirituality in each place, and also the healthy growth in numbers when they were preaching in their own churches and in the neighboring villages.

The trip out was long but seemed easy as we stopped, preached and picked up brothers and sisters who wanted to be present at the baptism. We visited the church for morning service and I talked to the candidates all approved by their local congregations and each would give a testimony of their faith, how it had started and grown. I had visited the traffic station and shown my license and local identity. Near the school I saw several teachers with suitcases; it was the end of the school year. They waited for a truck to take them farther on toward a desired destination going home. One, a man about thirty came over to ask if I could take him to Oruro when I finished the church services and baptism. I replied that I had a full jeep and until some of my group left an empty seat I could not promise anything. My riders were Indian and he was Spanish, so I don't think he liked my answer. My jeep was empty at that moment, but he had seen me come into town. Near the edge of town, I observed two brujos (brew hoes) seated, obviously waiting with a white llama on a short rope. They were sitting on a piece of property which I supposed would be used for a house. One may have been the owner. I was sure the men intended to sacrifice the animal for the spirits when the propitious moment came. They waited the spirit's call.

I was surprised when a city official ask me to come to the municipal building. I went leaving the believers at church.
I decided to walk over and see them. Usually they didn't work

211

on Sunday. At the mayor's office I was asked for my passport and other official papers. I didn't have them and explained why. They offered to telegraph the La Paz office and get an identity check and told me the price of the service. I thought it was a shake down and a way to extort money; I knew the emigration offices didn't work on weekends, so refused. They knew me here and the believers could vouch for me. I noticed an army boy waiting while we finished our conversation. As I rose to go he asked me to accompany him to the army barracks on the edge of the city, the Captain wanted to see me. We walked to the army base. There the same questions were repeated with the same answers, but there was no offer to send telegrams. After close questioning I was asked to place my hands on my head for a body search. I reluctantly complied, while I protested and pointing to my breast pocket said I had a card they should see. The tension had steadily increased and they froze for a moment as the captain rasped "Keep you hands up!" They relaxed when no weapons were found. So, I told him I would come back with the car after the baptism finished. Since I had come for that purpose, I had to complete my mission. They now knew who I was, but since I hadn't the proper papers they would have to take me back to Oruro and report to their commander. We agreed and they gave permission.   After the service where we had baptisms , we moved out to the car and I drove to the base. After the passengers were looked over, the jeep was searched, with the books and projector it required more time. A sergeant with pistol strapped to his waist was to sit in the front seat. A grinning corporal with a pistol-grip, submachine gun waited to get in the back. I objected strongly. I had passengers to carry back and they had searched jeep and people. The sergeant's handgun was enough. The commander agreed and ordered the corporal with the sub machine pistol to stand down. He was very disappointed not to get a trip to the city, so I gave him a Bible. In fact I gave out several portions of Scripture which they gladly received. My passengers got in and the sergeant occupied the front seat beside me. After an hour we passed a village where several passengers got out to visit the village for Sunday night service. Later we came to a truck stop where we met the teacher who had solicited a ride back on the frontier.

The sergeant remarked that he was the man who denounced me to the authorities. I had understood this from what some of the church people told me. I decided to 'heap coals on his head.' (Romans 20:12) I invited him to accompany us since I had several places vacated on the road.

He accepted gladly and as we continued on our way he expressed his amazement that the military should not have recognized that I was the regional pastor and strictly attending to church business. He came close to insulting the intelligence of the commander and the sergeant became ominously quiet. I defended the army's action, I was at fault. I didn't charge the teacher for the trip and felt rather smug about everything. However, in the city they allowed my national pastor, Eugenio Velasquez, to go home and took me to the army base. I told the pastor not to tell my wife. I thought I would be released promptly in the morning. It was night and the military decided that the hospital would be a better place to hold me. I was alone and went to sleep promptly. The pastor rounded up several prominent men to plead for my freedom, but since I was asleep the base commander had an easy negative. In the morning more Christian leaders came. The commander found no reason to detain me, but sent me to Interpol for the international police to establish my identity. They were interviewing a woman liaison worker from Brazil whom they suspected of contact with communist elements in the mines and were not interested in my story. I just had to wait. I spent an hour with them and on confirmation of credentials in La Paz I was released to go to the Reekie School where the resident missionary, Matilda Findley, lived. I was hungry and spent. I found the kids, but no wife. I explained to them why I was delayed and made a joke of it. I never mentioned where the guns were pointed. They didn't know where mother was. I was annoyed. Where had she run off to? Hazel had no clue to what was going on. I'll let her tell you.

When I said goodbye to Marshall, he wasn't sure when he would be home. He had been asked to preach on Sunday night at the East Church, named for the martyr Norman Dabbs. We all attended there when we were in the city. So the deacons knew that if he didn't get back in time, that I would be speaking in his place. So I did. Matilda had invited us to stay at her house the last two weeks before leaving, so I could dedicate myself to packing. Her maid was preparing our meals, and mine was still living in her little room at our house, and helping me to pack and get ready to go.

So on Monday morning, around 8 o'clock, Matilda came down to my room before I got up, and sat on the side of my bed. We had already packed 17 boxes with things that would stay in the storage room next to where I was sleeping. She asked me if I could find any of our old expired passports. (It was customary to destroy old passports, but due to the problems we had with ours, we always asked at the consulate that they void ours, and allow us to keep them.) I knew they were in one of the 17 boxes which were taped closed and stacked in two neat piles next door.

She had heard from the deacons. They told her some of the pertinent facts, and thought that old passports might solve the problem. When Marshall dropped the pastor who had accompanied him off at his house the night before, he had asked him not to tell me he was being detained. He didn't want me to worry.

We decided that we would start at the army post where she heard he had spent the night. When we went there, they said no, that he had been released at 8 o'clock. We called Matilda's house to see if he had turned up there. When they said no, we decided maybe he would go to our house, thinking that he would find me there. He wasn't there. So we went to the house of the accompanying pastor. His wife said, no that her husband hadn't come home either. Next we went to look for him at the downtown jail. As we crossed the square, we saw several of the deacons, and they saw us. So they scurried around the corner and by the time we got the car parked and went to look, they were nowhere in sight. So we went into the jail. One of our friends, a lawyer from the Salvation Army, was there in the jail, but avoided answering any of our questions, saying he was busy with a client. There again, they said he had been released. With that we went back to Matilda's house, to find Marshall and the children having breakfast. He was angry that I wasn't there to welcome him and comfort him when he came home after his ordeal! He had set up everyone NOT to tell us anything, and then blamed ME for the result!

There was such a tension, that I'm sure everyone had indigestion from that meal. When we had each recounted our stories, with tears, everything was alright. The packing finished and we were off to La Paz and home for more work and travel in the north. We had been brought through fiery trials, but it's never easy, especially as a farewell.

Please inquire of the Lord to learn whether our journey will be successful.

Go in peace.

Your journey has the Lord's approval.

Judges 18:5-6

Ready for furlough : Borden, Hazel, Karlene, Marshall, & Krystal

Our fourth period of work in Bolivia was directed toward the city of Sucre, a colonial city clothed in white. It was the original capital of Bolivia, set on a plain at the foot of twin moderately high peaks. One has a statue of Christ crowning it with out-stretched arms blessing the city; the other has a church dedicated to the Virgin Mary. Students often crawl on their hands and knees up the steps of stone leading to one of these shrines, during the week before exams. This is in the hope of receiving a blessing that will allow them to pass. Fireworks are launched from the heights for every holiday. High up the hill lay an ancient monastery with carvings of the martyred priests of Japan in its sanctuary and a thousand-year old tree in the garden that takes six men to reach around the trunk.

The city spreads over the different levels, descending from over 10,000 feet at the top, to 9,000 feet at the railway station at the bottom of the city center. Following the holy sites, on the hilltops, are many fine residences, the plaza, the shops and markets toward the middle. The University, Supreme Court buildings and the beautiful railroad station lie below the plaza. The road to the airport goes down from there, through a sprinkling of adobe houses to a tributary of the Pilcomayo River and up the side of another hill.

Chuquisaca was its first name, the *Departamento* (province or state) still bears the Quechua name to this day. Charcas was its second, the colonial name. Because the Spanish *Conquistadores*, white-washed their adobe homes it was soon called *La Ciudad Blanca*, the White City. It only came to be named Sucre for the general, who won the War of Independence.

On the lower side of the plaza was the Casa de la Libertad, where the 'Cry of Liberty' (The declaration of Charcas) was first heard in South America, triggering Simon Bolivar's rebellion against Spain. When Bolivar launched his *'Grito de Libertad,'* from the legistative chambers of the city, it re-echoed throughout the continent! He spoke to a conference of leaders from all over South America, calling them to stand against the repressive treatment they were receiving from Spain, which was suffering trauma from the Napoleonic wars in Europe. The worst thing was that even though Sucre's parents were Spanish, he could not go to be educated in Spain, and he felt like the local houses of learning were second-rate.

The legislative assembly chamber has the same elaborately carved tables, maroon velvet padded chairs for the legislature, the throne for the viceroy or president of the colony, etc. as when that cry was heard. In the patio a colorful garden and an enormous bust of Sucre carved from one huge oak tree trunk stands. Volunteers of the historical society will take you on a tour of the property, giving you all the anecdotes of General Sucre and his feats of prowess on the battlefield. The war hero passionately wanted to have a highland republic rather than be a fringe province at a great distance from Lima, the capital. Bolivar wanted to continue calling it Upper Peru. So, Sucre flattered Bolivar by naming the territory for him, and since he was backed up by the other leaders, he won! He also won the 'boss's daughter!' So he became Bolivar's son-in-law.

The capital city was named for him and the first university and seat of government were located there. Eventually, the other branches of government were moved by subsequent circumstances to La Paz, but they would never give up the judiciary. This gives Bolivia the distinction of having two capitals.

The large university was the only one for many years. The normal school and the school of medicine had a monopoly for a long time. Only in the 1970's did they establish these schools in other large cities where you could study those things.

The climate is warmer than the heights of Potosi, the ancient silver city of the world. It is cooler than Santa Cruz, the tropical city that bakes in the heat of the lowland sun and kinder than either. The banks of the Pilcomayo River and surrounding haciendas have a peach and orange-growing climate with a brief chill winter and a longer warm summer.

Here, paired with a national pastor, we were to be deacon and Sunday School superintendent with the object of planting a gospel work that would grow and be leaven and light to the ancient city and surroundings. We were to make changes that would endure.

Our house was four blocks from the central plaza: a pleasant walk for shopping or picking up the mail. The post office was in the next block and we never made it home with the mail. After posting our letters and picking up our mail, we always stopped and sat on a bench in the plaza to read it. The shade of the ancient trees provided a cool retreat. A neighbor across the street sold candy in the plaza, and we often ran into other friends there as well.

On the upper corner, across from the plaza, was the Cathedral. It brings many pilgrims to see the five foot high, one inch thick, solid gold statue of the Virgin of Guadaloupe. It is like a cutout with porcelain faces of the mother and child. Her cape was encrusted with ropes of pearls crisscrossed to make diamond-shaped frames. There was an enormous ruby, emerald or diamond set into each frame. A foot-wide strip down the middle was a collection of precious things that devotees had dedicated to the Virgin. Past presidents, other statesmen and high ranking generals had given watches, medals and other artifacts of memorabilia that had been presented to them by foreign governments. This was their thanks for her protection and guidance, when they prayed asking the Virgin to intercede for them.

Tourists from all over the world came to see, and security was tight as they were led through to stand and gape, five feet from the statue. It had been stolen once, they spent years finding and recovering it -- and they were not going to take any chances again.

There were three evangelical groups working in other parts of the city when we came. All were small and struggling. Sucre was the seat of Cardinal Meyer, a German national in the Catholic mission field of Bolivia.

We arrived in Bolivia from furlough in September and stayed in the guest bungalow in Cochabamba until they could appoint someone to accompany us to Sucre. We settled our kids into school and Borden into a room where he could do volunteer work with the Wycliffe print shop for a year between high school and university.

The Missions Committee met and paired us with pastor Cornelio Heredia. He was from the mines of Oruro, but had been a pastor in Potosi after we had begun the work and gone. He had married a local girl. They were serving in the mine at Llallagua and could not join us with their ten-month old baby for three months. They didn't want to leave the church just at the Christmas season.

We went together to Sucre and looked at places to live. We were trying to get things in line to move in ourselves; so we would be ready to help them, when they joined us at the first of the year. At a pastor's conference shortly after we arrived, we told everyone that they could walk from the lower side of the plaza four blocks, stand in the middle of the street and yell 'Marshall,' and we would hear them. However, we were unable to get that place, but rented the second floor of a house just around the corner.

The house was a real colonial gem with two-foot thick walls. We found that our electrical system had only two wall plugs and eight bare bulbs, one in each room, hanging from a long cord in the middle of the ceiling. The meter at the entrance at the bottom of the stairs had a five-amp capacity. We wondered if we could use all the lights and a fridge at the same time? Hazel knew we couldn't. What would the stores have as a substitute? We soon found out: nothing. They all said we would have to pick it up in Cochabamba. We were allowed to choose a new stove, a combination of electricity and gas. It would not only need more power than the meter could handle, but also would need a tri-phasic hook-up. Of course, it would have to be okayed by licensed inspectors, but we decided to wire it ourselves. So we made some basic calculations and found that we would need at least a hundred meters of wire.

Our first Sunday worship service, we: Marshall, Hazel, and Borden, without any furniture, sat around in a circle on our suitcases. We had brought along from Canada a tape of the Messiah. We decided to play it for our first Sunday worship service and were joined by a retired pastor, Francisco Tapia. It was almost over when the doorbell rang again. It was a normal school senior, a Baptist girl, who had heard from her family of our arrival, and came to our first meeting there. We felt the Lord's presence with us.

We went to Oruro to collect our furniture and shipped it to Sucre by rail. There we were able to buy a fifty-amp electric meter. However, when we got to Sucre, we were informed that we would only be allowed thirty-five amps because we were not industrial or commercial.

One of the reasons we had come was to minister to children from Baptist families going to the normal school or university who were often far from the influence of home and church. The dormitories were over-crowded and social life was limited and grungy. We had hoped to open a hostel to reach those students. We found a house where we could supervise live-ins, but were unable to come to terms and couldn't get the funds. Some young Baptists had made contact with other churches and after several years of attendance were quite involved. Naturally, they were reluctant to leave. Who would be open to the gospel in a fanatically closed town where the Cardinal's influence was great? Children came to see what we were doing. We held the meetings in our house, and a foreigner's house is always interesting to them. Our landlady, who lived downstairs, became annoyed by the noise and the children taking piano lessons. I had told her about our expectations on renting, but she was tired of the volume. Six months after we arrived, we did agree to rent a room opening directly onto the street, around the corner and up the hill. It was still her property and large enough to contain our booming children's work. Our landlady had extra rent and less noise above her. Our work continued to be children and teenagers for several years. We used plays, music, memory contests, films and other activities to teach them. We started another weekly meeting on the edge of town where the railroad employees lived and also had Vacation Bible Schools there.

Charismatic Catholics were one of our contacts for the first time. We had attended interfaith talks and spontaneous encounters with Catholic clergy both friendly and hostile on a number of occasions in our 23 years in Bolivia. Most were friendly, and yet a certain unease existed even with Canadian clergy or Americans of the Mary Knoll Society who were trying to modernize and activate the state church. A few encounters were hostile exchanges, and we were stoned or threatened on several occasions in other places. The charismatic Catholics in Sucre were young people who had local leaders and a youthful following. Their meetings were not unlike our own and were accompanied by guitar and newly-created songs, some bearing the same melodies but slightly varied words from our own. They came asking permission to use our facilities for meetings, but we feared that without supervision there would be smoking, dancing and perhaps drinking if they partied at the meetings and it would confuse people as to who was participating in these entertainments. Other Evangelical and Catholic groups, were in the city trying to appeal to the university students.

After three years the congregation was still almost all children. Local parents came when we presented special programs for Christmas, Easter, Missions month, or had visiting speakers. It seems that they thought that it was all just for the children. Some students from Baptist families visited while studying there. When those students graduated they went on to practice their professions elsewhere.

The children showed no reverence – they talked and giggled, ran in and out at will, and seemed to be taking in nothing. Marshall began to pray that some of the parents would come to stabilize the atmosphere. I was praying too, and wondered what I could do. About that time I went with some of those children to see a movie. I noticed that they acted the same way there. They visited with their friends, ran out at intervals to buy pop-corn or candy, argued over the dividing up of the candy, seemingly paying little attention to the movie. I remembered visiting a Catholic church in Costa Rica for the Christmas midnight mass. I had been shocked at how, while the Priest was up front saying the mass, people came and went, greeted all their friends up and down the aisle, sought out their favorite Saint and knelt to recite their rosary, make their supplications; this was normal behavior. They didn't know that reverence was expected of them.

I decided that if I put up some posters with Scriptures about practicing reverence in the meeting place, it might help. I thought right away of "BE STILL AND KNOW THAT I AM GOD." I knew there was one, too, about "THE LORD IS IN HIS HOLY TEMPLE: LET ALL THE EARTH KEEP SILENCE BEFORE HIM. I wanted to find about six texts I could put up on the walls. Then, with a little devotional, I hoped to impress them with the importance of being reverent in the meeting place. I wanted them to listen to the speaker, the words of the Scriptures being read and the music that we heard from a soloist or we sang together.

Actually, I got out my Analytical Concordance of the Bible and looked up the words; 'silence', 'reverence', and the like. I didn't find anything more.

I didn't give up. I figured the Psalms would be the likeliest place to look, and I decided to scan them quickly, and I was the one who was impressed! There was plenty about worship, and praise, and communicating with God; but all except the two I had memorized as a child, and could still quote without looking them up, were noisy. There are many references suggesting that we "Shout for joy unto the Lord" "Praise the Lord with the voice of the trumpet" in our worship services. Like the 150th: Psalm; verse one tells you WHERE to praise Him, verse two tells you WHAT to praise Him for, verse six tells you WHO should praise Him. And just listen to the verses in between: " V.3 Praise Him with the sound of the trumpet; praise Him with the psaltery and harp, V.4 Praise Him with the timbrel and dance; praise Him with stringed instruments and organs, V.5 Praise Him upon the loud cymbals; praise Him upon the high sounding cymbals." David invokes the people to praise the Lord singing at the top of their voices accompanied by a polyphonic orchestra!

So I thought I'd better limit my signs to the two Scriptures that I started with, and leave the other Scriptures for when we were planning a special program where they would need to speak up to be heard.

The last year we were there, before we left to go on furlough, there were quite a number of young people who wished to be baptized. We found out about a property, that had a tank that diverted creek water for irrigating their fields, situated about five kilometers from Sucre. It belonged to a relative of one of the families attending our services. They invited us to make an excursion of it for the baptismal ceremonies. There were about ten who took the preparation classes, but since they were mostly minors, we visited with each of their families to talk to them about this step of faith. Most of them had been baptized as babies, and we wanted to be sure the parents had given their consent. Of the ten only 6 were allowed to be baptized. Some of the parents accompanied us to see the ceremony. We had a picnic lunch afterward. What precious moments those were!

After that we went out once more for a picnic, and also for a one day-camp. No mother would permit her daughter to stay overnight. I understood that the congregation continued to use it from time to time for day-camps.

One of the young men in the congregation was in third year medicine. For a short time we had a little clinic at which he attended. He took blood pressure, treated and dressed small wounds, and gave an occasional shot that some doctor had prescribed. He also wrote a little column in 'El Centinela Boliviana', our Baptist magazine that carried news of the work all over the country. He began with the items one would need to set up a First Aid Kit for the home. Subsequent articles treated with other first aid measures, and recommendations for hygiene, disease prevention and healthy eating.

We didn't get to the national library until we had been there several years. The visit of a fellow missionary, Hedley Hopkins, triggered our inspection of this ancient site. We were allowed to leaf through historic letters in an enormous file five-inches thick. We were intrigued to read a collection of colonial letters from Phillip II of Spain to his Viceroy, discussing the ordinary daily affairs of empire. The signature, however, merely stated: *Yo, el Rey*: I, the king. Hedley compared it to God's declaration to Moses from the burning bush: "I am, that I am."

There were many impressive things, but one other really was outstanding. There was an ancient music box. The whole contraption was five-feet high, four-feet wide and maybe two-feet thick. The hand-rubbed mahogany cabinet was a lovely antique. You could see the whole works through the glass in front. It had about forty of the interchangeable little brass cylinders that you could insert to play. They were carefully guarded in a velvet lined drawer in the cabinet. They could be easily exchanged. They looked just like the tiny ones we have today, but instead of being about one-and-a-half- inches long, they were about ten inches. This artifact was one of the furnishings of a nunnery, so were all hymns. We were enchanted by its music when we were invited to crank it up and listen.

Marshall, unfortunately for family life, was on a number of national committees of the Bolivian Baptist Union, as well as being responsible for the missions further south, and was required to travel constantly, leaving the national pastor and Hazel to keep the local work on schedule. This was hard, even when the children were in boarding school or busy elsewhere. Life, truly, was generally hectic and busy for all. One year we were required to home school our youngest daughter, Karlene, in her ninth grade correspondence course. French was one of the heavy requirements. We got a tutor to help with the lessons she was required to do. For the oral requirements, we also attended an Alliance Frances course offered in the city. On our return to Canada, Karlene was the one student that the teacher could count on to try to converse with him, and some visiting French students.

We had the joy of receiving a youth caravan while in Sucre. We had been expecting them to arrive around 8pm, and had a meal prepared for them. However, they were nearing the end of the tour and demanded more stops along the way. Cornelio was planning on taking the boys to his house, and we were going to keep the girls at ours. Our pastor had waited until 2am before driving home. They got in after a long grueling trip at 2:20 am, all tired out. We had no transportation, and the kids were too exhausted to separate the baggage into boys and girls. So, they spread sleeping bags on the floor: boys in the living room, and girls in the meeting room, and slept with their clothes on until nine the next morning. By that time, the pastor was back and the breakfast was bountiful and appreciated.

All kinds of new youth were attracted, and they had a great time. Some Brazilian students at university started to attend sometimes, after their visit.

Our landlady rented some rooms on a second floor walkway accessible through our terrace to four girls who were dental students. They, too, were interested and made friends with our foreign visitors. We were not able to reach them for Christ, but they were very friendly and respectful. Before we left, we were able to attend the graduation exercises of three of the four. These were very interesting. All our university graduations have everyone attending with all their families, friends and professors and getting their degrees and honors together. There, at least in the school of dentistry, each student had an individual rite of presentation. One rented a hotel ball room and hers was followed by a buffet, reception and ball.

One used a university classroom and served a bottle of warm Coca Cola. The third rented a hall, and our landlady catered a dinner in her garden-ringed patio, featuring a specialty of hers, Pepper steak. I remember drinking lots of water. In all three cases, however, the formality of the ceremony was equal. All the family, friends, fellow students and professors were present, and the presentation of the diploma, and any honors, was made by the dean. The head of the Department of Dentistry along with some National Government Official administered the Hippocratic Oath, and pledged loyalty to Bolivia as well. Professors were allowed to mention something that had made this student memorable to them. Happily, there were only 7 who graduated from the School of Dentistry that year in Sucre. This made for beautiful, intimate memories for each of them.

Days before going on furlough, we organized 'La Congregation del Cristo Viviente'- The Congregation of the Living Lord. It was several years after we had gone that it was upgraded to a Church and was integrated into the Bolivian Baptist Union.

Sucre seemed friendly, but there was much work and little fruit--except for the children. They would grow up and some would be deacons and workers for the Lord, but that was a matter of time for growth. Meanwhile, our children were becoming adults. Passing the teen years is difficult anywhere. A good beginning was evident even in Sucre, reputed to be the hardest city in Bolivia for the Gospel. God had not failed us. The planting was to prosper and grow.

Everything

He does

prospers

Psalm 1:3

Long mountainous gravel roads wind in, out, up and down the country of Bolivia. The whole Andean Mountain chain shares this feature. The amount spent on roads and bridges is extremely high, and maintenance always a problem.   In Bolivia, the problem is compounded. It is the second highest country in the world. Only Tibet is higher. High altitudes are hard on all motor vehicles, and transport is more precarious and dangerous.   Roads wash out, crumble away, cave in; landslides cause rock falls and destroy the vegetation that holds the soil in place. To move from one city or area of the country to another requires good driving skills, strong nerves and precision negotiating turns and climbs as well as a good stomach for the dizzying descents, in short, STAMINA. Unfortunately, not all of us have such qualities and the day-long trips were rarely without a few incidents that families and friends would wish to spare from their experience. Lost meals, drinks, dust allergies, sun burns, intestinal problems were a regular part of excursions of any kind in Bolivia. So you pack for all kinds of problems: carry tissues/TP, food, medicine, wet-wipes, hats, sweaters, rain gear, and cool wear to strip down to if you're going down the mountains to the jungle side. But even then, you can be wrong.

Where the road narrows, the vehicle coming up hill against the grade has the right-of-way. But if a truck is coming downhill fast, don't argue and block the way. Better slow than 'dead right'.   The same applies to passing another vehicle. Good drivers notice when they are overtaken and some will give up their position as leader and be content to trundle behind just out of their dust trail, until increasing distance resolves the problem of breathing another's dirt. However, as everywhere, there are road hogs who will hold you behind by speeding up at every wide section, only to revert to type and velocity in the narrower sectors. Such an animal will ignore all horn blasts and shouts from the gray cloud following him. I say 'him' because women drivers are a novelty to most of them.

There were two roads of lesser importance out of Sucre we seldom took them, but the roads to Potosi, Cochabamba or Santa Cruz we traveled almost monthly. On one such trip I,

Marshall, was passing a curve in the lower near-tropical area when I heard the ping of a stone on the frame, not unusual on gravel roads, but I saw a little boy about six-years old draw back an arm and reach for another stone. I slowed and pulled over in a wide spot where I backed off the road. As I emerged from the driver's seat, the child ran into a thatched hut followed by a little girl about seven who had evidently been an observer. I followed the children announcing my presence with a 'Buenos dias' to the occupants and stopped before the boy and sister that were hugging each other and watching me with apprehension. I squatted down to be at face level with the children and said seriously : "You must not throw rocks at cars. You might break a window and that would hurt someone." They didn't answer, so I repeated my message again and rising turned to see a Quechua woman squatting at the hearth. I said a cheerful "Good morning ma'am," and walked out. A ten-year old girl was jumping rope in the hut's front yard, and she gave me a smile and giggle that said she thought I had done a good thing. I could imagine that the mother would use the incident to threaten the child. "You be good now or the *gringo* will come and take you away."

After some six or more hours of this kind of tripping you would arrive at a treasured spot where the Potosi-Sucre gravel road joins the Cochabamba-Santa Cruz paved road. Away to the left four hours uphill lay Cochabamba. Our Children's school at Tambo lay five hours downhill to the right through Siberia, a land of constant fog. There we saw the bare mud road in sunshine once and passed in twenty minutes, but normally we had to place one passenger on the hood to indicate left or right on the curves as we crept along the ridge.

The occasional cross marked the margins of the road as a reminder of those who perished at that spot at some past date. This custom of commemorative memorials beside the roads is universal in Bolivia. Four hours beyond Tambo lay tropical Santa Cruz, the thriving second largest city in the nation.

The prosperous village of Episana is located at the juncture of the Sucre/Santa Cruz road with three restaurants, the police station and a traffic control booth. There are a few inhabitants who attend to cars, sell gas and do repairs, and serve customers, for other needs.

We have finished the snacks and fruit brought to occupy all the car load of trippers for six hours. The day's breakfast and lunch are forgotten. Like desert travelers sighting the oasis, we pull up and pile out for a meal or refreshments at the Hilton, so named for the famous chain of luxury hotels around the world. The one in Episana is not part of the chain but is too insignificant to challenge for the use of the name. Meals and bathrooms before they went into business, were quite primitive. Almost anything looks good after six hours of travel in mountains. When the 'Hilton' came to town, they set a high standard and were greatly appreciated. In place of a wee smelly outhouse positioned over a running brook (to carry away the waste) the very best in porcelain fixtures graced their facilities. The modern plumbing did not last long and was soon broken by those who did not understand its use.

On the menu there were specialties of many kinds. What we preferred was the steak sandwich. A slice of fresh local French-type bread on each side of a thin, boneless steak, nothing else! We don't eat fresh salads without cooking, peeling or cleaning the raw ingredients with permanganate water. Most of the ice cream was forbidden and the candy too. On our arrival in Bolivia a friend had advised us about ice cream things. If the milk used is fresh it may not be pasteurized and if it is powdered it may be prepared with unboiled water. One leads to undulate fever, the other to amebas or tetanus. Every thing had to be recently cooked and still hot, or factory packaged for us to risk buying it. But there was no danger in the steak sandwich. They poured a bit of pan gravy over the bun of our sandwich, and it was delicious!

The inside decorations were moderately attractive. That is, people looked at them and laughed or passed off with a nod. They were signs rather like posters with scenery from other countries: high, green, snow-capped mountains with lakes; flower gardens around large houses; sea shores and waves. There were also religious pictures: Jesus thorn-crowned head, a glorious Virgin Mary surrounded with flowers or the 'Visit of the Magi.' Political slogans or wise/pious sayings vied with a few glitzy, voluptuous girls scattered in various inviting situations and positions. Jokes and innuendos were also expressed.

This truck stop is utilized by all the traffic that bridges the high prairies of the altiplano with the valleys and finally the jungle plains of the Amazon and Paraguay river basins. Each area has its special produce that the other regions need. Yet each must go through high mountain passes to reach the other zones. It produces regional pride and patriotism that often demeans other areas and their people within the nation. Different life styles, by necessity of climate, is a fact of life.

Communication and commerce are necessary. The roads make Bolivia a nation, but they pay dearly for their construction and maintenance. The Episana Hilton is one of the necessary points of provision. The village grows slowly with the addition of graders and other road equipment used to maintain its life and service to the travelers between the developed areas. So civilization creeps out from the cities: garages, gas stations, bus stops, stores, restaurants, schools, playing fields, and eventually a church or two will bring local people into the life of the nation with new conveniences and amenities as well as trials and temptations. Human progress is always on this kind of balance. We have the choice of how to use each new situation for our profit or hurt. God and our conscience are sometimes the only arbitrators.
Jesus said,

"I am the light of the world"   John 8:12

Crossroad vendors sell coffee and bread

229

Financed by gifts from an Ottawa church and pastors in
New Brunswick, Marshall was able to place in rural schools a
book called, The Man You Ought to Know. It contained a write
up of the life and ministry of Jesus, but although it quoted
Scripture, was not considered a Bible or holy book. The
teachers, except the communists, loved it, and called it a book
on 'morals.' A determined sum of books were given to a
school, and the teachers supervised the use of the books and
they were not to be taken home and lost or misused. The Bible
Society provided hundreds of books that saturated Potosi and
Sucre, two province's needs. The Catholic School System
secretary requested that the provision be open to their rural
schools as well. This was accepted on the basis of a few
requesting schools, but not all of them asked for books. Our
pastor and Marshall did the distribution personally, often with a
'God and Country,' speech of presentation.

As a colporteur for the Bolivian Bible Society, I, Marshall, was
frequently out selling Bibles and portions at schools and
markets. I would take books out during noon and recess
breaks and sometimes after the end of the school day. The
parents may have been hesitant about Scripture, but the
children were not. They bought little gospels with their
allowance. I heard one teacher scream at a group of first
graders, "You can't even read yet," in exasperation. However,
one old priest in front of a parochial school declared: "Boys,
boys look, Saint Mark, Saint Luke, here for you to read!" I was
surprised by his gracious commendation.

I decided to go to Cardinal Meyer, who resided in the city.
Carrying my books with me, I requested permission to speak
with His Grace and was permitted to go in. A cute, petite
German nun, admitted me to the office and I was able to
speak person to person with him. He was a large man and
balding; with his black cigar and round face, he could have
passed for an Irish politician. I explained my work as colporteur
at schools and showed him the books. Several bore the
imprimatur of the Catholic church. He asked me the price and,
as I told him, said, "We have them for the same price." He
tossed the New Testament, God Speaks to Man, in current

market Spanish, back in my basket. I said, "Why don't you put them where people can see and buy them? They wouldn't buy from a Protestant if you sold them visibly." He looked irritably at me and said, "You want to convert everybody!" I laughed, "Impossible," I said, "Too many are loyal to tradition." He nodded in agreement and I terminated my visit. I was told that the next month Scriptures were on sale in the Catholic schools.

While in Sucre we started meetings under the direction of a Quechua translator for the Wycliffe missionaries. He met in another spot under our encouragement. The number of Quechua-speaking believers grew. We expanded into the rural agricultural areas between Sucre and Potosi. I was at that time one of the outstanding volunteer colporteurs of the Bolivian Bible Society, as well as one of the founders of that national body. For many years in Oruro and in the missions of the south, I held the record for the most Scriptures sold each year.

About this time our pastor Cornelio Heredia, started a radio program with the young people helping. It was musical, but included scripture reading and a brief homily. It proved useful.

Several pastors in new areas of work in other provinces of Bolivia complained of the lack of Bibles to give away to the poor and needy in their districts. So a fund was supplied to satisfy this need through the Bible Society. Jaime Goytia the secretary of that Society laughed when I asked of its condition and possible need for more funds. "The ones who complained the most were the last to draw on the supply available," he said. For me it was another lesson in the need of prayer rather than complaints. If we wait on God's time, often the supply appears, but we have to keep checking for it. Believe He will provide, even as He promises.

Several rural congregations developed that required visits. As the younger generation attended rural and city schools, literacy increased the desire for reading material. The Bolivian Bible Society provided a wealth of Scriptures and other useful books that spoke to the needs of the common people. God's promises are read and believed. There are books that give life for they speak of that eternal life that God wishes all of us to enjoy.

Your word is a lamp to my feet Psalm 119:105

I, Hazel, have a fear of 'whooshes'. A 'whoosh' is the place in the road where a culvert goes from the ditch on the towering upper cliff side of the road, all the way across under the road and out toward the twenty-meter drop-off on the other side. Each time there is a torrential rain (every day between November and February, that is) the water comes dashing down from that cliff above into the ditch and eats away at the edges of the unpaved road. It washes away tons of dirt and gravel from around the culverts each year and may take as much as a meter off each side of the serpentine road. It happens all over Bolivia, but there are some areas where the road hugs a river bank, and there is a whoosh at every sharp turn. I used to dread the trip between Oruro and Cochabamba where several stretches of the road have an inner whoosh or an outer whoosh every 10 or 15 meters. Marshall delighted in zipping along at a brisk pace, while I feared a 10-ton truck rounding the next corner and forcing us into the cliff-side, or off to that long plunge down to the river.

"On one trip, our colleague Cornelio Heredia and I both had business in Cochabamba, and we had to hug that cliff-side on an emergency trip at night. I actually prefer to drive at night on that type of road. When everyone has their lights on, you can tell four or five curves before you meet them, that they are coming. I took the wheel for the first section and made very good time for the first hour, until we got to the switch-backs where the real work began.

"Then Cornelio took over. He is a very good, smooth and careful driver. However, the rush of getting ready for the trip, the duties of the day, and wrestling the Toyota jeep down that road, left my nerves in poor shape. I don't remember the nature of the emergency. I just know that I found it hard to try to close my eyes and rest, so I could take over again, when it was my turn. I started counting whooshes. At three hundred, I gave up and got into the back seat so that I could rest some. I knew the whooshes were still there, but I was finally tired enough to commit them to the Lord and go to sleep.

"Most of the ditches and drains are dry except in the rainy season. But they all erode at that time of year. They develop slopes and deepen ditches on either side of the pipe or channel under the road. Sometimes a mud slide will fill a ditch and water spills across the road.

Economy demands that all such pipes be as short as possible. They must accommodate one heavy truck, but why waste money for two way traffic, especially since the rains may have taken edges off the road anyway? To pass a whoosh, you hit the middle, even on a curve, but with ditches and cliffs on either side you can understand my fear. The whoosh is a frightening sight at fifty 'klicks' (kilometers) per hour on a gravel curve, looking down from five hundred meters above to the dry riverbed below. If it is flood season, it is even more frightening. One skid to the side would carry you straight down. While there is less of a dust problem in the rainy season, there are the washouts. So beware the whooshes.

Naturally, this type of hardship creates a certain camaraderie and helpers stop if troubles are detected. "May I help you?"; "What seems to be the trouble?"; and "Wow, you do have a problem!" Truckers compete fiercely yet help each other on a regular basis. An example of the third statement 'Wow,' occurred when we met a truck loaded with bananas beside the road obviously not going anywhere. When we stopped to ask if we could help, the driver, resting in the shade under the truck, said the axle had broken, and he had sent for the needed parts. The smell of ripe bananas filled the warm air. We offered him some food, and he loaded two large stalks of bananas on to our jeep top. After all, they would not be fit even for banana bread in another few days. He was giving away his load.

The date of the retreat in Oruro for the women of the Cruzada Femenil was coming up soon. We had planned with the women of Potosi, that Gloria Heredia (our pastor's wife) and I would both go. There would be room for three of the women from Potosi that we would pick up on the way. All of us had really been looking forward to it.

On a good day, the trip from Sucre, where we lived, to Potosi took at least five hours. Then it was at least another ten hours to get to Oruro where the retreat would be held. The weather reports told us that there was flooding in several sectors. It didn't look good for traveling, Gloria decided against it. We looked for someone to go with me, but everyone else had previous plans. I didn't feel that I could back out because the ladies from Potosi were counting on me. I started out after breakfast and made good time.

A little past the half-way point, I was startled to see, as I rounded yet another corner, a great line of cars. Instead of following straight on toward the approach to the bridge, the next car veered off to the right. He descended to the place where they used to ford the river, before they had the bridge. When I got out of the car and went to look over the situation, I counted 28 vehicles: cars, buses, and trucks of all sizes, between my Toyota jeep and the river. The Department of Public Works had found a way to go where the water was most shallow. There were several tractors at work towing those who couldn't make it alone and leading those who could.

I heard that the night before the raging river had taken out the bridge just as a big transport truck came by. It had dived off the bridge and lost its load. In the intervening hours, the water had gone way down, and the bright afternoon sun belied that the river might be capable of the violence of the night before. The only evidence was the twisted remains of the big truck still resting where it had landed below the bridge. A bale scattered here and there along the edge, where, by now, the water had left it stranded. I watched several of the trucks go through as I walked down the hill. I thought that I could make it, but that I should consult before trying. Those of the road crews that I talked to said that the jeep could certainly make it, if I wanted to try. They suggested that I wait and follow the tractors the next time they came back, since they had marked out the best way. I talked to others as I went back, but stayed with my decision to go ahead. So I pulled past the waiting cars, and plunged in!

Following the tractor was no big deal for most of the way, but there was one spot where the water went almost up to the window. The rest of the way was only hub-cap level. When I went up the other bank, there was a cheer, and I waved to the people that I'd left behind, and those I was passing on the way up the other side to the road.

I went at the best pace possible past the other bad spots -- there is one stretch of slippery shale on the way up where you feel so vulnerable -- and there is no guard rail. I arrived for suppertime at the home of one of the ladies with whom I was planning to travel. However, they, too, were having their doubts. There were other reports that whole kilometers at a stretch were underwater, and nobody was really very enthusiastic about making that trip at night. We needed to get going if we were to get there for 9 a.m. to begin the retreat. There were some young people, also, who had been planning to go to a special event in Oruro. They suggested that if I still wanted to go, they could help me with the driving. In the end, however, they too gave it up and we all went to bed.

The next day I headed back to Sucre. Downhill is easier. At the edge of Potosi city, where the traffic control booth is located, you have to get your travel permit registered. As usual, there were people hoping to find a car with room for them to travel, as the bus wouldn't go until later on in the day. The next in line was a school teacher, and I thought he could help me stay awake if I got tired.

We drove along quietly for some time while I found my way out of the city and onto the road again. Then we began to discuss how the weather had changed my plan to go on to Oruro. He made some remark about how brave I must be. I didn't understand what he meant by that. Then he told me that he too had come from Sucre the day before on a bus. He was there stranded at the ford for hours until the bus he was riding finally decided to trust the tractor to lead it across the river. He said that after I went across, most of the trucks and buses were willing to try the crossing. Many of the smaller cars gave up and went back home. By the time we made it back to that point, even the smaller cars who had stayed and waited, had been able to cross and were all gone. It was a fruitless yet memorable trip. Many of our activities seem fruitless, but we can't know how our efforts affect others and shape both our characters and theirs. An Old Testament promise is to 'establish the work of our hands', so, many of our perceptions about our effectiveness or lack of it as Christians are probably wrong.

Jesus said: "fear not ... I will be with you ... "

Matthew 10:26;   28:20

My father celebrated my sixteenth birthday and graduation from High school by hosting me to a flight in a single engine Piper Cub from a field several miles from our house. It was my first experience in the air. As we flew over our house, situated several miles outside the city, I thought I should like to live there forever. It looked so beautiful, neat and miniature from the sky.

My second flight was from Boston to New Orleans after my first year in Canada. I went to see an old friend from University days; I carried a diamond ring of quarter carat in my pocket; as a mustard seed of faith that I could persuade her to become a companion for my call to overseas work. It was considered and accepted after three weeks.

After my ordination and our marriage a few days later, my month holiday was over. On the fourth day of our honeymoon I flew away from Houston to Boston and finished my return to Canada by rail. From that time on flying became a delightful part of my life. We flew Toronto to Cuba to connect with an airline to Costa Rica for language study. We flew to Panama and Lima on the way to La Paz where I had been called to serve as pastor.

Pan American and Braniff, two reliable international carriers had good reputations, so we used them while our children were small. Flying inside Bolivia was riskier business. I remember a flight where we circled Mt. Illimani going to La Paz and as we gazed down on the impressive snow cap our cabin oxygen failed and a mask, at the end of a curled tube, was dropped from the ceiling above each seat. My two-year-old daughter passed out in my arms as I tried to share the flow of air with her. Hazel and Borden had a seat and mask each.

On another trip, alone, I was flying to Roboré in the eastern lowlands, but an engine failed on our C3. The smooth flight was interrupted by a sudden lurch on the right and a lopsided flight as we circled and started back. We were over an hour in flight and were likely over the halfway mark but the mechanics and parts are not on the dusty air strip of Robore, so we returned to Santa Cruz on one engine to land crookedly, running off the pavement into the grass, and dug in there. All passengers were undamaged and bused into the terminal with dispatch.

I cancelled the trip and took a bus home.

My colleague John Palmquist's house rested right under the approach to the airfield. He had hourly flights over his head. It was while staying there that I noticed that I had high sounds (tinnitus) in my ears day and night. I understand that John is affected by deafness, so I tend to feel that that is a cause. I only spent a few days there on trips through to the east, but he lived there for several years.

While on home leave in Wolfville, Nova Scotia, I started piloting lessons at Waterville, the nearest airport. I got a provisional license and frequently was invited to co-pilot private and commercial flights after that.

We had a mission aviation plane in Cochabamba and I was occasionally allowed to fly with them into small jungle and mountain strips unattended by any but villagers anxious for contact with the wider world.

In 1964 we flew to Salta, Argentina with our three children for a return to the north by ship from Buenos Aires. Formerly, all missionaries had traveled by boat, but the convenience of getting home quickly with small children persuaded them to follow our example and use air transport home. We took our only sea voyage home that time because our youngest was four and they were all experienced travelers. We would take the bus once we were on the flat pampas of Argentina. We thought we would avoid mountain sickness by flying out of Bolivia., We were wrong, it was a bumpy flight and first Hazel, then all the children lost their lunch. I had to clean up after them and almost lost mine as well. After that trip we returned to the constant use of planes.

We also had problems traveling north on another furlough year due to a pilot's strike in Bogota, Columbia. We spent several days in Bogota, seeing the sights and staying in a dismal little hotel.

The Airport Hotel Register called it *EL Hotel Aleman*, (The German Hotel) and we visualized a spotless environment, welcoming hosts and delicious meals. We found that the Germans had left long ago. The thin mattresses, that rested on a metal mesh, like a hammock of chain-mail over widely-separated slats, were extremely uncomfortable. The first night we played 'fruit basket turn over' until we found that Karlene was the only one light enough to sleep on the worst cot. For everyone else it was like sleeping on a ladder. The bathroom down the hall, had no door from the hall. Anyone coming down the hall had a great view of you washing up at the basins. There were three flush toilets, but the door on one of them served the shower as well.

And it wasn't segregated.

We were supposed to leave for Houston on Monday morning. We were called at our hotel by the airline saying that our flight had been cancelled. There had been a rash of hijackings and the pilots went on strike demanding more safety measures. Our route was via Panama and Mexico City. They suggested that we might want to call again before our flight time, and see if it had been resolved. So we were all packed up, and ready to go.

We called again just before we left, and we were told that the flight was going! We got a taxi to the airport, and found ourselves with all our luggage at the end of the line. up to the ticket counter. I must say that our kids amused themselves and didn't cause any trouble while Marshall waited in line. The people in front of him complained and threatened, and yelled at the attendants aggravating already frazzled nerves.

Marshall is a diplomat and a peace-maker by nature. So when it was his turn, he spoke in a quiet voice, and asked about the tickets for the five of us. It seems that arrangements had been made for one flight directly to Miami, avoiding the stop-over, and possible hijackers. We were only going as far as Panama, and would have changed planes there for the last lap with touch-down in Mexico City. This meant that we couldn't take that flight after all. Instead of ranting like the rest, Marshall explained our situation: there were five of us, we had disposed of all our local money, and checked out of our hotel. The man left the counter, to check in the offices behind him, promising to do what he could for us. What he did was send us to the most luxurious hotel in town, the Tequendama (the Hilton was under construction and opened a month later). He also supplied vouchers for taxis going and coming, supper and breakfast the next morning, when the strike was scheduled to end. We went to the hotel, and called a friend. We had only discovered he was in the city when we were in church the day before. He took Borden, Karlene, and Marshall to see the beauties of the salt mines: caves that look like art galleries filled with marvelous ice sculptures. Krystal and I stayed at the hotel, and since we had two rooms with bath, each spent a couple of hours taking a hot soaky bath. We followed that with a couple of hours of restful, blessed sleep that wasn't possible in that grungy hotel where we had been before. On the flight the following day, they found seats for all of us; but they put Karlene and me (Hazel) into first class, where we were treated like royalty.

The rest of the trip was without difficulty, except that there was such a tie up in the Mexico City Airport, that we circled for more than 30 minutes before landing. Then they wouldn't allow us to go into the airport unless we were disembarking there. Also, in Houston we were at the end of the line going through customs. They found that the pretty necklace of black and red beans that we had bought as a curio, had poison that could kill a baby, if it sucked on it. We naturally didn't object when they kept it. Several friends had gathered to greet us, but most had gone home by the time we got out, except for the family members.

The Potosi airport was one narrow dirt strip that took off down hill and landed uphill. I only used it once. I preferred the bus to that kind of danger. I love flying but disliked landing under such conditions. Yet the attractions of flying over mountains that take hours to circumnavigate is the magnet that holds all travelers. An hours flight instead of nine to fifteen hours of dizzying curves and dangers. The ill, the hurried, the fearful and those with children, all pull toward the shortness and ease of flight, especially if the price is right -- and it is. All flying in Bolivia is now beyond the pioneering stage and flight passenger volumes are way up. Like all travel there are risks and inconvenient moments. Bolivia enjoys good and courteous air travel.

I, Marshall had talked to Miss Cathy McGorman about the travels of the medical boat in Chapari that made regular trips to Trinidad in the Beni province, a tropical heartland of rivers, jungle and lush grasslands. Every time vacation time rolled around they were repairing the boat or it was staying home until the rainy season brought up the water level for easier travel. During our last term we gave up on travel with the boat and decided to hitch a ride on whatever came along and give the kids experience on board. This was the first water trip since the BA cruise to the Gulf years before. Going from school closing to Puerto Suarez, we found a barge piled high with gasoline drums, linked side by side with a power barge. The price was reasonable for the discomfort: 500 Pesos about US$25. It included food plus a seek-your-own-spot to sleep on the upper deck. Masaca would be the main course (a mix of Yucca root and fish mashed together) and fish soup, with river water or purchased water, coffee or tea to drink. It would take about five days to get to Trinidad. Daily flights guaranteed contact with Santa Cruz and Cochabamba where I had a Monday meeting. I bought the air tickets before leaving Cochabamba. We had a week of fun ahead.

Since we are concentrating on air travel, I will not bore you with the details of lazy days of fighting off mosquitoes, fishing, spotting all the dolphins, turtles, monkeys, reading, making friends with the crew. The nights were filled with fighting off mosquitoes, in spite of home-made mosquito nets of quite closely woven muslin designed especially for the occasion.

We arrived at a small island where they dumped us, assuring us that there would be a ferry at the other end of the island (a 5 km. trek away), and buses from there. We lugged our luggage the 5 km's along the path dodging into the encroaching growth when we heard the buzz of the next approach of a motor-bike for hire. Several passed us holding the driver, the passenger, who wanted to get on the river craft we had just left, and all his luggage. Then, before we could arrive by foot at the ferry dock, they passed us on the way back with passengers. They had been on the boat with us, and knew to wait for the taxis so they wouldn't have to walk.

We took a truck on the other side of the ferry. The only hotel on this holiday weekend offered three beds, but we were used to the floor by then. Our flight was for 11am Sunday morning, so we just passed by Sunday School, and brought greetings from our church. Then we each took our little motor bike taxi, and left for the airport.

There were long lines leading to each wicket to check in for the flight. There were far more people there than would fit on the plane, and though our tickets were prepaid, there were no seats left when we got to the window. The next regular flight was Monday, at that same time, when we were sure that we would face the same dilemma. So when most of the people had gone back to the city, we were ready to spend the rest of the time there, until then. We still had our sleeping bags and we would sleep on the protected part of the airport porch.

While the crowd was there, venders offered fresh fruit, and some cooked tidbits, and we found enough to have a nice lunch. Now that most had gone, we settled down on one of the benches. One of the men came to Marshall and mentioned that there was a private cargo plane that would be there at approximately 1:45. We could pay the fare to the pilot, and get a refund on our tickets later. Sure enough, when the plane got there, it was easily arranged, and it cost just about the same. However, he was headed for Santa Cruz, not Cochabamba. We figured that we could take the night bus, and be in Cochabamba by morning. We could still make it on time for our Monday night meeting.

Upon boarding we found that this was really the 'no frills' flight. They had delivered their cargo, and we were the return cargo. The DC3 plane had been stripped of all the seats, and any of amenities it had ever had. We and the other 15 people who boarded at the same time, sat on our luggage, and there were no seat belts, nor seat belt signs. We all joked about the fabulous accommodations. When one young lady got motion sickness, I tore a page out of my Cross Word Puzzle Book, and she used it as a tissue, to clean up.

Marshall decided to go up and talk to the pilot. Eventually, the co-pilot got up and gave his seat to Marshall. He came back where we were and was inspecting the inside of the plane. At every rib, he would follow it with his eye, the edge of it from top to bottom, and finally said, "AHA!" We wondered what it was all about, so he explained. "Ever since we stripped out the insides, we have been experiencing electrical shorts. I've finally found the short. If I had only the insulation tape, I could mend it, now."

Well, I am a kindergarten teacher, and I carry all kinds of things around in my bag. One was a string run through the center of five or six rolls of brightly colored insulation tape. I took it out, and said," Here! Take your pick!" So he proceeded to mend the short.

The co-pilot, when he returned the tape, sat down next to Krysi and asked if she knew who was flying the plane. Of course, she had no idea. He said, "Your Daddy!"

The pilot had invited Marshall to take over the controls, after the co-pilot left the cabin. He flew the plane about an hour, until the pilot took over to land.

We found a taxi at the airport, and we went to Hedley Hopkin's house. It was about 4pm. Hedley was surprised, but said immediately, "Now I know why I haven't been worried about my sermon for tonight – The Lord sent you to preach!"

We had a lovely afternoon, catching up on their news. We went to church in the evening, heard Marshall preach and still caught that night bus to Cochabamba.

They built the new airport in Sucre, while we were there, to accommodate the larger jet planes. Karlene was almost ready to get her driver's license, and we often went up there to let her do her practice driving on the runways, since flights were only once a day at that time. The missionaries were also beginning to use the air services more for local travel.

The Sucre Airport was dedicated on the 150th anniversary of Independence Day. Since Bolivia was named for Bolivar, born in Venezuela, there are special sentimental ties. Their President and his retinue with fifty air cadets were invited to take part in the festivities and were due to arrive at 11a.m. The Sucre airport was unique in that it was built on a slant and one end terminated at a high hill. Up until the very last day, they were still shaving slices off the runway's hillside edge. They cut a slot in the hump at the upper end. Half the people of the city and the surrounding countryside were present, and many doubted that the field was long enough for the huge international jets to land. They had come for the proof. Our Bolivian planes were not so large and our pilots were more experienced, so nobody was worried about our president and dignitaries. They landed first to be there when the guests arrived. Of course, the VIP's were all whisked away to a state dinner, but the most humble person was able to see them as they passed along the road and waved their greetings.

The local entrepreneurs had made banners, t-shirts, and

other memorabilia to sell. All the street vendors were ready, too. There were *anticuchos* (shish kabobs), fresh fruit, cotton candy, *buñuelos* (donuts), ice cream, and other sweets. Some stayed there and celebrated and sold; others straggled back to the city. They wanted to be in on the parade promised after the dinner. The Venezuelan pilot came through the slot to make a perfect landing. Everyone was jubilant! He landed as light as a dove, some said.

It brought to my mind the song, "The King Is Coming." How thrilling it would be if we were here to welcome Christ as He comes to meet and collect His own. Have you chosen to follow Him? Have you served Him in any way? Are you living in expectancy? Will He take you with Him, or will you be left behind?

Blessed is the one whom the Lord finds...waiting.
Matthew 24:46

Airports connect all major cities of Bolivia

When we left Bolivia in 1977 to go to the Middle East, many of our Bolivian friends felt betrayed. They felt that we were abandoning them. Actually, we went with the express intention of working ourselves out of a job. All our preparation pointed to preparing the Bolivians to take over the work. When we arrived we were amazed that the Prado Church called Marshall to be their pastor. After two and a half years, we moved on to Guatajata to take over the direction of a school that had been created to train teachers for the schools scattered around the shores of Lake Titicaca. We served there for a year and seven months (two school years) before furlough. We came back in 1960 for a year and a half in Oruro waiting for someone to volunteer to go to Potosi. After 2 years there we had another year and a half in Cochabamba, from which Marshall traveled as executive secretary of the Bolivian Baptist Union.

The next five years after furlough were spent in Oruro, and while we were home on our next furlough, Marshall applied for a leave of absence while he took the class work required to receive his Master of Arts in History. Twelve years and many obstacles later, he managed to finish his thesis and in 1978, receive his degree.

The following 12 years until retirement, and then for a few months each of the next three years, we worked in the Middle East. At retirement, we established residence in Moncton, New Brunswick, from that point the next year he planned a trip at the Lord's prompting. Then he wondered if I wanted to go somewhere the same year.

A construction project in Bolivia caught Hazel's eye. She applied, not knowing if she would be in Achacachi fixing a school roof, or in Vinto putting a cement floor, class divisions, doors and windows in the shell that was their educational building. There were only five who applied in all, so, to have a team, they all needed to go to the same place. Vinto was chosen.

Many of the older women of Vinto were married to retired miners who had gone to the valley's kinder climate (its altitude was 8,000 ft. while most mines were 12,000 ft. or higher), to escape the chill, and thinner oxygen. So she found many friends there. But I will let her tell it.

Before going, my ladies' society asked me to tell them about my upcoming trip. I suggested that when they were doing their exercises that they could pray for me. Some do that with exercise tapes, some just do their exercises as they clean house or work in the garden, and some just 'lift the weights' of their grandchildren. I told them I'd probably be hefting adobes (heavy, dry, mud bricks), and would need their prayers. However, I needn't have worried. June Marr Castellon came to spend the time with her ailing mother while we were working on her husband's church. But I talked to her before I left. She said the ladies wanted me to accompany them to the market when they shopped for the food they would prepare for the workers; keep account of the funds; and give them a Bible Study. So, I NEVER actually had to lift even one adobe!

There were only five of us, but there were between five and ten men there every day working with us. Dennis Shierman delivered us to the work site, and worked beside us most of the time. There were five to eight women who came to cook. Several of them brought their small children with them. That made about twenty to feed each day at noon. We all had a mid-morning break, and sometimes tea before we left at 4:30. If there were left-overs the local men often finished them off before going home at six or so.

The Bible Study was another story. When June told me, there remained very little time to prepare a study, but the Lord calmed my heart about it, and I went praying about what I would do. I imagined that when we had all worked to prepare, serve and clean up after the meal, we would all sit down together, and I would lead them through the Bible Study. However, they wouldn't let me peel a potato or snap a bean! While they were working they began asking me questions - the ones they were afraid to ask the pastor, and figured their husbands didn't know the answers to (I Cor.14:35). They couldn't afford that extra hour – they had to hurry home to cook and clean for their own families.

Dennis had arranged to show us some of the other mission work, which included a trip to the prison-children's ministry; The 'Come and See' Church (you could see what was going on because there was a roof, but NO walls); Hans Ellen's ministry —helping some of the believers and pastors supplement their income or enrich their diet by raising small animals. We drove by many of the city's Baptist churches, but didn't have the key or the time, to get out and go in.

Each evening, some key person from the Bolivian Baptist Union, or some other ministry there in the city was invited to speak to us about his or her work. A few shared the evening meal with us.

Miss Cathy McGorman, on her way from Tarija to a meeting in La Paz, was picked up at the airport; talked to us about her work; answered our questions; and made it back in time for her connection 45 minutes later. We wanted to visit the Chapare (the lowlands nearest to Cochabamba), but civil unrest prohibited it. So we left Friday afternoon to spend the first Saturday in Oruro. We hadn't warned anybody we were coming, so I didn't see a lot of friends. We did see The Risen Lord Church, and the Norman Dabbs church. At Reekie School, we found a meeting of the Education Committee of the Bolivian Baptist Union, and I enjoyed a few minutes visit with some old friends. On the trip back that evening, we stopped at Obrajes: a hot springs resort, for a short swim.

We had finished the cement floor, put in the windows and doors, and painted by the end of the first week. We faced a dilemma as to what we would do for the second week. We didn't have the time nor materials to do class divisions as planned. And they liked the big room the way it was. They had an enormous metal gate made for the back wall, so that a truck could drive in. The adobe wall was in bad shape, and they planned to get brick 'some day' and replace the adobe and hang the gate. While we were being hosted at other churches for our second Sunday there, the members who had helped us all week, were enthusiastically showing off the work that had been done. Taking advantage of the momentum, someone proposed that they take up an offering to pay for the bricks they would need for the wall. They collected Bs.600 (which equaled about $120) which was enough to put up a five ft. wall. So we put up the wall and hung the gate. It needed to be higher, and they did add more adobes after we left.

Sunday morning early, three of our party, caught a plane for another spiritual adventure: one week at the Baptist World Alliance meetings just beginning in Buenos Aires, Argentina.

We joined a Canadian group that had already arrived, and had a tour of the city that the others had enjoyed the afternoon before. The evening service in the Central Baptist Church was crowded with other Congress attendees.

Monday—all day long was the Women's Department Day. A downtown theatre was the place where it all happened, just a few blocks from the Obelisk, a land mark in central BA.
. The parade of flags, news of what work the representatives of all the Societies who were present had done the week before, the choirs and visual presentations of many nations became lovely memories to be called up and savored even today. Noonday saw ALL of us walking the few blocks to the Obelisk, where there was a program. All of us were armed with gospel tracts, New Testaments and Bibles to hand out freely, and encouraged to share our testimonies with those who spoke to us. The evening was a real extravaganza with more live presentations from the countries present. I think that the Indonesian presentation of some of Jesus' parables was the most impressive for me.

Throughout the rest of the week, during the general meetings, the day began at 10 am with Bible studies. Church leaders from around the World directed these studies in smaller groups using the facilities of local churches. The one nearest our hotel was Presbyterian, and we were invited to help serve in their soup kitchen afterward.

There were activities each day at noon. Evangelistic outreach took us to some other sites: The Casa Rosada (the palace of the president of Argentina), hospitals, senior citizen homes, orphanages, and jails. There were workshop groups for those interested in crafts, and other hands-on activities. I spent one noon working on making a church bench. The pieces for it had been pre-cut, and groups of three worked to put them together. I stepped in when someone had to leave before their project was finished. Then the other two moved on, and I painted it by myself. I think that all 50 were being made and sold at cost for new congregations there in the city.

Then, in the afternoon, there were workshops on every imaginable subject. Some were simply Bible studies on some specific subject or Book of the Bible, others on how to direct a Bible Study, evangelistic outreach, church music, and I went to one on the history of Baptist work in Argentina.

I was surprised to hear someone call my name, the very first day when I was registering, and see a man from the Norman Dabbs church in Oruro. He had moved to BA several years before and took me home to dinner to visit with his family. They also wanted to give me things to take back to their families in Bolivia, but since I was not going back there before going home, I put him in touch with those who were, and I trust that they were able to arrange it.

I ran into dozens of friends: some I had studied with in Texas at Baylor University, Southwestern Seminary, Golden Gate Seminary in California, or language school in Costa Rica, or worked with summers at Ridgecrest, a Baptist retreat center in North Carolina, or Daily Vacation Bible School in Washington and Oregon, two from our church in Moncton, New Brunswick, and others that were on the tour from Canada. The most interesting one, though, was a roommate of my daughter Krystal, who had been in her wedding. She was a missionary in Argentina, and like Krysi was a 'missionary kid'. Her parents had worked in Mexico.

All this made for a really memorable few weeks. All of which point up the value of being a Baptist Volunteer overseas. You should try it!

Servants obey your masters ... not with eye service as men pleasers, but as servants of Christ, doing the will of God from the heart...   From Ephesians 6

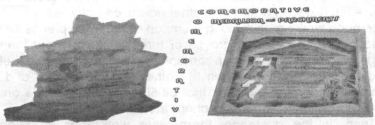

Parchments of recognition from churches to their founders

It had been a generous proposal made from an important man in a key position in an organization I loved. I knew I would be hard put for an answering letter that could explain my reaction. There were so many thoughts that one could not express in something so formal as a letter. My mind wandered over some of the outstanding experiences in my life of seeking to do God's will.

I had invested my life, after army service, in returning to work as an orderly at Providence Hospital and returning to Baylor University. I saw my slender hope of becoming a medical doctor disappear in the post-war rush of veterans. The older men, who had the same hope, made a demand on med schools that created a three year waiting list. It produced the need of top grades for pre-med students like me: a boy whose math and composition were weak, even though my Biology, Zoology and Genetic studies were strong. Chemistry was the balancing point and Organic and Quantitative Chemistry were proving to be math saturated. The head of the Science department warned my father, who warned me, of the coming elimination. It could not help my situation. I failed with the majority of the class. In the ensuing turmoil of seeking new goals for my life; I became a committed Christian. After a double major in History and Political Science, and a double minor in Sociology and Spanish, I graduated; a '49er searching for gold. I went to California to a seminary for mission studies. I returned for studies in Norman, Oklahoma in the Summer Institute of Linguistics promoted by Wickliffe. I thought I was going to India, but the language I was given to analyze was Modern Turkish. I did not notice it as significant.

Now I had been working for ten years in that language in Istanbul. The executive Secretary offered us the opportunity of returning to Bolivia, where we had lived for 23 years. They wanted me to teach in the Theological Seminary in Cochabamba. Should I consider going back before retirement to teach during my last year? I had avoided any long term teaching efforts while there, preferring to give an occasional short course and to teach by doing, setting examples in being God's helper. Yet to pass a year teaching among friends, in a beautiful climate, with beautiful people you love, is no small temptation. Prayer, consultations with Hazel and a visit to Bolivia were needed to discern the Lord's will. What would the answer be? What should I write? How could I be sure I was doing the right thing? These are the kinds of questions we all ask ourselves at some crisis point in our lives.

It's not good form to resist the suggestions of an executive. One should, at least, find and state the negative reasons as an explanation of refusal. The time required to prepare semester teaching materials was only one of many. There were retired seminary professors, who would have lessons and experience, if the need was acute. Otherwise, it was simply an accolade. The number of people fluent in Spanish was great in the US and Canada; the number of knowledgeable Turkish speakers few. National teachers were appearing and even in the old days it was never difficult to find teachers for our seminaries and Bible Schools. It was a position sought after by many. Few courted the difficult task of breaking into a closed religious society. My choice under God was obvious to me, but how to say it?

Dr. Robert Berry   December 8th, 1989
7185 Mill Creek Drive
Mississauga, ON.
L5N 5R4

Dear Bob,

Thank you for your letter of November 30th. It was a very considerate gesture and I do appreciate it. My first reaction was, 'But I haven't finished the net yet!' You see, in every house I've lived in since I joined the mission, I have had a fishing scene. Most of them showed a net. In Jesus time, the net was already recognized as more effective than a single line. His followers were fishermen. I have many friends who favor the single line, one-by-one soul winning. I've used that method, but I'll take the net every time for getting in a harvest of fish.

I helped construct such a net in Bolivia. It is called the Bolivian Baptist Union and it contains functioning committees and Juntas, which we established and ran by example and shared precepts. It was not easy, and I was often disappointed and frustrated in regard to the slow progress and poor results, which some of the committees yielded. However, when I left for Turkey to answer a call from God, the net in Bolivia was functional and largely national in composition.

I would like to visit Bolivia and examine the net and see what strengths and weaknesses exist in the structure. I'm trying to build a net in Turkey. It will doubtless be smaller and simpler, but the principles will be the same. I have two years to retirement and would wish it four years for the net's sake. I am often frustrated by the slowness of human nature, both others and my own, always afraid to venture and risk for God. As I measure the task and look at my strengths I realize that only God can help me complete such a plan.

Part of my need is a look at how things are functioning in Bolivia after 12 years absence. At the same time, I can exercise my gifts and leave a blessing by taking a short visit there, visiting the country juntas and some of the newer mission areas. I will be able to encourage and stimulate many of the brothers. By bringing news of far countries and God's providence there, they will be encouraged to pray for all our fields.

I went to Bolivia in default of the call I felt to India: the call that brought me to Canada. My call to Turkey has borne fruit in many ways, and we are networking individuals and organizations into relationships for usefulness for God. So our feeling is that while a visit to Bolivia seems desirable, the work in Turkey is at present our chief concern and the leading edge of God's purpose for us until we finish the CBM phase of our life.

While I'm writing this, let me also say how much I appreciate what our organization has done in the way of effective personnel and group support. Your networking here is continuing to improve, and I think that many innovations in mission have come about through your efforts as a team and as individuals. I value my links with CBIS and hope to see it continue to grow and network into Eastern Europe and USSR.

We would like to go to Bolivia for six weeks and then go on to Turkey via Canada. Then we will only take such things as we need for Bolivia and leave the rest here for our return flight to Turkey. In that way we would arrive at the end of August in time for university classes in Marmara where my job has been confirmed by phone call from the school's director.

We are looking forward to participation in the newly organized Asian-side International Fellowship. When I left, they expected my return and help in leadership.

I'm willing to lose two month's salary for the privilege of visiting Bolivia on my own expense, but I do not wish to terminate my work in Turkey. When my retirement date is completed, I would like to transfer to volunteer status. I intend to remain very active while the Lord gives strength and opportunity.

Thank you again, for your kind offer. I know it was made with my best interest intended.

I pray for your continued success in the work God has given you and for the financial growth of CBM and the Canadian Churches that form our support.

Your friend in Christ,

Marshall Thompson

Net fishermen on lake Titicaca

It was 13 years since we had left Bolivia. We wondered how much the society had changed by 1990. How was the Bolivian Baptist Union doing now that they had control? We had heard good things about the work and were looking forward to seeing friends. Our return was prompted by a verse in Acts15:36. Paul said to Barnabas, "Let us go again and visit our brethren in every city where we have preached the word of the Lord, and see how they do." Marshall had applied for permission for a preaching tour in Carangas and South Bolivia to the Junta of Evangelization and Missions and he was accepted.

We purchased the tickets for the 14th of June because the plane was full on the date originally targeted. So arrival time varied by one day, but better one day early than late. We had three weeks to encompass a lot of land.

We, Marshall and Hazel Fay had been to another mission field for over eleven years teaching English in Business School and a University in a Middle Eastern mega-city. There we had discovered that local Christians were leaving for Europe and North America, as they had since the First World War. Those remaining in the churches were a small group of pressured few.

Under secularism old Islamic attitudes were hidden, but contempt for minorities still held most hearts. With the waning of Communism, and the Iranian revolution flooding the country with Islamic fundamentalist propaganda, secularism was viewed by many as immoral and this perception had brought many back to Islam. It was slow uphill work to bear the Christian message there at this time.

The chief executive thought that the year remaining before Marshall's retirement could be spent teaching in the Cochabamba Seminary. Marshall advanced an answer before they made their trip and returned with a situation report. The board decided we two could remain a month on salary since we paid our flights, but because Krystal was expecting a baby in July, Hazel decided to leave Bolivia a week early so she could have time with Krystal and get acquainted with our latest grandchild.

After an all night flight from Miami they waited in the Santa

Cruz airport, Viru Viru. While Marshall made arrangements for the luggage, customs, and money exchange. Hazel Fay hovered near the main desk to see who would pick them up. Marshall was beginning to worry about who to contact and how to get the bus to the city when Fay overheard a man who was asking about the arrival times the next day. She looked and realized he was our contact man.

She spoke up: "We're here, Don Fidel, we came a day early." He paid no attention and asked the clerk again when tomorrows plane from Miami would arrive. Fay tried again, and finally touched his arm:

"Don Fidel! We arrived today. There was no room for us tomorrow. We are here now." Fidel turned. His face showed shock.

"Señora Fe! We don't have a reservation for you. I have business in town." Then his look of consternation changed and he gave each of us a big Bolivian 'abraso': a bear hug.

"Welcome to Bolivia. We'll find a place. Give me one of those bags! Let's go to the car." Off we went!

"The ride to town was filled with the sight of blooming trees and cane fields. The highway was being enclosed by adobe buildings; businesses painted to show their success. Large signs announced the name and specialty of each place. The build up and prosperity was notable. The money was also stable after years of using thousands of pesos for even the simplest purchase. By changing the name to Bolivianos and cutting zeros off the end of the inflated pesos with financial guarantees by the world bank and major powers; they were using responsible spending to maintain stability. As a result, business was profitable again.

Santa Cruz is not only the fastest growing city, but also, the most beautiful in the number of parks, esplanades and new buildings. It is as large as La Paz, the seat of government administration: executive and legislative. Some feel that Sucre, remained as capital in name only, since those branches of government moved to the population center, La Paz, and only the judiciary remained.

Now a balance was being achieved. Each large city had a different climate and product and each had discovered the mutual support that brought betterment for it. The fierce micro-nationalism was changing to a wider pride in Bolivia.

Santa Cruz typified the new. Immigrants from other provinces out-numbered the native born. Foreigners, too, flocked here: Chinese merchants, Japanese and Mennonite farmers, Brazilian importers and students, along with the best and worst of the outside world. Ethnic churches were started and growing.

On the trip into town, we were greeted briefly by Emigdio Veizaga and other Bolivian Union leaders working in the city. Fidel Cueto, our driver made appointments or reminded them of meetings together. We were dropped off at a mission group house and the car taken to a garage for some work. The local Board of Missions and Evangelism made the plans for the trip, but the mission was lending a jeep, to make the traveling easier.

Fay called up friends and got addresses. They had two days to catch up on 13 years. While Fidel saw to fixing the car, we found friends who took us to see new works in several parts of the city. We ran into a couple of Canadian Baptist Volunteers from Yarmouth, N.S. and enjoyed hearing that they were running a soup kitchen for needy school children of Santa Cruz.

The next day we started out on the 'new road' to Cochabamba. The first few miles were paved, but before we got to Porta Chuela where the pavement stopped, something in the car sounded terrible, and we pulled over and stopped. We got a passing truck to tow us into town, and Fidel left us sitting in the plaza, while he went to find a garage, and get the car fixed. If we had accompanied him, the price would have doubled.

I had my knitting with me, so we sat in the park and waited for the verdict. Seems something had broken and Fidel had to catch a truck into Santa Cruz and come back with a part before they could fix it. We had reservations to stay in a hotel at the other end of the unpaved part of the road. They were preparing supper for us and holding rooms for us. However, the afternoon passed, and when we finally got the car back, we grabbed a bite to eat on the way, and hurried out onto the now darkened road. Soon the pavement ran out and we bounced from side to side and up and down. I felt betrayed! They hadn't told us just how new that road was. The stumps and boulders were everywhere in the middle, and going down river beds that had only the markers to indicate that someday a road would go between them. The flight from Miami had begun at midnight and there was a loud movie on the TV that was practically in our laps, so we hadn't slept too well then. We hadn't caught up the night before, so the men were suggesting that I sleep in the back. However, with the constant bouncing, I felt like someone was beating me and I hardly closed my eyes.

We arrived at the Hotel at about two in the morning, and I would have stayed out and slept in the car if they had allowed me to, but they insisted I go in. I must admit I DID sleep finally. All too soon Fidel was there to waken us and start on our way again. At last we were back on the pavement.

Fidel had scheduled a meeting that evening, and we were supposed to arrive in Cochabamba by 5 PM. So when we arrived about the half-way mark and happened upon an accident, they asked if we would take a wounded man to the city with us. Our jeep was piled high in the back and there was no place where we could have stretched him out, much less made him comfortable. And I know that we might have been involved and not been able to travel if they had insisted that we stay as witnesses (when we really had not witnessed anything). The driver's assistant, who admitted that the chauffer had lost control because of speed, thought we could take him to report the accident and get the company to send help. The pickup truck had rolled completely over and looked totaled. We cleared off a six inch space opposite us, but he would have been wedged between on-end suitcases. I, Marshall, decided they would be better off traveling together on a truck he saw coming up the road below us. The whole evangelistic tour-plan might have been thrown off. But we've never gotten over the feeling that we were like the priest and the Levite in the story of the Good Samaritan. We reached the city about four hours later, grimy, disheartened and late for the meeting.

We stayed at the Jordan Street property and visited those who lived behind in the second building. Mrs. Tococari was in charge of the guest rooms above the offices and printing press areas that faced on the street. Fidel talked Joan Rutherford into trading the jeep we had brought from Santa Cruz, for another one in her charge. It did need a lot of work, and if we lingered for long waiting for repairs, the tour timing would be thrown off again.

Our stop in Oruro was brief, but we were thrilled at how the church that had begun during our last stay there had grown both in leadership, maturity and numbers. They had named it the Quinta Capilla (the Fifth Chapel) and it was the fifth because there were four Baptist churches before. It had even begun country work on its own.

We hurried on to Tupiza where a young student and his little family had just arrived, for their practical work before their last year in Seminary. I think that we knew more people than they did, and the evening service brought many of our old friends to hear about the work that we were presently doing. We prayed for the continued growth of the congregation that we had seen from it's beginning. From there we proceeded to Villazon on the border with Argentina. Marshall was not feeling well, but preached that first night. There were to be baptisms the next day, and we drove out to look at the stream where we were going to be. It was the middle of July (which was mid-winter). With the strain of travel, lack of rest, and the cold, Marshall lost his voice.

Different people took us home for meals, but Marshall was not interested in food. We went to look for some strong cold medicine for him. When he had eaten a little rice, our hostess insisted he rest until the evening service. He still could not speak, so I told them about our work in the Middle East. Fidel preached and there were decisions. Fidel and I did visitation, and Marshall rested. Then in the afternoon he refused to be left behind when we went for the baptisms. While we made the preparations, we left him in the car. We had to break the ice at the edges next to the rocks where the sun never reached at that time of the year. When it was finally time for the people to begin the service, we bundled Marshall up warmly and he stood in a sheltered place and looked through a V in the rocks to see Fidel do the baptisms. The bright sun held no warmth, but the mood of the meeting was a warm, friendly one. That evening there were more decisions, after I spoke and Fidel preached.

Because it was an all day trip to Tarija, we rose early the next morning. The scenery is dramatic where the river cut through, and exposed the strata across the road. It looked like raw, roughly cut bacon, with strips of red and white that stretched for many kilometers.

The believers in Tarija had many improvements to show us. One little house church where we had visited many years before, was having the recognition service of its girl's missionary auxiliary. They asked me to present some of the awards, and it made a lovely impression. They were meeting in their well appointed building. We met some who had come to know the Lord, and even been raised to leadership positions since our visits years before, as well as the old veterans of the work.

Then they took us to the recently established house churches and congregations, who are NOW struggling to reach their friends and neighbors for Jesus. Visits in the homes of old friends brought joy in seeing those who were children born since other visits, now presented their children and even some grandchildren! Some old friends had established contacts with another Baptist group, and established more congregations. They invited us to tea and took me to their beauty salon for a 'make-over'.

From there we headed north to Potosi. There were three groups in the city where we had gone 28 years before to plant a church. After about two years there, the congregation had been organized into a church. Then after another two years it had dissolved. Only the efforts of a couple of the young people had pulled it back together. It had it's ups and downs over the years, but now, there was the oldest church near the market, one newer one beyond the army post where we used to live. and the third below the train station: all three were packed out when we visited them.

When we arrived, Fidel had word that his wife was ill and decided that he could trust the congregations to take care of us, took the car, and went home to take care of her. He actually left us in a hotel , so as not to show favoritism. (I think he thought there might be a little rivalry among the three congregations.) I believe that was the most uncomfortable night of our whole trip! The bed was like a not-quite-wide-enough hammock with insufficient covers. If we needed anything, we were supposed to just call the on night clerk.

However, we found ourselves pulled by gravity toward the center of the bed and had to cling to the sides to have room to breathe. Though we arrived quite late there were several old friends who came in a few minutes to welcome us -- they offered to take us home, but Fidel insisted that he had made this arrangement and couldn't back out now. Since he had planned the whole tour, we were all somewhat intimidated and did want to cooperate, so nobody objected. When we were feeling the chill, we could have used a hot drink, and a hot water bottle, (we had brought one with us.) We prowled around looking in the tiny lobby and the kitchen nook where he heated water trying to find the night clerk. We never found him, and couldn't get the hot plate to heat, so we went back and put on some more clothes to keep warm. We managed very little sleep and probably looked haggard when our friends came to take us to breakfast. We moved into the lady pastor's quarters (she had gone to visit her family during the winter break). In their zeal to have everything just right they had freshly done the floors. Candles melted with kerosene made a good floor surface and an unbearable smell. However, the warmth of welcome and wealth of blankets overshadowed that discomfort. Our first meeting was at the church near the market. It seems that there was a holiday, and the ladies prepared a meal for us and we made a day of it. People came from all three congregations to be present. We struggled to remember names, ooh-ed and aah-ed over the children of those who had been children when we had lived there, and took pictures of everyone.

The next night we went to the church in the building where we were staying. It was a smaller place, and was stuffed, but only with their own members. Remember Humberto? His little sister Feliza and her husband Mauro, who were the ones who were key players in the awakening of the church, when it almost died two years after its beginning, were also movers in this congregation. Their little girl Sarah, was one of three or four namesakes discovered during that trip. Her middle name was Hazel.

My memory is not clear as to when we went to Cornelio's house church. There, too, they were packed in tight. When Cornelio had been pastor of the church after we went away, he had also found his wife there. We remembered his wife as one who came faithfully to church bringing all her younger brothers and sisters.

Later when we went to work together in Sucre, they came from Llallagua, and we came from temporary quarters in Cochabamba to make the team. Their first little girl, Marisol, was 13 months old I think, and we worked to establish the Church of the Living Lord for three and a half years. It was constituted as a church about a month before we left for furlough.

One of the things that we remembered was how musical he was. He had composed words and music for several hymns that had been published. Their first Christmas in Sucre, Gloria was waiting for her second child. They had been visiting a local doctor and when, just before Christmas, she started labor, they bundled Marisol up and went off to the hospital for the birth. Though the doctor had been seeing her, they had not been living in the city long enough for their social insurance to pay the bills, and no one wanted to take her in! His Christmas carol, was straight from the heart, since he, too, had experienced finding 'no room in the inn (hospital)!' We were invited to bring our children's choir and present a Christmas Concert over the radio. Along with 'Silent Night', 'O Little Town of Bethlehem', and 'Hark the Herald Angels Sing'; he sang, ' No room in the Inn". After 13 years, however, he was letting his daughters do the singing. His youngest, had won awards in their folklore festival for three straight years. While there we translated a hymn that I had brought from the Middle East, and we played and sang it during that service. During this visit, he was working for World Vision, registering needy children in the neighboring villages for the school supplies, uniforms, medical help, etc. that perhaps some of you may have sponsored.

Baptisms were planned for Sunday morning, when the three churches all brought the ones to be baptized in the Olympic pool that was at the foot of the hill where we had baptized at the camp site beside the volcanic vent, mentioned before. We actually ended up at a smaller pool, where many picnickers had come to spend the day. One friend lent us his patio for our meeting, and then we went and while there were some people who stayed in the water playing, others came out of the water, and watched respectfully while Marshall and Fidel did the baptizing. One of those who wanted to be baptized, was Roxanna, Cornelio's middle child, who had heard about Pastor Thompson all her life, and wanted him to baptize her. All the pools in this area were hot springs, so even though the air was chilly in mid-winter, the water was very pleasant.

The next day we were off down the hill to Sucre. We had been in rented quarters all during our service there, so it was nice to see the church in quite a large building, and the piano we had left for them to use, was there and I got to play it! The pastor's apartment was upstairs, but some of the rooms he used during the week, were also used for Sunday School.

The next day, I flew to La Paz to attend the convention of the Women's Cruzada. Kay Rowe met me at the airport in the Alto of La Paz. We picked up some supplies on the way to take to the Convention, and then went right through the city straight to the bottom of the hill to one of the new churches. It was built into the side of the hill, and I think had five stories. Like most conventions, the ladies talked and sang all night long. The programs were well prepared, and the reports of the different societies demonstrated such diligence, dedication and devotion, that I was thrilled to be there. A number of those leaders we had worked with had gone on to their reward, but new ones had stepped in, and we praised the Lord for the advances that they had made, and the blessings that He had showered upon their work.

Kay took me out to Guatajata, and we had a nice visit when the Convention ended. We saw all the new development around the lake side, and marveled at the beauty of it. One thing that we lamented was the lack of the balsa boats that the lake is famous for. We saw a few that had been left to rot in the shallows. All the fishermen were into motorized craft. Kay was due to retire the next year, but was considering going early because of some family, and health concerns. We prayed together that her decisions would be wise ones. Sunday morning I was in the Prado church, meeting in the mezzanine of one of the buildings that was responsible for the collapse of the church building where we had worshipped during our first years there. There were very few of those present that I could recognize. If they remembered me, it was that they had been children when I was there -- and so looked very different -- what I mean is unrecognizable! Fidel's wife, Fortunata, was present, along with many others from the convention. She had special recognition, since her daughter was married to the current pastor.   All the ladies brought greetings from their churches and ladies societies, and received the greetings from the Prado congregation, too, to take back to their home churches.

I then boarded the plane that would take me back to North America, where a new grand baby was awaiting my visit .

Marshall had stayed in Sucre, still visiting our old friends there. He will tell you about the conclusion of his trip in the next chapter.

Singing and making melody in your heart to the Lord   Ephesians 5:

Roxana Heredia, a pastor's daughter is baptized in 1990

I stood on the La Paz Prado Boulevard, near the corner of Camacho Street and stared in disbelief at the gap between two high ten or more storied buildings. The gap included a crater that descended at least three stories beneath the paved sidewalk and street. An awful gap in the most fashionable and modern part of the government city. A sacred spot that once held the oldest and largest Protestant church in the country. I stood alone for Hazel had returned to the north for the birth of Joy, a grandchild. As the daylight faded and city lights livened the scene I crossed the street to a stand-on-wheels that offered pizza and other fast foods. I ordered a slice and he had a portable micro-wave oven to heat it up for me. I walked backwards in time in my mind's eye to the time when the temple stood and Manuel Zubieta was pastor. The Canadian Baptist Institute was functioning as a school in the three story building behind the church. A strictly church centered effort, it had prospered, added grades and outgrown its facilities. A school with a name to honor the mission that founded the gospel work in the city and country. It was financed and taught on a wonderful national level, but the church structure was trembling.

One morning, they came to school to find that the dividing wall between the church and the neighboring hotel had fallen into the patio. This disaster convinced them that it was time to seek a safer place. Before the desired property was found, cracks appeared under the cement walks, revealing deep crevices and hollow spaces dozens of meters below. It became too dangerous for children to attend. New property was sought and bought by national efforts again. The school director and pastor admitted that being a principal was easy. He paid the salaries and gave the orders and got quick obedience. However, being pastor of the church was difficult. There was never the same prompt response to suggestions and recommendations made for the congregation. After the school moved to a property on Mexico street, the church physically imploded. The owner of the last built neighboring edifice was sued in the Bolivian courts for the implosion, again without the participation of the mission. The   courts had ordered the perpetual use of the new building's mezzanine for the demolished church, without charge until they were able to replace it's building. The vast hole held a one story mud brick edifice lining the back wall of the property. It was for the Janitor and care taker of what was left of the open property. He cleaned the part of the mezzanine floor set aside for the church. The lot connected to the new building through an outside door.

From a church of several hundred it had become a place where less than one hundred believers gathered on Sunday. I had my opportunity to talk to them about gospel work in the Middle East. They were attempting to collect sufficient money to rebuild. It has proved to be a long and arduous task.

My mind went further back to my first introduction to the Prado Baptist Church. I received the call to pastor the church while still a language student in Central America. It was really starting off BIG. As a young seminary graduate I moved from a small rural circuit of churches in New Brunswick to the largest Protestant church in the nation of Bolivia. I had the benefit of a year's language study in a reputable school in Costa Rica. I had a tailored black suit required of all pastors at the time. I had a dozen sermons prepared in the second term for the eventual preaching opportunities. Most students needed them while finishing the second year of required on-the-job language study. Neither teachers or students expected the people they trained, or trained with, to do what I was forced into: full time preaching and pastoring on my arrival in Bolivia.

The church had been through troubled days and could not agree on a national or foreign minister known to them. I was unknown and no one had anything against me. As they could not find another solution, they accepted me as a candidate sight unseen, who, at least, had no enemies. Their letter arrived the day before we left for Bolivia. There was no opportunity to answer the letter before we arrived four days later. I struggled in prayer over my decision during the trip. Could I unite the people? All our preparation had been to let the 'national' do it. We did enjoy the stop-overs in Panama, and Lima. But it was always there niggling at the back of my mind.

We were surprised by a truckload of members of the Prado Church, waiting to welcome us when we arrived. About 30 of them gave us *abrazos,* took care of the baggage, the baby and the bird. They loaded us and our bags into the pickup truck, and they got in the big truck for the trip down the hill into the city.

They were not used to a new missionary who could speak the language upon arrival. In a consultation with a couple of the deacons, Lucho Araya and Estanislao Blanco, they told me that they would take care of the preaching until my Spanish improved. It didn't work out that way.

Here's what happened. A group of seminary graduates came to make a presentation on a Wednesday night at the church. From there they were to visit the highest Baptist church (16,000 ft. above sea level) at a mine center in Milluni and invited me along. Since I didn't have to preach that Sunday, I could accompany them for two nights. It was an exciting venture out with young men, who would be friends and colleagues in the work, in the future. It snowed on the last day of August while we were up there. I came back in high spirits late Saturday night to my lovely wife and nearly six month-old baby boy. We were to stay in the Wormald's apartment behind the radio building while they were away for their two months at low altitude. They would not have to look for a house-sitter while they were gone, and there would be time to renovate the parsonage apartment behind the church.

Upon arrival, Hazel asked me pleasantly: "Do you have any of those sermons you worked over in language school?" I looked at her blankly, "I think so, why? "

" I hope you can find them, you're preaching tomorrow."

"But Lucho said he'd be preaching." She shook her head,

"He was operated on this morning for appendicitis!"

I preached every Sunday from that time on. Lucho Araya was a month getting back to church meetings. Several of my national friends took note of my mistakes in Spanish and gave me a list to work on after each sermon. It became the only language study that I had time for that second year.

I tried to get the deacons to come for early prayer as Charles Spurgeon of London had done in his successful church in the nineteenth century. Only a few ever arrived early and they were always in a hurry to leave. I wrestled alone with many of the evident church problems, but God helped me.

We had moved into the second story of the building behind the huge church edifice. The Church had a large sanctuary with a set of accordion wooden panels that could be opened to unite it with the Sunday School auditorium. The adult Sunday School classes met there regularly. When those doors were opened 600 people could be accommodated for the Christmas concert, or any extra large evangelistic meetings. There were several rooms behind the podium of the Sunday School; below there were two rooms, and above the youth had 'The upper room' which they used for their meetings. and considered their own domain.

The three story building behind the church had the children's Sunday school rooms and a kitchen. Those rooms doubled for committee meetings and dining area for social times. There was another entrance, that led to the bathroom facilities. That door also gave access to a fair sized storage depot where the Guatajata missionaries brought their purchases when they came shopping about twice a month.

The staircase there lead to the second floor which held the bookstore, and the pastor's office and apartment. The third floor held a large room with lots of glassless windows, where we could dry the clothes on a rainy day, and an apartment used by the Guatajata missionaries, when they needed to spend the night in town.

A narrow walkway of about two meters wide connected the steel-barred street gate entrance to the second solid sheet-iron gate that opened onto the patio and back building. I had enough ground to dig flower beds: planting both front and back and to tend the terraces behind the second building, It made things look cared for and orderly.

The people needed to be brought together in some common goal. Praying, I felt we should beautify the interior of the building. A large picture of the Bible under a lamp was shown with the verse "Thy word is a lamp unto my feet, and a light unto my path." in Spanish. It was in need of repainting and the sanctuary walls showed plaster where paint had flaked off. The ceiling was a dull color with water marks. The place had a shabby look. Someone suggested the mission should paint it. I told them the church belonged to the Bolivians and they were getting help in the form of a salaried pastor. They owed the price of one salary to the mission and should hire a city missionary to do needed work there. There were only two Baptist churches in a city of a third of a million people. We put up a thermometer to show our giving and started painting on what the church gave.

Later we did hire a pastor, Modesto Alliaga, to start meetings around the suburbs. Pride and self confidence grew out of our success. People could see our progress inside the temple and outside it. God was blessing.

I did get the deacons involved in a one day a week mission preaching and several new meetings grew up. There were open air meetings on *San Pedro Plaza* near the church. In the *Garita de Lima*, above a large market, a five story church building stands today as a result of that work.

A meeting in the Aymara language was started above the city, La Portada, where the flat lip of the *Altiplano* stretched outward. The Southern Cross Radio had land for a transmission tower there. The little rooms held supplies, transmitter and twice a week meetings for Bible study and preaching. Many of the people came from the area near the airport and they started meetings there. Then we had two churches on the *Alto de La Paz*. Today, it holds a population as large as the city of Oruro and has five more Baptist Churches to tend its growing multitudes.

I bought a map on which I labeled the areas where meetings were starting and encouraged our people towards the spots where no churches existed. And meetings grew in each new developing area of the expanding city. We tried to build a ring of churches around the center of the city. A few of the meetings and gathering points for meeting were temporary and failed to develop. Today, many that did grow, are larger in attendance or in membership than the Prado Church, which gave itself credit for mothering so many churches. I wondered, as I considered the demise of its physical plant, of the efforts of many pastors, foreign and national. Where had it gone? The answer would be revealed on an updated map of living churches and in the lives of the increased membership and faithfulness of the believers there. They bear witness to the presence of God in their lives and the sure foundation that is present in Jesus our Savior. As we live our physical lives we know that, we too will some day, leave a hole or empty spot in the fabric of our own families', our friends' and neighbors' lives. Though we are not physically present any more, our influence and work for the Lord will have a bearing on the lives we have left behind.

In October of 2005, at a reunion of ex-missionaries, their children, and Bolivian friends transplanted in North America -- Canada and the USA -- pledged their resolve to help raise the funds to rebuild the Prado church. The same man, Dr. Juan Aguila, who initiated the mission outreach of the Bolivian Baptist Union, the first year we were in Bolivia, was one of the moving forces in starting the ball rolling. He and a half dozen others who live in California were present. Two couples came from Washington DC., Lucho Araya of the appendicitis, Nora his wife and Augusto Clavijo and Carmen. Luis Castillo, who I had in an English class 50 years ago, came from Madison, Wisconsin. Another outstanding pastor, Dr. Jaime Goytia, who worked for Bible Societies for many years, came all the way from Bolivia. Missionaries were there as well. We are involved in praying for the Prado church, that it will again, one day, be a power for Christ in the heart of the Capital City of Bolivia.

I will build again the ruins . . . Acts 15:16

Large buildings surround the gap in the Prado Boulevard

Most people assume that the life of a missionary has many narrow escapes. By this they mean life threatening situations. They think you unusually brave or perhaps careless in your value of your own life and those you love. Let me assure you that this is not so. There are places and times when everyone is more careful. When there are road blocks for political reasons or marching protesters you always proceed with caution. You avoid contact with hostile people. All Bolivians do. They know the local scene better than the analysts and reporters do, so you consult them as to the best manner of reacting. Running away is, after all, a universal survival tactic.

When the men show fear, or a defiant mood, then, I go on high alert and stay home when possible. If you are traveling you try to act like people should when a gun is pointed in your direction with orders to do something. You stop, talk pleasantly, obey promptly and it is surprising how effective that can be in tight situations. Usually you will not fit the profile of the persons they are guarding against. This will be the case 98% of the time. If you do fit the profile you submit graciously with a smile and expect your friends or diplomatic people to get you out later. Courage is sometimes to accept your momentary state as reality and to trust God and human kindness to get you through any risks.

There are also places where extra caution is always best observed. Borders are one, as I have already shown. Yungas and Chapare roads are another. They receive heavier and more sustained rain than the high plain and therefore are more subject to road washouts. Most descend from the high passes at five thousand meters to about two thousand. The tropical vegetation here is not heavily rooted for water is abundant and they will not hold the soil of the roadside. I was a member of the Methodists' High School board of directors in La Paz (My father was a Methodist Steward in his home church.) They trusted my interest in their work. The director was Murray Dickson who was a respected friend. Several years after that his car was involved in a cave-in that threw the car hundreds of feet down a slope. He was evidently thrown clear, but another greater slip took him as he tried to climb up. It was a great loss.

One of our men, John Czerepka, after an all day trip on the road to Chapare, explained it "I look down, mist and rain all around. I feel good. We take road home, I look down, no mist, green and steep mountains everywhere." He whipped off his hat and held it over his heart to say, "I pray."

I traveled to the Yungas of Inquisive several times a year. Once I had planned a trip there when my children were home from boarding school and, typically, I wanted them to share some of the work we do for God. I was to travel with a pastor, Eugenio Velasques, who had been admitted to the pastorate of Oruro Moderno, the north church. Several deacons were to accompany us. Hazel was going to go, but at the last minute our youngest, Karlene developed a pain in her side. Hazel decided to take her to the doctor while the rest of us traveled. Her mother has told you the story of her appendicitis.

We traveled down the high passes and showed Gospel and Moody Science films in the jungle villages. We carried our portable generator with us. It fit neatly in the back of the jeep and the passengers sat around it. It could be removed or left inside the jeep with the rear door open for ventilation. It also screened the sound of the little gas motor. Some of the villages responded by spontaneously giving us sacks of Yuca, a tropical root used in cooking; plantains, a cooking banana; Cherimoya, a custard apple and citrus fruit. I protested the bounty because we were getting ready for our departure to the north. Eugenio, however, said that he would take it for use at home. I didn't realize that he had left his job in the mines with only enough money to pay the moving of his goods. He was facing a ,month without money or food. The Lord was providing all his needs on this one trip. We even found a bag of food dropped in the middle of the road from some commercial truck used in the traditional commerce between the high Prairies of the Andes with the jungle hill country. Salt, dried meat, corn and potatoes exchanged for tropical fruits, wood and coca leaves.

We finished our film showing rather late, after a dawn to dusk day of driving and visiting. It was now after ten. We finished the presentation and preaching, answered questions, held consultations. We gratefully started back to the village an hour away, where we were staying. The stars shone fitfully casting bizarre shadows on the winding road. The children and deacons were sleeping in the back. Eugenio and I spoke rarely as I concentrated on driving. I misjudged a shadow on the high, ditch side of the road and swung away from it. My front right wheel went over the cliff side edge of the road, throwing the weight of the car, with the top rack piled high with produce, on the outer right side of the small vehicle. Our velocity carried us forward as I tried to get the yawing machine back on the road. It stopped just on the verge and the motor stopped dead. Then, weight backed us up a few feet before stopping again. Something had kept us from falling back over the cliff. The car leaned over at a 45 degree angle. The driver and the hood stood high and the back left side hung down steeply. I was evaluating our situation, it was not good. I was, perhaps, resting on the point of balance that kept the car on the road. I could imagine vividly what would happen if the jeep plunged down the lush slope. The water rich stems would not hold the weight and the generator motor and projector inside the vehicle would crash from side to side on any descent. The people in the back would be mince meat! I could not afford to move out of my seat, lest It destabilize the car. We could not open the back door over the edge, it could only be opened from the outside. The occupants would have to exit over the driver to the only safe door. One at a time the brothers obeyed my request. They climbed over me and out the door which I held open with my foot propped against its heavy weight.

One man said "I wasn't afraid until I got out of the jeep and saw how it balanced on the edge of the road. The front wheel was in the air a foot above the road." My two near teenage children came out last. All lives were saved. Now, the car and equipment must be salvaged. Still in the drivers seat I put the jeep into four-wheel drive and tried to ease it out of its position. The wheels spun. The projector and lighter stuff was passed out and placed on the roadside. My children had stretched out on the road and had to be moved to a safer place to sleep. One man set off for the settlement to bring some digging tools. The others took turns clearing the tires paths with the straight rod used to raise the jack. We couldn't see to get below the jeep and did not know what was holding it up.

It was still dark, hours later, when the brother appeared with the tools, a spade, and we had an easy path for the wheels to move forward. The pastor stood on the front bumper to weigh down the front wheel to get traction. The brothers pushed from the fenders. The motor roared and we slowly emerged from the arms that supported it. The cliff didn't fall away directly at that one spot. There was a pillar of eroded looking clay that had supported the rear right end of the car. This alone kept us from falling. We were saved 'by the skin of our teeth', as Job 19:20 expressed it.

We had a prayer of thanksgiving, reloaded the car, woke up the kids to get in and drove thirty minutes to arrive at our billets for the night. The next day we started our return. There were several spots where the road had fallen away and we had the passengers walk across and the pastor guide the driver across the narrow remains with hand signs, shouts of encouragement and applause by all before they seated themselves for the continued return. Such narrow escapes build a spirit of affection and appreciation among the believers.

This was the most memorable of the narrow escapes that seemed to happen on a regular basis while serving in Bolivia. There was a constant stream of events and plans that went wrong at some point and there was no way to predict if it would be either stolen equipment, delayed packages, or canceled meetings that would cause new adjustments and changes of plans or venue. We all live in a world of uncertainty, so we need Jesus as our firm foundation to face life anywhere.

Fear not, you are worth many sparrows. Luke 12:7

The BBU jeep visiting a rural school on the high prairie

I got the news from Hazel that a tour of Bolivia, to celebrate the 100th anniversary of Baptist work there, was to be led by Mark Parent. I had known him as a three-year-old when he had arrived with his folks, Hazen and Hazel who had come to Bolivia to work as missionaries.

They were guests in our home for their first week in Bolivia. In later years, we were often guests in their home when we went to La Paz for committee meetings. Then Mark served as pastor at First Moncton United Baptist Church for several years where we were members after our retirement. I thought a tour guided by a 'third culture kid' would be unusually interesting and was easily persuaded to go along. Other TC Kids that went in the group with us were Jean and Dorothy Buck, (79 and 81 years old respectively, who gave a tour of the Reekie director's house where they had grown up), Mary Haddow, and of Mark's generation, Gloria Stairs Tranquilla, who took her daughter, Giselle, along to see where she had grown up. It had been twenty-- one years since we had left the work there in 1977 and now in 1998 we could visit again. But we went in style like tourists. Would it look any different?

The price was reasonable and the itinerary took us to the important places that we wanted to visit. The time spent would give anyone a good look at the field of work and the different climates and cultures present in Bolivia. I was intrigued by the variety of activities.

We got a prodigious amount of instructions with a list of shots. We would be staying in three star hotels, rather than with friends, fellow missionaries or pastors in their homes. Health is always a valid concern, so we went for our punctures and pills. We got orientation: printed and in Santa Cruz, Bolivia, face-to-face! We were being grounded in history and health; a good preparation for outsiders new to the country. I found it fun to listen to and was allowed to add an experience here or there in the sessions to illustrate the importance of the subject . We were in a lovely hotel where I went swimming twice a day. The meals were much better than I had expected, but only about half were native dishes; the rest were home and international cuisine. It was largely buffet, so you could choose what you wanted to eat in the quantity you were comfortable with. You could take a taste of everything you wanted to try. If there was any room left, you could go back and get a whole helping of something that you really liked. You weren't stuck with a big heaping plate of food that would be wasted, if you didn't like it. There was no need to 'grin and bear it'.

There were rest stops, shopping times and visiting options. The Bolivians were on their best behavior, warm, friendly and appreciative of us joining them in celebration. Important men and women took time to meet us and explain their plans and concerns, both past and future. I wondered if other tours were as thorough and interesting.

Starting in Santa Cruz, the second largest city, a small party of us chose to visit some of the Mennonite farms on a half day drive north-east to new lands being opened up. Others stayed and shopped or rested. We attended a Youth rally at the Good Shepherd Baptist Church (Buen Pastor) and also a special presentation at the Evangelical University there. On Sunday we went to a new church where an American Latino pastor preached and welcomed us. We met Fernando and Maria Luisa de Galindo, (our maid-daughter of early Bolivian days) met her extended family and caught up on her life. We visited a new congregation where she attended that night.

After the week in Santa Cruz, we made a connection in Cochabamba for Sucre.

The church in Sucre has two different congregations. There is one made up of University students from the many schools: normal, medical, pharmacy, dentistry, music, law, etc. Many came from Baptist churches elsewhere in the republic, and witnessed and won friends to swell the numbers. The other group was made of Quechua speakers, who, while we were there, had Wycliffe missionaries in their congregation. They were revising the Bible in Quechua, and their work brought a whole new generation into the church.

Gloria Stairs gave a piano concert, which was attended by members of both groups. Her daughter accompanied her with the flute. Afterwards, a number of friends came to give us an update on their lives. We took the tour group to another feature of Sucre that has write-ups in all the tourist guide books -- the Cemetery. All who went with us confirmed its beauty.

Hazel had been looking forward to visiting Cornelio Herredia and his wife GLoria, with whom we had worked to establish the Church of the Living Lord in Sucre in 1974. However, upon arrival in Santa Cruz, she had inquired of Enia Arana, another pastor's wife, and heard that Gloria had passed away just 90 days before. So, it was a nostalgic rather than a happy time for her.

From there we flew on to Cochabamba. They held a dinner theatre, on Saturday night at the Calama Street Baptist Church, showed all the local musical groups with the latest in hymns and choruses, served with our meal, at full blast. It was rather informal, so that our friends who remembered us and were present could stop by and have a wee chat to catch up on each others lives. It was an open air affair, and sometimes hard to hear above the musical background.

The next morning was Easter, and we rose early to join the march to the Coronilla with all the other Evangelical churches in to city taking part. We met in one of those large inflatable tents that would hold 20,000 people. There were about 15,000 present. Again we were the focus of the blaring amplifiers. It was a very inspiring service, and the growth in all the local churches was overwhelming.

Enia, pastor Emilio's wife, had gone into the transportation business (since it was hard to make ends meet with their meager pension) and had handled our local transportation. She met us at the airport in Santa Cruz when we first arrived. She saw us off when we flew to Sucre. She was there again to meet us at the airport in Cochabamba, and drove us around for the rest of our stay.

In Cochabamba, the Sunday School we attended was a small mission, established by, Grace Tapia de Garcia, the wife of pastor Juan Garcia. She had established the work, and left her family home, when she passed away, to be used for a church when it was established.

In the evening, Enia took us to the church that she and her husband, Emilio, were establishing beside their home. It was a one room building into which they had crowded about 70 people. We sang heartily with a worship team, but were deafened by the ever-present amplifiers. We were in the back corner, so Marshall had to climb over many people to get out, but he had to, it was just too loud. He 'swam' through the sound and when he went out the door, found there was another amplifier about 8ft. away. It was aimed at the door, to add to the blast. He went across the patio, and down a narrow alley walkway between the house and patio adobe walls, 20 meters away and stood on the street, and enjoyed the rest of the concert. He could hear perfectly well from there! However, he experienced some hearing loss from those three extensive exposures to such intense sound.

Sunday afternoon we saw off a convoy of bicycles: The Youth convention was cycling the whole 230 kilometers uphill to Oruro from Cochabamba.

The next day we left for Oruro, where the pioneer Archibald Reekie had arrived on April 20, 1898, 100 years before.

Canadian Baptists were represented by 80 Canadians, consisting of several groups with different leaders.

There were 24 in Mark Parent's group that we came with.

The Presidents' group was made up of the presidents of Canadian Baptist Ministries, and all the related Canadian Baptist conventions: Convention of Atlantic Baptist Churches, Baptist Convention of Ontario/Quebec, The Baptist Union of Western Canada, The Union of French Baptist Churches, the Atlantic Baptist Women, and Baptist Women of Ontario/ Quebec. Several brought their spouses.

Miss Cathy McGorman brought five ladies from the Atlantic provinces as a working group. They were away at the crack of dawn traveling on public transportation, visiting small societies away in the distance: ordinary ladies talking to ordinary ladies about what Jesus had done for them. They discussed some problems common to both countries, and how each had sought to solve them as Jesus would have. They did some crafts together, each teaching the other. They ate what the ladies supplied them and usually were after dark getting back at night. Mark's group often stayed in the same hotel, but we seldom saw them.

There was a working group representing Christian Education led by Marilyn McCormick. They called themselves the M & M'S, because all their first names started with 'M'. When their translator turned out to be June Sekella, they said, that just the 's' that made them 'plural'.

There was a group from the West that included John and Helen Palmquist. There were several other ex-missionaries John's twin sister who served in India, Jean Palmquist, Art Wormald, Douglas Moore, Gunther and Rhinhilde Rochow (he represented the Canadian Government) Ruth Dryden and Muriel Bent (both went early, and did a lot of the preparations there.) Dennis and Judy Shierman, June Marr Castellon, Joan Rutherford, Hans Ellen of course, had this to work on in addition to their "normal" load. Visiting from India was David Sarma.

There were Evangelistic services, preaching on the streets, and in the parks, "How to..." workshops on many aspects of Christian Work, Bible Studies, musical presentations in the churches of the city, conference rooms in some hotels, and Reekie School.

One event was the presentation by the Bolivian Federal Government of their highest award, 'The Condor of the Andes', to the Bolivian Baptist Union in recognition of the contributions made during the 100 years of service there. Quoting from a letter I wrote at the time: "The Departmental Governments of La Paz, Cochabamba, and Oruro as well as the Federal Government, all decorated the Bolivian Baptist Union with all the pomp and splendor imaginable. Many of the authorities, speaking of their districts, also spoke of the contribution made by Mary Haddow -- who while she served as a Canadian Baptist missionary -- is also a Bolivian by birth! Lest you worry -- they didn't start a new Mary worshipping cult -- they only wished to express their heartfelt thanks for her bringing them the Gospel."

Mary, whose father and mother were pioneers of the work, had also given her own entire career to it, was chosen to receive these honors in the name of the Bolivian Baptist Union. There was limited seating, but all the ex-missionaries were invited.

We were expecting our son to arrive, and his bus was late, but we mentioned it at the door (since we were holding the invitation) and when he arrived, he was admitted and witnessed a part of the ceremony. Borden went on to visit other sites that were meaningful to him, when that celebration of six days was over.

In another ceremony at the pavilion at Reekie School, the

Bolivian Baptist Union honored churches that had been organized over 20 years.

Then they presented medallions to all the pastors who had been in service for 20 years or more.

Then to our surprise, they had also had medallions made for missionaries. Several members of Dr. Sid Hillyer's family were there for the event, and one son accepted the honor in his place. We had served for 23 years, but since we had gone to serve elsewhere, were quite surprised that they had included us in those who were awarded medallions. Some of the pastors, too, who had already passed on, had children or grand-children who accepted the honor in their place.

For the main event in Oruro, they wanted to accord the place of honor to us again, but we chose to move out of the focus of sound to the edge, and escaped that blast for the rest of the events we attended. The one big negative point on the whole trip was that everyone turned the volume to maximum.

"The next Sunday, 19th of May it all culminated in the BIG PARADE! Though people had come from the extremes of the Republic, there were only small groups representing those churches. However, from the immediate area, some had their whole congregations. So when they started the parade, there were thousands of people present. Seeing how they filled the Coliseum I would judge that there were between 12,000 and 15,000, to march from the center of the city, about 20 city blocks, out to their inflatable tent, that would also hold 20,000."

Our tour group was fairly near the beginning of the parade, just about a block of flags, standards, banners, the BIBLE, VIP's, authorities of the Bolivian Baptist Union, civic dignitaries of the city of Oruro, the Federal Government, others, The Canadian Baptist Ministries Presidents' Team etc. preceded us. Then came the rest of the Canadians. With all us elderly Aunties in mind -- a mini-bus was provided at the end of that group. Some rode the whole way, but I managed to march with the rest for about the first eight blocks... descending when there were about four to go. "

They were expecting about 15,000, too, but civil unrest with blockades on major roads, prevented the arrival of many from the South, and the Orient of Bolivia. We had invited the other local evangelicals, as well, to join us for that Sunday Service, and we had about 10,000 present. They recognized that Reekie had opened the door, and they had entered at a later date to bring people to salvation in Jesus.

"I marched in with the rest of our group when we reached the coliseum. Then I realized what I had forgotten: the little ring-pincushion favors in the minibus. I had brought them along to give as keepsakes. I'd been working on them for months, and this was the moment I had waited for to give them away. I went to the bus and found it locked, and the driver gone. "Well, the big bus is at the end of the parade, so I'll walk back to meet it." I said, and started out. However, it was very hot, so I stopped under the shade tree, to watch the rest of the parade go by."

"What a thrill I would have missed if I had sat and rested inside! When the Canadian Baptist Institute passed with it's baton twirlers, I realized how tired they were as one dropped her baton. She would have left it, but some young bystander picked it up and returned it to her. There were shouts of encouragement. The tree I had found was near the entrance, so the leaders of the groups often shouted, "Take heart! We're almost there!" "The goal is in sight" or "Be brave!" When I had heard them a few times, I got the people sharing the shade to help me urge them on.

"Here again, as people recognized me, they stepped out of the line a moment to catch up on the news, take pictures, and present their children.

"As the groups went by we heard many new cheers:
'Who died for us?' (and the answer rang out) 'JESUS! '
'Who rose from the dead?'   'JESUS!'
'Who's coming again?'   'JESUS!'
Or "Who died to save us? ... 'Jesus! Glory to His name!"

Besides the school bands and the Southern Cross Radio sound van, many churches had musical groups. The people just before and just after them often sang along with them on 'Onward Christian Soldiers' and other marching songs, and hymns of the resurrection (it was just one week after Easter), and many of their own compositions. One combo had even written a Centennial hymn!

The most impressive part was that they just kept coming: some churches were very small, some had 30 to 50, and the four big local churches had a couple of hundred apiece, but they just kept filing by. Little ones marched by mom and dad, and the babies bobbed up and down in the 'ahuayo' on mother's back."

Since Sunday is the day that most people have off from work, most take the family, and go visiting, or on an excursion. So those who were not in the parade, were out on the street to witness it. Now looking back, I see the parade as the highlight of the whole celebration. "

Quoting again: '"That last service was awesome. Inside the coliseum the worship team included forty young ladies who had been practicing all year long, the art of accompanying the music with tambourines. They were dressed in simple long golden dresses, and the tambourines had long golden streamers, which added a visual beauty as they kept time swinging the instruments: sometimes above their heads, sometimes waist high, and sometimes in complete circles - in a level of artistry unsurpassed in the entertainment world. They added a graceful, lovely visual image, as well as a fitting accompaniment to the band, and the congregational singing. Gloria and Giselle Tranquilla (daughter and grand-daughter of Lorne and Florence Stairs), joined Hernan Orsi, (grandson of Pastor Donato Saldias) in a musical presentation with piano, flute and violin.

"Special speakers were Neilson Fanini, President of the Baptist World Alliance from Brazil, José Missena of Chile, and Samuel Escobar of Argentina.

"After that service, we went for lunch and then departed for La Paz. It was still light enough to see the snow-cap of Sajama from the road, when we had a flat tire, and had to stop and fix it. Of course, we didn't arrive until very late to the city.

"On Tuesday, there was a social meeting for the La Paz women, at which the missionary ladies were honored.

"Wednesday, our whole tour group took a trip to Guatajata, where all the missionaries who had served there were honored. Besides Mary Haddow, there were John Palmquest, Marshall and Hazel Thompson, and Gloria Stairs (who had lived there at about the age of six.) Some were asked to say a word." My shame was that I didn't have enough of my little favors left to give them to all the women present. They had a big dinner 'on the grounds' like old times, and we toured The clinic which had been named for Mary Haddow.

After that we visited some historical ruins, geological wonders, and did some shopping. However, the spiritual wonder of the multiplication of the church under the leading of the Holy Spirit, was the most outstanding memory that I hold of Bolivia in 1998. We pray that the same kind of increase will happen under His guidance in the second century.

Behold I make all things new   Revelation 21:5

THE GOOD NEWS
LAS BUENAS NUEVAS

Jaime Goytia S.   (Himno Centenario - Unión Bautista Boliviana)   Jaime Goytia R.

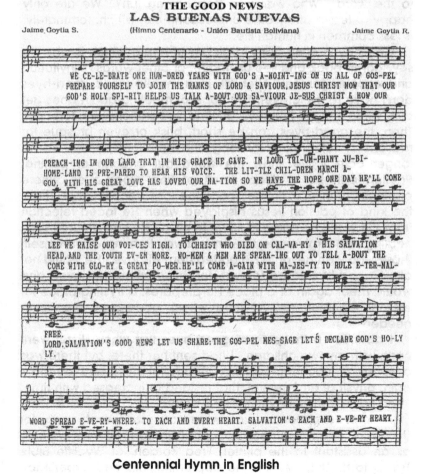

Centennial Hymn in English

For most of our lives we leave someone behind or we are left behind. Parting ways is a part of life in a mobile world. We early learn that people come and go. Some are fun and we like to see them. Others, perhaps, not so much. Our first experience is probably involved in visits to or from nurses, parents, or grandparents. There are special people we visit or receive visits from, some carry gifts. Then, fun times come to an end and we or they say good-bye. Sadness tends to stick to the word. Who wants to stop having fun? We are only happy to leave after some unpleasantness; which, fortunately, is less common in human life.

Good-byes often carry a gleam of hope. Which is why we say "come back and see us again," or other words of invitation and encouragement. After all, in a mobile world good-byes don't have to be forever. The hope of meeting again does get dim when longer journeys or time separations are forecast. Then, the good-byes can be short, brisk or even brusque for reasons of self-control, or long and emotional, when we no longer care if we show the world our anguish of parting. Passion can be a direct result of final good-byes, where partings are infinite, timeless, and the loss irreconcilable. That's the kind of passion Jesus displayed when He faced rejection from the world he came to save, to which He had brought such healing and forgiveness, that finds a way to bring, after Himself, those who wish never to be parted from His love. He would not allow good-bye to be forever, for those whom He loved and would meet again at a place He prepares: a trysting place for eternal togetherness. A world where good-byes are never needed.

I discovered the pain of good-byes first when Hazel went north with my two children. I had sent her there, but there was a sense of vacuum, lacking, incompleteness and constant pain, physical and mental, that resided or increased with time. I had never known anything like it before.

A later experience was when our son went north for University. I kept him near in Cochabamba for a year working as an assistant to the printer, Fred Borden, at Wycliffe Bible Translators. It gave him the apprenticeship and experience printing Scriptures in the tribal languages. It enabled him to get a job at a friend's press in the north, but I felt a continuing pain and, yes, sorrow I had rarely felt before. Hazel experienced something like that when the second child, Krystal, left to join him. The third experience for me was with the youngest when she became interested in a young man totally unsuited for her life companion. It was a good-bye which did not develop to parting, yet promised as much, had God permitted it to mature. Love attaches and parting brings pain. God is good for there is a place where parting will no longer be a threat to our tranquility. Not that we love less, but that love brings a bonding with others that permits no good-byes.

Bolivian good-byes are elaborate, they include many words, gifts, dedicatory plaques or sheepskins. Scripture is amply quoted and a tremendous meal is all part of the good-bye: they want to make sure you remember it and them. It presents joyful sorrow and acknowledgement of mutual love and respect; a recognition of shared values.

I found that good-byes include countries, climates and even pieces of land. Once, flying over my family home, I felt such a depth of emotion, I could hardly stand it. It was almost like heaven. I can still see it in my mind's eye, but that loved beauty ceased to exist while I was elsewhere. I have successively loved places, buildings, people in other parts of the world.

Each with its beauty and its problems. None of these could I keep intact as they were. Nor would I wish to, until they reach a state of mature perfection I can only imagine: a gem of reality to be preserved forever. It will be a relief to enter that steady state, changeless world which our Scriptures offer those who believe and obey.

Good-bye is not forever; in Jesus, among the redeemed, it is no longer a necessary word. There are no good-byes there, forever.

Behold the dwelling place of God is with men.

Revelation 21:3

283

Thompsons: young and old!

After the first term in Bolivia 1960

Birthdays still come and go